P9-EEO-241

INNOVATIONS
IN GOVERNMENT

INNOVATIVE GOVERNANCE IN THE 21ST CENTURY

GOWHER RIZVI
Series editor

This is the second volume in a series that examines important issues
of governance, public policy, and administration, highlighting innovative
practices and original research worldwide. All titles in the series will be
copublished by the Brookings Institution Press and the Ash Institute for
Democratic Governance and Innovation, housed at Harvard University's
John F. Kennedy School of Government.

Decentralizing Governance: Emerging Concepts and Practices,
G. Shabbir Cheema and Dennis A. Rondinelli (2007)

April 2008

INNOVATIONS IN GOVERNMENT

Research, Recognition, and Replication

SANDFORD BORINS

editor

Sandford Borins (signature)

ASH INSTITUTE FOR DEMOCRATIC GOVERNANCE AND INNOVATION
John F. Kennedy School of Government
Harvard University

BROOKINGS INSTITUTION PRESS
Washington, D.C.

ABOUT BROOKINGS

The Brookings Institution is a private nonprofit organization devoted to research, education, and publication on important issues of domestic and foreign policy. Its principal purpose is to bring the highest quality independent research and analysis to bear on current and emerging policy problems. Interpretations or conclusions in Brookings publications should be understood to be solely those of the authors.

Copyright © 2008

ASH INSTITUTE FOR DEMOCRATIC GOVERNANCE AND INNOVATION
HARVARD UNIVERSITY

All rights reserved. No part of this publication may be reproduced or transmitted in any form or by any means without permission in writing from the Brookings Institution Press, 1775 Massachusetts Avenue, N.W., Washington, D.C. 20036, www.brookings.edu.

Library of Congress Cataloging-in-Publication data

Innovations in government : research, recognition, and replication / Sandford Borins, editor.
    p.   cm. — (Innovative governance in the 21st century)
    Summary: "Answers questions on the future of government innovation and its effect on citizens and democratic governance by presenting a comprehensive approach to advancing the practice and study of innovation in government. Discusses new research on innovation, explores the impact of programs that recognize innovation, and considers challenges to replicating innovations"—Provided by publisher.
    Includes bibliographical references and index.
    ISBN 978-0-8157-1377-7 (pbk. : alk. paper) 1. Political planning.
2. Organizational change. I. Borins, Sandford F., 1949–
    JF1525.P6I56 2008
    352.3'67—dc22   2007052018

9 8 7 6 5 4 3 2 1

The paper used in this publication meets minimum requirements of the American National Standard for Information Sciences—Permanence of Paper for Printed Library Materials: ANSI Z39.48-1992.

Typeset in Adobe Garamond

Composition by Cynthia Stock
Silver Spring, Maryland

Printed by R. R. Donnelley
Harrisonburg, Virginia

For Lila and Roy Ash

Contents

Foreword

The Innovations in American Government Program at the Kennedy School's Ash Institute was set up in 1986 in response to widespread concerns about the dangers to democracy arising from citizen apathy and consequent loss of trust in government. Over the years, the institute also has sought to restore citizen confidence and trust in government through the Innovations in American Government Awards Program, which recognizes, celebrates, and replicates the best innovations in government. Since the program was launched, 400 outstanding government innovations have been recognized, and the institute has awarded in excess of $20 million to disseminate and replicate these innovative ideas.

Perhaps it will not be an exaggeration to claim that the attempt to make government effective through innovation is fast becoming a worldwide movement toward effective good governance. The program has been widely replicated, with sister programs in Brazil, Chile, China, Kenya, Mexico, Peru, the Philippines, and South Africa, and awards programs such as this have emerged as a major tool for promoting government innovation. Nor can one deny the Innovations in American Government Program's transformative impact on the way in which the public purpose is realized and governance delivered.

Governance today is no longer what it used to be twenty years ago, even though the public purpose of government has remained the same. Today, the combined resources and expertise of government, civil society, and the market are harnessed in co-producing the governance of society. Although it is perhaps commonplace, it bears repeating that these innovations in government have helped to bring about a paradigm shift and fundamentally altered the way in which societal governance is delivered. These innovations have demonstrated that the governance of society is no longer the sole prerogative of the government—the public purpose is today being advanced through the combined effort of all three sectors in society; governments have adopted the principle of competition and are outsourcing many tasks to take advantage of the competence offered by outside providers; governments are using market incentives (instead of setting up new agencies) to advance public policy to change public habits; departments and agencies have cut across their bureaucratic jurisdictions in order to provide seamless service to citizens; governments have become flexible and cost-effective by introducing cost budgeting and simplifying procedures; governments now emphasize outcomes and not merely outputs; they are delivering quality services through the introduction of the International Standards Organization (ISO) benchmarks and have unleashed a plethora of innovations such as the citizens charter, public sector service report cards, and participatory budgeting; governments are vigorously delegating, devolving, decentralizing, and deconcentrating their power and control of the purse, recognizing that problems are best solved by those who deal with them; and governments, through the extensive application of information technology, have cut the cost of transaction and are delivering service to the door steps of citizens.

It is easy to see why government innovation has caught the imagination of government and the citizens alike around the world. Innovations are not exported from "donor" countries but rather are "homegrown" in response to local problems; they are ideologically unencumbered, not necessarily tied to market-based solutions or hostile to the market. Because innovations address real problems facing citizens, their application usually confers a perceptible and immediate relief to the citizens. It is therefore scarcely surprising that government innovations are fast becoming a global movement.

The celebration of the twentieth anniversary of the Innovations in American Government Program is also the occasion for both retrospection and looking forward. We are delighted that many of the government innovations that have been recognized are now widely regarded as standard operating procedure. The program shows that public servants are prolific innovators. And what is really remarkable is that, unlike in the private sector, public servants innovate not because of financial incentives or personal rewards, but because of a public service ethos—the simple desire to serve the citizens. Many governments are today more efficient, transparent, and accountable than they were twenty years ago; they are nimble, responsive, and cost conscious, but they are also able to solve problems and respond to the differentiated needs of diverse citizens. At the same time, however, it cannot be denied that efficiency and equity have not always gone together. Going forward, much remains to be done. We must ensure that governments fulfill their core responsibilities as guarantors of social justice; that government innovations must strengthen and nurture our democratic institutions and processes; and that the habit of innovation remains deeply ingrained in the culture of public service. But if the past twenty years of recognizing innovation in government tells us anything, it is that the country—and the world—is up to the challenge. In that spirit, the Ash Institute looks forward to a future of highlighting, celebrating, and seeding innovation and democracy domestically and globally.

I am particularly grateful to Professor Sandford Borins, the author of the classic study *Innovating with Integrity: How Local Heroes Are Transforming American Government* (1998), who has generously given his time to edit this volume and to lead a group of eminent scholars to reflect on the successes and challenges of government innovation. I am also completely beholden to the contributing authors who are all members of the Innovations community and have supported our work throughout the years. This book, of course, would not have been possible without the help of my colleagues at the Ash Institute. Christina Marchand worked tirelessly and enthusiastically with the authors to ensure that they all met the grueling deadlines. Thanks also to Marty Mauzy, Tim Burke, Carla Chrisfield, James Cooney, Jessica Engelman, Dan Gilbert, Eric Goodwin, Gizelle Gopez, Maureen Griffin, Kate Hoagland, Bruce Jackan, Rebecca Kalauskas, Emily Kaplan, Kara O'Sullivan, Jason Pryde, Andre Rolle, and Susan Valaskovic. I am lucky and privileged to have them as colleagues. At Brookings Institution Press, Chris Kelaher, senior acquisitions editor, provided helpful advice, and editors Katherine Scott and Elizabeth Forsyth, with Janet Walker, managing editor, assisted in giving the final product consistency and precision. To all, I am deeply indebted.

GOWHER RIZVI
Director, Ash Institute for Democratic Governance
 and Innovation
John F. Kennedy School of Government
Harvard University

1

Introduction

SANDFORD BORINS

The Festschrift, or tribute volume, is a well-recognized academic genre: an opportunity for colleagues, admirers, and intellectual fellow travelers to pay tribute, in print, to the scholarly achievements of an eminent member of their field. At its best, the Festschrift aspires to more than eulogy. It uses the occasion of a retirement or other significant milestone to advance the state of knowledge in the discipline. The homage to excellent scholarship takes the fitting form of further scholarship and new research. Though we are honoring a distinguished program that has come of age, not a venerable scholar who has reached retirement, our goal for this volume remains that of a Festschrift. Collectively, we hope to advance the state of scholarship on innovation in government, in tribute to a program that has fostered, and continues to foster, both the practice of innovation and its study.

A Festschrift generally begins in retrospect, with valedictory accounts of the honoree's illustrious career. The sense is of summation, of the final words of a chapter soon to be closed. We, too, will look back, but our focus is at least as much on the present and the future, as our subject enters its third decade with ambition, productivity, and relevance undiminished.

The Innovations in American Government Awards Program began in 1985 with the first in a series of annual grants from the Ford Foundation to the Kennedy School of Government to conduct a program of awards for innovations in state and local government. The foundation's objective was ambitious and, in an era of "government *is* the problem" rhetoric, determinedly proactive. It sought to counter declining public confidence in government by highlighting innovative and effective programs. At a time of public-service bashing and highly publicized governmental failures, the program would seek out, and publicize, the good news in government.

From its inception, however, the program recognized the need for more than mere boosterism. The grants also included funding to disseminate information about winning programs, thus encouraging replication, and dedicated funds to support research on innovation in government. These three strands—recognition, replication, research—are the source of the program's continuing influence and vitality.

The first ten winners were announced in 1986. Since that time, the program's scope has widened dramatically. In 1995 applications from the federal government were made eligible for consideration. In 2001 the Ford Foundation transformed its annual grants to an endowment of $50 million. It also built on its successful experience in the United States by providing support for innovations awards programs in Brazil, Chile, China, East Africa, Mexico, Peru, the Philippines, and South Africa. The Kennedy School program, meanwhile, has become instrumental in the Global Innovators Network, established to help government innovators in all these countries, and beyond, share their experiences. Finally, in 2003 Roy L. Ash, who reshaped the Bureau of the Budget into the Office of Management and Budget and served as its initial director under Presidents Nixon and Ford, provided a generous endowment to create the Ash Institute for Democratic Governance and Innovation, of which the awards program became a part. The new name reflects a new focus on the principles and practices of democratic institutions, both in the United States and internationally—a change in perspective and priorities that is proving no less timely than the Ford Foundation's own founding initiative.

Two Decades of Innovation

The original impetus for the Innovations in American Government Awards Program may well have been defensive. In retrospect, however, it seems clear that the Ford Foundation's emphasis on innovation was also prescient. The twenty years of the program's existence have witnessed waves of change of almost unprecedented magnitude, driven by the twin engines of globalization and information technology, with innovation as both forerunner and consequence. With the spread of the Internet and its ancillary communication technologies, the conversion of the former Soviet Union and its satellites to more market-based economies and more democratic modes of governance, and similar shifts in developing countries throughout the world, billions more people are now participating in the global economy and in democratic governance than two decades ago. These seismic shifts have affected, and continue to affect, virtually every corner of the private sector, making innovation a condition of survival (Friedman 2005).

The public sector has been equally transformed, though perhaps in ways more visible to students of government than to the average citizen. Analysts have categorized these changes under a number of rubrics, including "New Public Management," "Reinventing Government," "Administrative Reform," and "Citizen-Centered Governance." Although there has been considerable debate among practitioners and academics about the precise meaning of these terms, there is now some consensus that they denote changes in the structure of government institutions, applications of new technology and private-sector production methodologies, an emphasis on defining and measuring the performance of government, and new patterns of involvement of the private and third sectors in governance. The noted public administration scholar Donald Kettl (2005) has gone so far as to define the sum of these phenomena as nothing less than a global public management revolution. And it was in the throes of this revolution that the awards program came of age, its applicants often literally the vanguard of reform or reinvention. What is more, the program itself became an agent in the process it was witnessing, its "three Rs" of recognition, replication, and research further disseminating innovative ideas and practices and promoting a culture of innovation within the public sector that has now become a virtual creed.

The "Kennedy School School": Two Decades of Innovation Scholarship

Clearly the Ford Foundation envisaged the important role scholarship had to play in enabling the replication of innovations (through analysis, contextualization, and conceptualization), but it may not have foreseen the contribution the awards program itself would make to that scholarship through the database its applicant pool would generate. The raw material that database has provided to scholars, coupled with the foundation's generous research support, has in fact produced a significant and distinctive body of writing about innovation in government, in effect the Kennedy School school. To understand how it has done so we need to look briefly at the awards program's structure and methodology, before returning to the place that the Kennedy School school has staked out for itself in the field of public administration scholarship.

The design of the awards program itself has created incentives for gathering a large amount of valuable data. This is true of both the large number of initial applications and the amount of detailed information elicited about the best of them. To ensure that the net is cast widely, the awards are not limited by either policy area or theme. The initial application form is short and easily completed, asking only for a brief description of the program, the nature of its innovation, and information about clients, budget, achievements, and replication. Program staff publicize the awards extensively and watch the media closely for emerging trends and leaders, proactively contacting public servants who are mentioned. The participation of the Ford Foundation and Harvard University made the awards program prestigious from its inception, and the enthusiastic endorsement of the Clinton administration, beginning in 1995, further raised its profile.

As the applicants are narrowed down to semifinalists and then finalists, the program requires more information about the innovation, including detailed financial and evaluative or audit data, as well as particulars of the innovative process itself (the genesis of the idea, the organizational structure used, and the process of gathering support and overcoming opposition). The finalists are all subjected to a two-day site visit by a recognized expert in the field. The judges read the site visit reports and hear presentations by the finalists. The winnowing process thus produces a substantial body of information about the top-ranking applicants (Borins 1998, pp. 12–18).

Because the awards program casts its net so widely and generates so much interest, we can be confident that its pool of applicants represents the range of trends in innovations in government. One way to categorize innovations is by policy area, and the awards include all policy areas. When the awards were restricted to state and local government, there were substantial numbers of applications in such areas of subnational government activity as environment and energy management, community building (policing, housing, economic development), social services, and education. Expansion of the program to the federal government added traditional areas of federal responsibility such as defense and economic regulation. As trends manifested themselves, the applicant pool reflected their influence. So when community policing became a growing trend, there was an upsurge of applications in that area, proving the effectiveness of the program in maintaining its relevance.

A second way to classify government innovations is in terms of their comprehensiveness within their own jurisdictions, and by this measure, too, the applicant pool has proved representative. Government-wide innovation denotes an initiative established centrally to be put in place in all departments. This category would include various aspects of administrative reform such as procurement reform or performance reporting and evaluation. All of these have been amply represented, at both the local and federal levels. The program also receives applications arising from organizational "turnarounds," that is, instances where departments that were notably poor performers develop innovative practices while in the process of dramatic self-improvement. The third and most common type of application comes from local innovations that affect part of the operations of a given agency or agencies. Although these applications are local from the point of view of the applicant agency, when viewed nationally they become important markers of trends in a given policy area.

The database the program has generated is thus sustained, continuous, broadly inclusive across the fullest range of innovation types, and—at the level of the finalist applicants—fine-grained. Its strength can be judged by the range and quality of the scholarship it has supported. Michael Barzelay, in *Breaking through Bureaucracy* (1992, rev. 2002), drew on it to undertake a detailed study of Minnesota's reform of an administrative support organization and used this to develop an early conceptualization of New Public Management. Eugene Bardach, in *Getting Agencies to Work Together* (1998), used the awards to identify a number of successful interagency partnerships and, on the basis of subsequent interviews, developed a set of smart practices for interagency collaboration. Jack Donahue's *Making Washington Work* (1999) took a number of award-winning federal programs as subjects of further study, using these cases to demonstrate how successful innovations could be realized in the complicated Washington environment. Robert D. Behn, in his article "Management by Groping Along" (1988) and his subsequent book *Leadership Counts* (1991), drew on cases from the innovation awards program to conceptualize a model of public management by "groping along," in which innovative agency leaders set out a broad vision and then respond adaptively to changing circumstances in order to realize it. Sandford Borins's *Innovating with Integrity* (1998) examined the overall characteristics of a large sample of the best applications to the program, as well as the particular characteristics of programs in a variety of policy areas, to generate a quantitatively based typology of innovative processes, organizations, and leaders. And this is only a partial list of authors whose writings make up the Kennedy School school.

Beyond their drawing on a common database, however, what characterizes the authors of the Kennedy School school? When we analyze this substantive body of work it becomes clear that these scholars share a set of intellectual premises. First, they uniformly conclude that the innovations they have studied have improved the performance of government and are valued accordingly by the public. Second, they challenge the stereotype of the risk-averse bureaucrat awaiting orders from her political masters and instead collectively paint a portrait of entrepreneurial public servants making their own efforts to determine public expectations and needs and taking the initiative to meet them. Third, they see innovation as an equal-opportunity phenomenon capable of being initiated at all levels of government, from the elected politician to the frontline worker. They are, in short, innovation optimists who see in what the public administration scholars Christopher Pollitt and Geert Bouckaert (2000) have termed "micro-improvements" an important subject for research and an important source of knowledge for practitioners. It is a position that marks them as dissenters from much of the scholarship in the field.

Research on innovation in government can, of course, be seen as a subfield of public administration scholarship. In the last two decades, many public administration scholars have focused their attention on the government-wide innovations that have characterized the New Public Management, and their findings have generally been critical. We might call them the innovation skeptics (or pessimists). Steven Kelman (2007a) has discussed the reasons for their criticism. These include hostility to public management practices that draw on management practices of the private sector, hostility to contracting out or entering partnerships with the private sector, a judgment that respecting traditional public-sector process constraints (equity, fairness, probity) always outweighs enhanced effectiveness, public satisfaction, or cost efficiency, and a view that innovative or entrepreneurial public managers are undemocratically usurping the powers of elected politicians. Concentrating their critical fire on systemic reform initiatives, these scholars have generally ignored the local initiatives, agency turnarounds, or successful local examples of systemic reform that have been the focus of attention for the Kennedy School school. Indeed, Pollitt and Bouckaert's (2000, p. 191) comprehensive study of public management reform closes with an admission of precisely what is missing from this analysis:

> And yet there is another side to public management reform, which has a more solid and sensible persona. The pressure, the rhetoric, the loosening of the old ways—all these have combined to give many public servants the opportunity to make changes which make local sense to *them*. Such "improvements" may occasionally be self-serving, but often they are substantially other-directed and result in gains in productivity, service quality, transparency, fairness, or some other important value. . . . [O]ne of the major limitations of our approach—and the approaches of many others who have concentrated on big reforms and big ideas—is that they capture very little of this micro-improvement. As some of the most successful reform leaders in several countries have recognized, a crucial ingredient of a successful reform strategy is that it should create and sustain conditions in which small improvements—many of them unforeseen and unforeseeable—can flourish.

Where the academic analysts of comprehensive reform have generally tended to ignore or dismiss the significance of successful local innovations, other scholars have criticized research devoted to them as being hostage to the "best-practices" tradition, with all its associated limitations (Lynn 1996; Overman and Boyd 1994). The point here is not that the innovations are negligible, but rather that they are unreliable, unstable, or insufficiently analyzed as possible models. The general critique of best-practice research is threefold: it rarely attempts to verify self-reported claims; organizations lauded for best practices today may, without warning, fail tomorrow; and best-practice research focuses solely on the characteristics of successful organizations, rather than comparing the successful with the mediocre and the failing. In a statistical context, the latter point is referred to as selection on the dependent variable. In regression analysis, it is desirable to have as much variation as possible in observations of the dependent variable; in this instance, organizational performance. Best-practice research, by focusing only on well-performing organizations, violates this principle (Kelman 2007a).

The first two criticisms, as they apply to the Kennedy School school, can be addressed through reference to the awards program's audit process, which rigorously verifies applicants' self-reported claims. The program also revisits previous years' semifinalists, finalists, and winners and has consistently found a very high percentage of them still in operation and flourishing (Borins 1998, p. 115). Selection on the dependent variable remains a more salient criticism of any research using applications to the innovation awards program. Such research may fail to compare successful innovations with unsuccessful attempts, and it may fail to compare organizations that produce innovations (successful or otherwise) to those that do not. We offer two partial lines of defense. The awards program explicitly asks successful applicants to detail what obstacles they overcame and how they did so and which obstacles remain. At the very least, this information points to reasons for unsuccessful attempted innovations. Additionally, the awards program consistently draws a number of "turnaround" cases. By definition a turnaround is a before-and-after experiment in a given organization, allowing the researcher to compare a set of policies or practices associated with failure to those associated with success. The problem with individual turnarounds, however, is that they are usually overdetermined: turnaround leaders typically implement a package of reforms, and it can be difficult to establish which are necessary and which of all possible subsets are sufficient.

Despite these defenses, the critics of the Kennedy School school of innovation research do have an undeniable point. It has focused its attention on successful innovations and has had little to say about the populations of agencies within which these success stories have unfolded. Our response is to identify this and several other key areas as fruitful ground for new research initiatives. We clearly have important questions still to answer. One of the main goals of the awards program has always been replication, but do we know whether successful replication is in fact occurring? Or what factors are most likely to lead to it? The program focuses on individual innovations, but there are instances when a particular organization produces a number of them. What characterizes an innovative organizational culture in a large government agency?[1] Can this, too, be replicated? The awards program itself has now been replicated internationally. Is the experience of the programs in other countries, and the data generated, similar to that of programs in the United States, both in terms of the nature of the innovations in a given policy area and of the innovative process? The contributors to this volume all seek to advance the state of government innovation research in these directions. Their desire to do so, and the range of their inquiries, is itself a tribute to the vitality of the Kennedy School school.

The chapters that follow not only demonstrate a range of analytical approaches and critical concerns but also share a common impetus to raise "big-picture" questions. Many of the contributors explicitly address issues of methodology and conceptualization. Others offer international comparisons as a means of widening the context for discussion. All seek to build on the foundation of the case-based deductive research that is one of the awards program's most important legacies. And all demonstrate their continued adherence to the innovation optimism that is a hallmark of the Kennedy School school. We write here in the belief that understanding how innovations in government happen continues to be a serious challenge to scholarship and an important source of practitioner knowledge. In this, we hope we pay fitting tribute to the spirit that has animated the Innovations in American Government Awards Program from its inception.

Book Overview

Edited books often lack coherence, including chapters that are loosely oriented around a common theme and are presented in no obvious order. That cannot be said of the chapters of this book and their order of presentation, which present a coherent narrative.

We begin, appropriately, with origins. In the next chapter, Jonathan Walters provides a history of the Innovations in American Government Awards Program's first twenty years. He opens by discussing the Ford Foundation's intentions in establishing the program as a response to skeptical political and public attitudes in the mid-1980s toward the public sector. He shows how the Ford Foundation and the Kennedy School built a partnership whereby the Kennedy School would manage the awards program on behalf of the Ford Foundation and the Ford Foundation would support research on innovation spearheaded by

---

1. Paul Light (1998) studied a sample of twenty-six nonprofit organizations and government agencies in Minnesota that displayed innovative organizational cultures. He could not find large government agencies that met his selection criteria; the seven government agencies that did were atypically small, autonomous, and market-driven.

the Kennedy School. Walters then recounts the evolution of the program to include federal government involvement, its achievement of endowment funding from the Ford and Ash foundations, and its new focus on democratic governance. The chapter concludes with a discussion of future challenges, in particular that of maintaining a strong link between recognition and research.

Chapter 3 moves from organizational history to intellectual history. In it, Steven Kelman evaluates the Kennedy School school of research on innovation in government and its relationship to traditional public administration scholarship and mainstream organization theory. He finds that the Kennedy School school indeed constitutes a distinctive body of research but also finds that it has not built bridges to either public administration scholarship or to organization theory. Kelman is critical of much traditional public administration, in particular because of its focus on, and occasional glorification of, the constraints on public servants, and sees the Kennedy School school, with its emphasis on public servants' taking the initiative to improve government performance, as a valuable alternative. Kelman concludes with some recommendations for future directions in research on government innovation, in particular utilizing the concepts developed in organization theory and employing methodologies such as laboratory studies that use practicing civil servants and statistical studies that include in their samples innovation failures as well as successes.

Subsequent chapters all extend the work of the Kennedy School school in a variety of new directions, including innovations in democratic governance (chapter 4), innovations overseas (chapter 5), innovative organizations (chapter 6), the dynamics and sustainability of innovations (chapter 7), the replication of innovations (chapters 8 and 9), and innovations within a population of organizations (chapter 9).

Chapter 4, by Archon Fung, is particularly relevant to the awards program's evolution as the Ash Institute for Democratic Governance and Innovation. Fung begins by arguing that, to a great extent, the program began with a focus on innovations within the four walls of government agencies—in effect, innovations in production processes for government services. He then draws examples of innovations recognized by the awards program to show that in fact a considerable number focused on the role citizens could play as co-producers in areas such as environmental management, health care, and policing. Fung continues this theme by looking at innovations in public consultation such as deliberative polling, study circles, and citizens' assemblies, many of which have come to the fore outside the United States. He concludes by discussing some of the challenges inherent in citizens' participation and how they can be resolved.

Chapter 5, by Marta Ferreira Santos Farah and Peter Spink, follows logically from Archon Fung's. It focuses on Brazil, a country where the strengthening of democratic institutions and the construction of citizenship are important

aspects of innovation in government. Building on the work of the Center for
Public Administration and Government at the São Paulo School of Business
Administration (EAESP-FGV), where the Ford Foundation has supported the
Innovations in Subnational Government Program since 1996, they discuss patterns and processes of innovation in that country. They also look for answers to
the question of whether the Brazilian experience is similar to the American, in
terms of both the nature of the innovations and the nature of the innovative
process (for example, sustainability and replication). They find that although
innovations are deeply connected to the social, economic, and political characteristics of each country, they are also able to communicate across language, cultural, and political boundaries.

The awards program's basic unit of analysis is the innovative program. Going
beyond individual programs, however, we have observed from studying the
applications that some organizations give rise to a series of innovative programs,
leading us to hypothesize that they developed a culture that is particularly supportive of innovation. One such organization is the U.S. Department of Labor
under Secretary Robert Reich (from 1993 to 1997), which was both a frequent
applicant and a frequent winner during the first three years the awards program
was open to the federal government (1995 to 1997). Jack Donahue, the author
of chapter 6, was assistant secretary for policy and counselor to the secretary of
labor at the time. Drawing on his own recollections, he explains the factors that
created and sustained innovation in the Department of Labor: excellent political
appointments, management systems that gave senior executives latitude to be
innovative and made them accountable for results, and a culture that encouraged innovation at all levels of the organization. Donahue also focuses on
Robert Reich as a person of passionate conviction with a great willingness to
take risk who thus fostered an innovative organization.

Chapter 7, by Eugene Bardach, deals with the processes by which innovations that create interagency collaborative capacity are established and sustained.
Bardach's 1998 book, *Getting Agencies to Work Together,* had as its empirical
basis an analysis of nineteen cases drawn from the Innovations in American
Government Awards Program. In his research for this chapter, Bardach revisited
the cases he analyzed a decade ago and found that some were still thriving, others were coping, still others were being buffeted by external forces, and some
were dying. Bardach then discusses smart practices for establishing interagency
collaborative capacity (ICCs), for example, strategies for acquiring resources,
building momentum, and sequencing developmental steps. He then considers
the sustainability of ICCs in the face of a variety of external shocks, such as the
loss of political support following election turnover or a change in fiscal circumstances, envisaging a dialectical process of challenges and responses. Bardach

concludes by suggesting an entirely new direction for further research on developmental processes for ICCs, namely, computer simulation.

Chapter 8, by Robert D. Behn, deals at a conceptual level with replication, which is one of the primary goals of the awards program. Replication poses a challenge to both the exporter and importer: for the former, to articulate a causal explanation of why the innovation works, and for the latter, to go beyond a superficial understanding of the innovation to grasp its essential components and how they can be adapted to a new context. Behn also analyzes the vocabulary of adoption to draw distinctions among diffusion, transfer, propagation, and replication. Much of what is involved in an innovation is tacit knowledge; the ultimate challenge to the exporters of public-sector innovations is to communicate tacit knowledge, and the challenge to would-be importers is to understand it and then apply it to their own context. Behn illustrates his argument by contrasting the successful adaptation by many New York City agencies of the Police Department's CompStat (comparative statistics) performance strategy with less successful attempts by many city governments to emulate Baltimore's CitiStat version of that strategy.

We continue the focus on replication in chapter 9. Jean Hartley examines the Beacon Scheme, which is an English central-government program to recognize, reward, and disseminate excellence and innovation in local government and other local public services by sharing knowledge about good or promising practices by local authorities and their partners. Hartley's chapter is based on extensive research on the Beacon Scheme conducted at the University of Warwick. The research project examines award applications, learning from the innovations and the nature and extent of improvement. The research has looked at all 388 local governments in England to determine which apply for the scheme and why, thus providing an example of innovation research that looks at an entire population, rather than just the innovative organizations within that population. Hartley outlines a model of knowledge transfer that has similarities to Behn's discussion and then applies it to knowledge transfer in the program. A key result is that local governments found "open days" held by Beacon award winners to be the most effective means of dissemination and the most likely to lead to the transfer of tacit knowledge. The chapter concludes with a report on what local governments learned at Beacon Scheme events, changes they implemented as a result, and their assessments of the success of such changes, thereby providing evidence not only on the diffusion of innovation but also on the extent to which the innovations affected performance.

Our book concludes with two chapters from different, albeit complementary, perspectives. In chapter 10, Gowher Rizvi, director of the Ash Institute, reviews the contributions of the innovations awards program and Ash Institute to improving the performance of government and speculates about their future roles. He discusses the importance to society of trust in government and how democracy is the form of government most likely to produce public trust in the future. He shows how the Ash Institute's new focus on democratic governance, both in the United States and abroad, responds to the challenges of governance, especially in diverse and pluralistic societies. He then summarizes the key themes that have emerged from the innovations awards: collaborative arrangements, not only within governments but between government and civil society; citizens as consumers; market incentives; and flexible management techniques. Rizvi sees innovations as means to the ultimate objectives of government, namely, enhancing the quality of life for citizens, guaranteeing social justice, and strengthening democratic governance. Innovations must be judged by their ability to fulfill these objectives.

In chapter 11, Sandford Borins, drawing on the previous chapters, illuminates future directions for research on innovation in government and governance. These include research on what is happening at the leading edge in terms of both governance and government, in particular, research involving international comparisons, in both economically advanced and developing countries; research about the developmental dynamics of innovations; research about the diffusion of innovations, which depends on information about the populations within which innovations are introduced; and research on the relationship between innovation and improved performance at the organizational level. He concludes by discussing how data already gathered by the Innovations in American Government Awards Program could be used to explore some of these questions and suggests additional data that would have to be gathered to answer the others. Thus, there is a full agenda for research on democratic governance and innovation, and the Ash Institute will play an important role in the next generation of that research.

2

Twenty Years of Highlighting
Excellence in Government

JONATHAN WALTERS

"Stagflation," gas lines, and Americans being held hostage in Iran were just a few of the more depressing lowlights of the American experience in the late 1970s—an America that was, not incidentally, still in the process of recovering from a disastrous war. In an infamous speech in 1979, President Jimmy Carter described it all as a "malaise."

And so when, in 1980, Ronald Reagan famously declared it to be "morning in America," lots of Americans were ready to listen. But if it was a new, more positive dawning for America, American government still wasn't having a particularly good day.

"A Pretty Good Pounding"

While the soon-to-be president may have been high on his country's and countrymen's prospects, he was anything but when it came to government's role in helping to ensure that promising future. Another of his famous declarations among a string of them aimed at government: "We must not look to government to solve our problems. Government is the problem."

"Government was taking a pretty good pounding in the late 1970s and early 1980s," says Mark Abramson, who has recently stepped down as head of the IBM Foundation for the Business of Government and in 1983 was in the process of helping to create a new organization called the Council for Excellence

13

in Government, in part to counteract the overall impression that American government was not a particularly high-performing institution. "Government certainly wasn't being recognized for the good things it did," says Abramson.

Reagan's skepticism about government's role in the nation's progress translated rather powerfully into policy, especially as it related to intergovernmental relations and affairs. As the president took aim at a host of New Deal–era programs generally, he focused on intergovernmental policy and fiscal affairs very specifically.

Even as he was pushing responsibility (and costs) for various government programs down to the state and local level, he was also eliminating General Revenue Sharing, a block grant program started by Richard Nixon that had funneled millions in no-strings-attached federal dollars to cities and states.

It was an interesting confluence of forces: decreased confidence in government (the Harris poll's "alienation index" from that era indicates that a fluctuating but solid majority of Americans felt isolated from and neglected by government), along with a steady squeeze in intergovernmental transfers (outside of entitlement programs), in concert with a steady increase in the work that states and localities were being called on to do.

Reaganites called this "the new federalism." Advocates for states and localities called it, more colorfully, "shift-and-shaft federalism."

Whatever one's characterization of the new approach to government and intergovernmentalism, the equation arguably added up to this: Americans—led by their critic in chief—were losing confidence in government, at a time when state and local governments were being asked (or required) to do more of the public's business, even as the federal government's fiscal transfer spigot was being cranked closed.

It was against that backdrop, says David Arnold, that he took a new position as a program officer with the Ford Foundation in the spring of 1984. "This was the height of the Reagan years, and Ford was trying to figure out how to respond. I was brought on board to help develop a governance program."

The Ford Foundation, says Arnold, was interested in improving the image of government, particularly state and local governments, which, when compared to the private sector, were being generally painted as incapable of reinventing themselves in the face of stiff new challenges. The Ford Foundation wanted to set up some program to counter that popular wisdom, says Arnold, and was ready to invest millions of dollars in the proposition.

Ford had started to get interested in the cause as early as 1981, says the president of the Ford Foundation, Susan Berresford, who at the time was vice president for U.S. programs. "It came with the beginning of the Reagan administration, which brought this huge shift in authority for programs to the state and local level." The idea, says Berresford, was to try and counter the public perception of states and localities as "less innovative and more subject to corruption. The foundation just didn't believe that."

Arnold says that on his arrival he was handed a memo outlining the possibility of some sort of program aimed at highlighting and celebrating the fact that state and local governments in the United States could rise to the challenges they faced and that the country was peppered with smart, energetic public officials perfectly capable of figuring out new, innovative ways of doing the public's business.

To vet that general idea, Arnold canvassed a wide variety of government interest groups, ranging from the National Academy of Public Administration to the National Civic League. "I went to all the 'goo-goos,'" says Arnold, "the good government groups, to ask their opinion about how Ford might invest in improving the U.S. state and local government brand. As I talked to people, we developed some overarching ideas that we thought might be worth pursuing." And one of the ideas that kept surfacing was that of recognizing specific states and localities across a wide range of program and policy areas for doing a particular job in a relatively new yet proven-to-be-effective way.

At the same time he was talking to the "goo-goos," Arnold was also touching base with schools of public affairs and administration nationwide, from the LBJ School of Public Affairs at the University of Texas at Austin to the Maxwell School at Syracuse University.

At Harvard's John F. Kennedy School of Government something seemed to click. "At the Kennedy School there was real intellectual interest in this topic," says Arnold. "People like Graham Allison [then dean of the school], [the faculty members] Pete Zimmerman, Mark Moore, and Walter Broadnax—they picked right up on the fact that there weren't really any good case studies about successful innovation in public management or on how innovation takes place in the public sector. There was literature on private sector innovation, but not much from the governmental arena."

If Arnold found a group receptive to the notion of learning more about how the public sector innovates, the Kennedy School cabal was decidedly cool toward the awards side of the program. "Our initial response was, 'We don't do awards,'" says Pete Zimmerman.

In fact, at the time virtually nobody did awards, at least not on a national and across-policy scale. Mark Abramson notes that, at the time, the Fund for the City of New York had a modest program that recognized a handful of high-performing city employees. Likewise, various organizations representing specific public-sector professionals would recognize certain stars. "But there was no award that crossed all policy boundaries and that actually recognized specific jurisdictions," says Abramson.

But if Ford wanted awards and the Kennedy School wanted case studies and research, neither side had foreclosed the possibility of working something out, says Zimmerman. He called Arnold to discuss how the two organizations might blend their respective goals into one program.

Among those involved in the discussion was Walter Broadnax, now president of Clark Atlanta University, who says that a flurry of draft proposals and some shuttle diplomacy helped to hone the concept. "We met with Susan Berresford, and she said she wanted a program that would bring attention to the important domestic issues of our time, while recognizing those men and women who were dedicating their lives to struggling with these problems."

As discussion progressed, faculty at the school started to swing around to the notion that a marriage between an awards program and a school of public policy and administration might work, in particular because such a program would mean a steady flow of fresh new cases about government, especially government success stories. "In the past most of our cases were about failure because academics are just more interested in failure," says Arnold Howitt, who was one of the faculty members involved early on in discussions about the Ford proposal. Not only were most of the existing cases at that time about failure, says Howitt, but they were also getting pretty stale.

In the end, says Zimmerman, the Kennedy School proposed a deal aimed at satisfying the requirements of both Ford and the school, while hewing to the overarching cause of the concept: "We negotiated a trade," says Zimmerman. "We said, you give us money for research and case studies, and we'll administer an awards program."

Based on that understanding, says Broadnax, the Kennedy School shipped off a proposal that included money for both academic research and case studies and also for an awards program that would grant ten $100,000 prizes to innovative government programs, as requested by Ford.

"And then we didn't hear anything," says Broadnax. "I got scared. I was afraid that what we'd proposed was just too huge."

It was a late spring afternoon in 1984. Broadnax was sitting at his desk, sifting through his pile of regular mail. Tucked among the routine correspondence was an envelope from the Ford Foundation. He tore it open. Inside was a check for $1 million made out to the Kennedy School. "I'd never seen a check for $1 million before," Broadnax says with a laugh. It was the official launch of the Innovations in American Government Awards Program.

The Scramble

Money in hand, it was time to build both the administrative and the intellectual infrastructure for the program. Some of the fundamentals had been decided.

The organizational home for the program would be the Kennedy School's State, Local, and Intergovernmental Center (which would later become the Taubman Center).

The awards would recognize innovative programs in specific jurisdictions. Susan Berresford notes that the emphasis on rewarding programs as opposed to people was very intentional. "Even though it's more media friendly to give awards to people," says Berresford, "we decided to recognize programs, because very often more than one or two people are involved in pushing a successful idea." Ten winning jurisdictions would get $100,000 apiece.

But beyond that, significant questions loomed, including how to find potential candidates, get them to apply, and then winnow down the applications. And just what was "innovation" anyway?

Howitt says a small working group started meeting weekly to hammer out administrative details and to think through exactly what the program ought to be recognizing, along with what the application and selection process should look like.

Especially helpful to the team on the organizational side was Teresa Cader, a former Kennedy School MPA (master's in public administration) and now a nationally recognized poet. Cader was recruited by Zimmerman not only for her knowledge of government but also for her extensive experience running a statewide competitive arts awards program. "We started in September 1984," says Cader. "We knew we were running a competition, but we had no idea how many applicants we might get or the design of the process for culling through them. A lot of it we just invented as we went along."

Among the working group's first jobs was hammering out an application, both the physical design and what it would be asking for, says Howitt. "We had to develop the criteria and then decide on how to organize the application. So this extended brain trust would have lunch together once a week and argue about this stuff. In the case of the criteria, we wanted to make sure that this was not going to be an award just for some clever policy idea. It had to be a program with a track record, an operating history. So it couldn't be brand-new."

In other words, says Pete Zimmerman, whatever "innovation" meant, programs that applied had to be able to show actual results. "Early on we had the sense that applicants had to show tangible performance. It couldn't be that they showed promise," he says.

As for the application itself, it had to be simple to fill out so that potential applicants wouldn't be discouraged from applying. The format that the working group settled on was one "you could fill out in an hour," says Howitt. Another decision the working group made was that applications, ultimately, had to come from the top. To be considered, applications would have to be signed off on by the chief elected executive of the jurisdiction applying. "It was our way of elevating the visibility of both our program [and] also the program within its own governmental setting," Zimmerman says.

In the end, the working group settled on a short set of criteria for assessing programs that they hoped would attract the kinds of applicants they were looking for. Programs had to be the first of their kind or at least best in class among jurisdictions pursuing some relatively new idea. They had to be able to show results. Finally, they had to have real potential for replication. "The idea of replicability was a natural," says Howitt. As a basic criterion, replicability would mean that what a jurisdiction was doing had to have implications beyond its own borders. And not incidentally, he says, replicability helped to fulfill Ford's goal that the awards would have broader impact beyond the winning jurisdiction.

Going Live

With basic criteria hammered out and an initial application in hand, it was time to go public. Broadnax, who had been named director of the new program, and Cader, its administrator, both started attending meetings of a variety of government interest groups, ranging from the National Conference of State Legislatures to the National League of Cities. The program also took out ads in professional journals and trade publications.

The response to the new program's proposition was surprisingly positive, says Cader. "We went out to a lot of association meetings around the country and talked about the program, and people were actually very interested and excited. After all, how often do people from state or local government get offered anything?"

While Broadnax and Cader worked the outside, Zimmerman worked the inside. "I was running the school's Executive Education Program at the time and so I had a good edge on a network of bright, ambitious public-sector practitioners. We did a bunch of mailings to them." And the ability to "dangle $100,000 in front of them didn't hurt at all," he says.

"The first step was to generate interest so people would play," says Broadnax. That was gelling nicely through the winter of 1984 and spring of 1985. "The second part was to build the infrastructure to review an unknown number of applications."

Building that infrastructure dove-tailed well with the Kennedy School's goals of getting faculty involved and tuned in to the potential research and teaching opportunities that would come with canvassing the country for new and proven good ideas. Since the school had always used a case study approach to teaching, it was a natural fit, says Broadnax, and a group of young and bright faculty members seemed very interested in what the program turned up. Again, some overriding principles drove the design of the selection process, says Cader. It had to be intellectually rigorous and also "transparent and fair."

The working group decided that teams of two or three Kennedy School mid-career MPA students working with faculty would review initial applications in specific policy areas and cull a total of about 100. The applicants that made the cut would be sent a more involved set of questions. (One indication of state and local enthusiasm about the awards, notes Cader, was that there was virtually no attrition among applicants that were asked to go through the more involved second-round process). Those applications would undergo even more intense scrutiny by Kennedy School faculty, to winnow the field to around twenty to twenty-five finalists.

How to settle on the winners, though, was a trickier proposition. Zimmerman says the Kennedy School did not want to be involved in the business of "picking winners," so two other key decisions were made. First, the program would create a committee of outside experts drawn from related fields, ranging from former state, federal, and local elected officials to outside policy experts. Second, to ensure final quality control, topic experts would be assigned the task of visiting the programs being considered as finalists and reporting their findings to the selection committee.

"I remember going to a little café on Brattle Street with Terry Cader," says Arn Howitt. "We spent about three hours inventing the rules for the site visits." Among the pair's overriding concerns: "How can one person know whether or not they're visiting a Potemkin Village? How can they verify a program's claims? How likely is it that they'll be screened out from talking to people who might not think the program is the greatest idea since sliced bread? That's when we decided to ask the applicants to identify critics [and] tell us about any news coverage or other independent reviews that might have been done of their programs."

As those kinds of details were being worked out, David Arnold suggested a meeting with a former Michigan governor, Michael Milliken, whom Arnold had gotten to know while on staff at the National Governors Association and thought might make a good chairman for the proposed national selection committee. A small group of innovations program staff went to Mackinac Island for a meeting with the former governor.

Milliken accepted the job. Now the call went out for selection committee members. "We put some real muscle on the committee," says Walter Broadnax: "Max Sherman from the LBJ School, Richard Capen, who was publisher of the *Miami Herald,* and Dorothy Ridings, journalist and past president of the U.S. League of Women Voters."

As details of the program fell into place, all it needed was applicants. "It was scary as hell," says Broadnax of the wait. "Because there were two worst-case scenarios: The first one is that we'd get fewer than ten applications. The other was we'd get 10,000."

By the day before the deadline, several hundred applications had been received. Another 800 came in just before the deadline—so many that courier trucks were clogging the local streets—and the ultimate total for the first round, in 1986, reached 1,500. The initial culling process worked well, and Kennedy School faculty stepped up to the plate to do the site visits and reports. Governor Milliken thought that, in addition to poring over site visit reports, it would be important for the national selection committee to hear directly from the applicants, and so a day was set aside for finalists to make presentations in Cambridge. Ten winners would be announced the following morning.

Thirty Winners Later

And so the program went for three years, with ten winning programs chosen in 1986, 1987, and 1988. What the first three years proved, clearly, was that there was no shortage of governments nationwide actively engaged in new kinds of problem solving. And it highlighted some truly ground-breaking work by people who otherwise would have continued to toil in obscurity.

Toby Herr, executive director of Project Match, a small welfare-to-work program based at the Cabrini-Green housing project in Chicago, infamous as a haven of chronic poverty and out-of-control criminal activity, a 1988 winner, says the recognition the program garnered was huge. "We were just a little demonstration program supported by the state, working with Northwestern University. The award put us on the map." And also, not incidentally, in the *New York Times*. In fact, Project Match became something of a welfare-to-work Mecca for others interested in the whole field of moving people off public assistance rolls and into full-time work.

Ellen Schall, who in the mid-1980s was head of New York City's Department of Juvenile Justice, says the awards program gave her something else she wanted: credibility within city government. She describes having to fight with upper-level executive staff to get Mayor Ed Koch's signature on her application because in upper executive circles her case management approach to working with young offenders was viewed as small, amorphous, and insignificant. "It was hugely ratifying," says Schall, who is now dean of the Robert F. Wagner Graduate School of Public Service at New York University and also serves on the national selection committee.

While the program was raising the visibility of individual award winners, it was also starting to pay immediate and significant dividends for the Kennedy School, according to those closely involved in the effort, such as Arn Howitt and Teresa Cader. "I think it changed the school dramatically," says Cader. "I think it established Harvard as a center for connecting scholars and practitioners. And I think faculty were stunned that they had so much to learn from practitioners, really smart people doing really important work out in states and localities." Furthermore, she adds, the program was a constant and refreshing reminder to students in the school's MPA program "that there were people out there doing very interesting things to promote good government" and, in the process, offered hope to students that a career in government would not consign them to dreary bureaucratic routine.

At the very least, the program established a new and positive flow of people and ideas in and out of the school, believes Arn Howitt. "I think it vastly surpassed expectations when it came to being inspirational for young students or those in the midcareer and executive education programs." In fact, the Kennedy School's newly started Executive Education Program began drawing people from the pool of winning applicants, he notes.

Broadening the Scope, Refining Lessons

In three years, the program had proved its potential as a way to find and highlight interesting work in states and localities and also to bring academics and practitioners together in a way that clearly energized each. What remained to be seen, though, was whether any concrete, identifiable lessons could be gleaned from winning programs about innovation and how those lessons might be translated effectively into both teaching and broader research.

Wrestling with that evolution in the innovations program would fall to a new leadership team, Alan Altshuler and Mark Zegans. Altshuler had arrived at the Kennedy School in 1988 to head up the new A. Alfred Taubman Center for State and Local Government. He asked Zegans, a recent Kennedy School graduate who had been working on a major budgeting project in Boston, to take over as director of the innovations program and think about how to push it further toward fulfilling its potential. Both had an acute interest not only in identifying examples of good government but also in figuring out how to make those examples into something of larger and more lasting value than a one-day event, with sporadic media coverage.

"So the program came to the end of the three years, and Ford had invested a couple of million bucks," says Zegans. "And what we'd found at the end of three years was some interesting people and some innovative programs. Ford liked that result but wasn't sure about where to go next, so we decided to take a year off." For one year, the program would accept no applications. Instead, program staff decided to use the time to analyze lessons learned so far—not only

those lessons that winners had to teach others in the public sector and in academia but also lessons about how the innovations program itself might be
redesigned to increase its reach and its influence.

Zegans says he made three discoveries that year that he thought might offer
avenues for progress. First, the winning programs had not been marketed effectively to government interest groups—governors or mayors, for example, the
very people who arguably stood to gain the most from learning about new and
successful ways to do the government's business.

Second, the effort had been fairly insular—that is, there'd been no effort to
reach out to other universities and academics as a way to begin creating a
broader community of interest and perhaps help to kindle a very specific academic interest in the notion of innovation as a discrete area of study.

Third, the concept of turning winning programs into good case studies had
languished.

Given the promising programs that had been uncovered so far, given the
potential for a wider broadcast of best practices, and given the potential for a
national, academic focus on the art and science of innovation itself, the awards
program was relaunched in 1990. Zegans says he and his staff pushed especially
hard on getting the word out to potential applicants in an effort to maintain the
healthy number of programs that had applied in past years. "Staffers like Caro-
line Marple and Liz Gianakos worked their tails off," says Zegans of the reener-
gized effort.

While the new push on attracting applicants was gearing up, Altshuler and
Zegans were also steering the program in a new direction by refining the application process in a way that would try to identify programs that represented
core changes in institutional practice versus smaller, quirkier notions championed by one or two people in an organization.

Indeed, some critics of the early awards perceived that too many went to
small "boutique" programs. The poster child for such small feel-good applicants
was the Prison Pet Partnership Program, a finalist in 1986, which was not
exactly predictive of a major overhaul in how the country planned to handle
criminal justice into the next century. However, it can sometimes be hard to
predict what might be a harbinger of huge changes, and a quick scan of early
winners turns up plenty along the lines of a 1988 winning program out of Vermont, an information technology system that connected a network of libraries
throughout the state. Although such a relatively small experiment in a small
place might be viewed as "boutique," it could also be seen as an example of an
early, civilian-level application of the not at all "boutique" Internet.

Thus, starting in the early 1990s there was a conscious push to recognize
programs with a little more immediate heft. Examples of the new approach

included programs such as Wisconsin's welfare-to-work effort, which would become a model for the welfare overhaul undertaken by the administration of Bill Clinton; CompStat, for computer comparison statistics, the data-driven approach to fighting crime in New York City, which would lead to a wave of "stat"-based change in public management in policy and program areas ranging from social services ("JobStat") to contracting out ("VendorStat") to managing entire cities ("CitiStat"); and Vermont's Restorative Justice Program, an early exemplar of a diversion-from-incarceration program that offered alternative sentencing for nonviolent minor offenders.

As the program regained momentum, Altshuler and Zegans also began a strong push in cooperation with Ford to reach out to other schools, organizing conferences at the LBJ School of Public Affairs, Duke University, the University of Washington, and the University of Wisconsin. In the process, says Zegans, the program was able to tap into experts on government and government transformation such as Robert D. Behn, now at the Kennedy School; Paul Light, now at New York State University; and Don Kettl, now at the University of Pennsylvania, each of whom would fix his academic sights on studying the nuts and bolts of how to improve government performance.

The effort to reach out to other academic institutions paid off with one other important benefit, says Zegans. It vastly broadened the pool of potential site visitors—an area of particular focus for the relaunched awards program. Zegans understood the value of strong site visit reports, so enlarging the stable of potential experts would serve the program well, as would the program's practice of sharing some of the best site visit reports with newly appointed site visitors.

At the same time, the program restarted the case study machine, much more actively mining winners and turning them into academic fodder, in particular, for the school's Executive Education Program.

It wasn't long before the notion that innovation was a discrete area of study that might catch on began to prove itself. *Innovation in American Government: Challenges, Opportunities, and Dilemmas,* coedited by Altshuler and Behn (1997), brought together a diverse set of scholars and practitioners—from Mark Moore and Malcom Sparrow to Ellen Schall and Olivia Golden, who held high-level positions in both local and federal social service systems (Golden recently stepped down as head of operations for New York State and has returned to doing research in social services at the Urban Institute)—to investigate a broad range of issues and ideas related to innovating in the public sector, both in theory and at the street level.

Sandford Borins looked at the human side of innovation in his 1998 book, *Innovating with Integrity: How Local Heroes Are Transforming American Government.* Michael Barzalay's book *Breaking through Bureaucracy: A New Vision for*

Managing in Government (1992) focused on a single award-winning program from Minnesota that was itself aimed at encouraging government to embrace change, new ideas, and innovative ways of doing the public's business.

In 1999 the Kennedy School, in conjunction with the Council for Excellence in Government and the Brookings Institution, published *Making Washington Work: Tales of Innovation in the Federal Government,* edited by John Donahue.

More recently, the IBM Foundation for the Business of Government published *Understanding Innovation: What Inspires It? What Makes It Successful* (Walters 2002), a look at lessons learned from the first fifteen years of the innovations awards program.

While innovation in government was emerging as a discrete area of study being fed and supported by the awards program, the program was creating one other very important spin-off, says Bill Parent, associate dean and director of the University of California, Los Angeles, Policy Forum, who took over as director of the innovations program from Marc Zegans in 1994 and ran it until 1999. "The thing that I liked most about the program was that we'd helped to create this wonderful and interesting network of professionals and intellectuals who really wanted to study all these issues and work together."

Transition

As the awards program matured, two shifts in particular are worth noting. In 1995 the awards were expanded to include the federal government, a move pushed by Zegans and Altshuler and supported by Michael Lipsky, program officer at the Ford Foundation from 1991 to 2003 (he is now a research professor at Georgetown University's Public Policy Institute and also senior program director with Demos).

In fact, Zegans had approached the Bush I White House in the early 1990s and invited them to participate. He says there was some interest—mostly from those working on President George H. W. Bush's "thousand points of light" initiative. But it wasn't until Bill Clinton was elected president that the federal connection was made. "Clinton was in the White House and had embraced what we thought was the innovations spirit with his reinventing government initiative," says Lipsky. "We had ties to the Clinton administration. So we thought there could be synergy between the program and Vice President Gore's reinventing government initiative. If we could link to his reinvention initiative, it would marginally enhance his efforts and also would support ours."

As the program expanded beyond state and local borders in the United States, it had already begun to have influence internationally. In 1993 an innovations awards program was created in the Philippines following an initiative to push more power and responsibility down to local government. Brazil followed with a similar program in 1996 (for a more detailed discussion of the Brazil program, see Marta Ferreira Santos Farah and Peter Spinks's discussion of it in chapter 4, this volume) based on a similar shift in national policy. Those countries would be followed by South Africa, where local nongovernmental organizations pushed the effort, and then by Brazil, Chile, China, Mexico, Peru, South Africa, and the East African region. The program also had one significant spin-off domestically: a separate innovations awards program for American Indian nations, Honoring Contributions in the Governance of American Indian Nations (Honoring Nations), at the Kennedy School's Malcolm Wiener Center for Social Policy.

Into the Sunset?

As much as the program might have been catching on, though, it was never meant to be permanent. Walter Broadnax and Peter Zimmerman both say that the Ford Foundation was clear from the very beginning that its commitment would be limited.

Still, enough people saw the merit in continuing the program, including key players like Alan Altshuler, Marc Zegans, and Bill Parent, that when, in 1999, discussion with the Ford Foundation turned to wrapping things up, an alternative proposal was made to the foundation. "I remember having a conversation about the future of the program with Michael Lipsky," says Altshuler. "And Michael said, 'Why don't we go for twenty years, end the program, and declare victory.'" Altshuler countered that for what it would cost to go the full twenty years, Ford might consider endowing the program.

Even as the awards program faced the sunset, other challenges were emerging. Finding a regular and meritorious batch of programs that represented real innovation was getting harder every year. In fact, the reason the awards program had begun aggressively to identify and then recruit programs that it thought were worth highlighting was that the number of good new ideas coming in over the transom through the regular application process was dwindling.

Charter schools, for example, clearly represented a new and intriguing experiment that was beginning to catch on nationally in the late 1990s, and so the awards program researched the origins of the idea and discovered that Minnesota had been the first state to test such schools out. It took some persuading to get the state to apply for the award, says Altschuler; it was a winner in 2000.

While it was becoming tougher to find applicants, academic interest in innovation also seemed to be softening at the school, say those both inside and outside the program.

Today, speculates Altshuler, innovation as a discrete area of study is not necessarily that popular among faculty, many of whom see political science or economics as more promising intellectual ground to plow. Also, given the proliferation of centers at Harvard, he says, the candidate pool of faculty members interested in connecting with one or another can only be stretched so far.

At the same time, site visits were being farmed out more and more to topic experts outside the Kennedy School, and fewer of the award-winning programs were being written up as case studies. But even as the school and the program were growing apart, the Ford Foundation still saw enough merit in the concept to make the decision to endow a center at the Kennedy School that would allow for the indefinite survival of the Innovations in American Government Awards Program.

In 2001 the foundation offered a $50 million endowment, to be matched by $20 million in Kennedy School money. Part of the school's match came from Roy L. Ash, the cofounder and president of Litton Industries, who had served as director of the Office of Management and Budget in the Nixon and Ford administrations.

Part of Ash's vision was that a center be established to look at the broader issue of democratic governance, something that, arguably, was a precondition of innovative government. "After all, you don't really want to study innovation in totalitarian government," observes Altshuler. "And so he didn't just give his money to expand the innovations program. The idea was to study innovation within the framework of democratic governance."

The Ash Institute for Democratic Governance and Innovation was officially created in 2003 to try and meld the two concepts.

Meanwhile, in an effort to distill out higher-quality applicants, the program had already begun to scale back the number of finalists and winners it would recognize, from twenty-five and ten, respectively, to fifteen and five. (The program currently offers three other "sponsored" awards in the fields of affordable housing, children and family services, and government transformation, the latter at the international level, chosen via a similar innovations awards process. The three programs are funded by the Fannie Mae Foundation, the Annie E. Casey Foundation, and IBM, respectively.)

Future Challenges

Assessing the program's impact over the past twenty years is hard to do. Those who were part of the program at the beginning argue that it had a significant and positive influence on the Kennedy School's reputation, direction, and national standing.

At the same time, even though the awards certainly have raised the profile of good government nationally, some bemoan the fact that it has not ultimately garnered wider popular acceptance—and media recognition—as the premier form of public-sector recognition.

And there is continued concern that the lessons that could be gleaned through the program's recognition are not being synthesized through academic research, in part because of a continued lack of resources for research and in part because of a natural drifting apart of the program and the Kennedy School and its faculty over a twenty-year period.

Still, longtime insiders such as Altshuler argue that the program's promise remains significant. He cites the work being done by faculty members such as Associate Professor Archon Fung at the Kennedy School, who is currently studying the area of citizen participation and democracy, as an example of an important potential future direction of both awards recognition and study for the institute (see chapter 4, this volume, in which Fung makes the connection between citizen participation and innovation).

Given the axiom that democratic government is good, adaptive, and innovative government, Altshuler and others argue that the nexus between democracy and innovation is clearly a vital area of potentially fruitful study, well worth pursuing into the future, an area of study that could help to rebuild the connections among the Ash Institute for Democratic Governance and Innovation, the Innovations in American Government Awards Program, and scholars at the Kennedy School and elsewhere.

3

The "Kennedy School School" of Research on Innovation in Government

STEVEN KELMAN

This chapter seeks to position the "Kennedy School school" of research on innovation in government[1] in the context of two broader, though different, literatures: public administration literature and mainstream organization studies literature. Kennedy School school research has many virtues, but these do not include extensive intellectual engagement with other scholarly traditions. Situating the literature in a broader context will help us appreciate both its contributions and its limitations, while also helping to suggest an agenda for future research.

When one reads the Kennedy School school literature on innovation in one fell swoop, what is most noteworthy about it is that it presents an overall approach to public management, not just an account of public-sector innovation. That approach has several elements. First, it focuses on public-sector performance improvement as the key question for public management. Second, it

---

1. I characterize this literature in the first instance as research supported by the Innovations in American Government Program and using award winners as some or all the empirical basis for the work. The "Kennedy School school" includes literature by Kennedy School faculty at the time of writing (Altshuler, Barzelay, and Moore) and scholars at other institutions at the time of writing (Bardach, Behn, Borins, Golden, Levin, Sanger). One important book supported by the Innovations program that I do not discuss here at any length is Eugene Bardach (1998), probably the best work on interorganizational collaboration in government, but somewhat out of the mainstream, in terms of topic, of other work from the Kennedy School school.

identifies excessive orientation to constraints, and on rules and clearances that reflect those constraints, as crucial impediments to innovation and, hence, performance improvement. Third, it defends a creative—that is, innovation-promoting—role for career public managers. Finally, it sees the energy and mission orientation of public officials as crucial drivers of the innovation that occurs in government, despite impediments to it.

The first theme is that organizational innovation is less encouraged in the public than the private sector (Behn 1997), for reasons orthogonal to the account that is standard in the public-choice-style literature to the effect that because government organizations are monopolies, there is less pressure on them to perform well in general—where "so-called public servants have a captive market and little incentive to heed their putative customers" and where, therefore, citizens are "subject to endless exploitation and victimization" by bureaucrats (Savas 1982, pp. 134–35); this theme that more generally has not been emphasized in Kennedy School writing on public management. Instead, innovation is less encouraged for two reasons. First, "People in government fear nothing more than newsworthy failure. . . . When new initiatives fail—and inevitably a large proportion do—they become highly newsworthy, with a focus on who is to blame. In such cases, the 'standard practice' defense is unavailable" (Altshuler 1997, p. 39). Second,

> A deep ambivalence typically exists about the idea of encouraging civil servants . . . to seek better means of pursuing public purposes. Innovation requires discretion, and the dominant tradition of U.S. administrative reform has been to stamp out bureaucratic discretion. The roots of this tradition lie in the country's constitutional heritage, which assigns the highest priority to keeping government power in check and firmly rooted in popular sovereignty. Within the framework of this heritage, the two primary sources of legitimacy for public action are preexisting law and (for those who would enact new law) electoral victory. Permanent bureaucracies, which never stand for election . . . should be closely supervised by elected officials and held accountable for strict adherence to precisely drafted laws.

Out of these two premises grows a system for managing in the public sector centering on extensive use of rules and hierarchical clearances, which hurts innovativeness in particular and public performance in general. This is a central theme in Michael Barzelay (2002), the empirical material for which was based on a 1986 winner of an Innovations in American Government Award: a program in Minnesota, called Striving Toward Excellence in Performance, which sought to improve the performance of central overhead agencies such as those doing purchasing, hiring, and the motor pool by making them customer funded, often involving customer choice to choose a private provider, and by separating control from customer-service activities. Alan Altshuler and Robert Behn (1997) argue that in the traditional model, more rules and controls, rather than innovation, are seen as the remedy for performance deficiencies. Barzelay presents the traditional system of public management, which he calls the "bureaucratic paradigm," as having been seen by its Progressive-era promoters as simultaneously a way to promote good performance and also to prevent evils such as corruption and favoritism. They believed it would promote good performance because they accepted a Tayloristic account of organization that promoted development of "the one best way," enshrined in a rule (or standard operating procedure) for the best way to do a job, along with a Fayolesque belief in the efficiency of clear chains of command; they believed it would ensure that constraints against bad things happening were respected because it removed room for individual discretion that could be abused. Barzelay's "post-bureaucratic paradigm," by contrast, calls on organizations to be structured around maximizing value produced for the organization's customers. He argues that doing so requires more attention to innovation and less to rules: "A bureaucratic agency sticks to routine. A customer-driven agency modifies its operations in response to changing demands for its services" (Barzelay 2002, p. 8). Barzelay doesn't so much denounce the traditional focus on rules as much as suggest caution about it (p. 131):

> From a post-bureaucratic angle, arguments premised on existing rules and procedures should be greeted with a reasonable degree of skepticism. Arguments premised on rules should be challenged and the issue reframed in terms of achieving the best possible outcome, taking into account the intention behind the rules, [and] the complexity and ambiguity of the situation. . . . In this way, problem solving rather than following bureaucratic routines can become the dominant metaphor for work.

A similar theme appeared, more dramatically, in Martin A. Levin and Mary Bryna Sanger (1994), the first book to appear that was based on the experiences of a large group of innovation award winners. "Bureaucratic routines, with their formal rules and procedures, developed to ensure accountability, also suppress the legitimate exercise of executive initiative" (p. 11). Levin and Sanger, slightly differently from Altshuler and Barzelay, argue that rules and hierarchy privilege constraints over accomplishments. In this environment, Levin and Sanger honor the "bureaucratic entrepreneur," one with a "bias for action" (they cite Peters and Waterman 1982). They praise "creative subversion" of the rules (p. 14) and, citing Gifford Pinchot III's (1985) pop management tome *Intrapreneuring: Why You Don't Have to Leave the Corporation to Become an Entrepreneur* and the famous example of the development of Post-it notes inside 3M (along with Nike's ad slogan), subtitle a section of one of their chapters "Circumvent Formal Rules and Regulations: Just Do It!" (p. 222). They argue that oversight to prevent unethical or inappropriate behavior is the responsibility of the top executive leadership in the organization.

The second part of the overall Kennedy School approach to public management involves a defense of the legitimacy of the participation of unelected public managers in the political process of choosing valuable ends for their organizations to pursue, as opposed to the notion that such choices are the job of "politics," and that nonelected officials should limit themselves to "administration." The key argument for this view is in Mark Moore (1995), probably the best-known work of the Kennedy School school, which was supported by the innovations awards program though it does not specifically discuss any innovations award winners.

Moore starts with an empirical reality: senior managers face ambiguity in deciding how to lead their organizations, and, "Importantly, the ambiguity [concerns] *ends* as well as means" (p. 62; emphasis in original). But he moves from empirical reality to normative claim: managers should, as part of an overall strategy for leading their organizations, nominate and seek to gain political support for ideas about how best to use their organization's assets. His argument on behalf of this idea is actually surprisingly brief: "managers' knowledge of the distinctive competence of their organization," along with "what they are learning through their current operations about the needs of their clients and potential users," legitimate this role (p. 75). Moore contrasts this view with a "classic tradition" in public administration scholarship according to which managers need not pay attention to "questions of purpose and value or . . . the development of legitimacy and support," because "these questions have been answered in the development of the organization's legislative or policy mandate" (p. 74). Moore argues that his conception "elevate[s] public sector executives from the role of technicians, choosing from well-known administrative methods to accomplish purposes defined elsewhere, to the role of strategists, scanning their political and task environments for opportunities to use their organizations to create public value." Also, and important from an innovations perspective, it "changes their administrative job from assuring continuity and efficiency in current tasks to one of improvising the transition from current to future performance" (p. 76).

Another topic the Kennedy School school literature addresses is the public-sector innovation process itself. The first contributions to this strand in the literature are Robert D. Behn (1988) and Olivia Golden (1990). In research supported by the innovations awards program and partly based on ET Choices, a Massachusetts employment and training program that was a 1986 innovations awards finalist, Behn developed the idea that innovations are initiated by managers "groping along." Rather than innovations resulting from "strategic planning" by means of a process of working backward from where they want to be in the future to where they are now, the objective is to develop a policy, an "'optimal path,' for getting from here to there" (p. 647). To do this, managers undertake "a sequential process of adaptation in pursuit of a goal. The manager tries some approaches, achieves some successes, adapts the more successful approaches, and continues to pursue his goal" (p. 657). Golden examined all the innovation award winners for 1986 (the first year of the program) to see which they followed more closely: a strategic planning or a "groping along" approach. Her findings supported the "groping along" model: innovations did not typically begin with legislation; the innovative idea was "rarely fully present at the beginning but develop[ed] through action"; most of the innovations "were characterized by rapid implementation instead of extended planning"; and the innovations changed considerably after first launch. The distinction between "strategic planning" and "groping along," again with support for "groping along," also appears in Levin and Sanger (1994). However, the larger sample-size analysis in Sandford Borins (1998) provides less support for the "groping along" view: he codes 59 percent of the innovations as "closer to the comprehensive planning pole," and 30 percent "closer to the groping pole" (p. 52).[2]

How, then, is innovation possible in the public sector, given the disincentives? Behn (1997, p. 49) suggests that people who are motivated to innovate are "driven by mission associated challenges and internalized professional norms" (see also Kelman 1987; Bardach 1998). Borins (1998) has a noteworthy finding when the question posed is *who* the source of the innovation was (rather than what circumstances provided the impetus for it). The largest group (48 percent) of innovations came from career civil servants at or below the agency head level (23 percent came from the agency head, 18 percent from an elected official); Borins characterizes these career civil servants as "local heroes" and states (p. 38) that he was surprised enough at this finding so that it served as the title of his book. It is natural to assume, though Borins does not explore this, that these people were driven in their efforts to innovate by mission orientation and public spirit.

2. Borins's study of the development and implementation of innovative programs is the most careful piece of scholarship the Kennedy School school has produced. He examines 217 of 350 Innovations applications that achieved at least semifinalist status between 1990 and 1994, a large enough sample to permit statistical analysis. (Other categories, such as non-semifinalist applicants, were eliminated because of resource constraints.) He devotes some attention (pp. 13–15) to issues of the representativeness of the sample, although unfortunately he devotes only brief attention to the exclusion of noninnovative organizations or to unsuccessful innovation efforts, and the analysis did not take advantage of the opportunity to test for distinctions among semifinalists, finalists, and winners. Borins's data come from a fixed-response survey of respondents for each of the semifinalists; all data therefore are self-reported.

Another obvious answer to the question of how innovation is possible in the public sector is organizational crisis—the organization is in deep trouble and has no choice—an answer, revealingly, often made for the private sector as well (Kotter 1996). On the basis of respondent self-reports, Borins (1998) reports that the impetus for 30 percent of the innovations came from a "crisis or publicly visible failure," a number he (I think rightly) regards as interestingly low, although the impetus for another 49 percent was reported to be various kinds of internal problems with the organizational status quo that fell short of the level of crisis.[3]

The Kennedy School school makes a number of pathbreaking contributions. The most important is to provide significant weight behind a performance turn in government and in the study of public management. Second is its serious consideration of the political context of public management.

Kennedy School school work should be seen as an instance of what I have elsewhere (Kelman 2007a) called the "performance turn"—the view that improving public-sector performance is the most central issue in public management—in public-sector research and, even more important, in public-sector practice.[4] This is a crucial development in public management practice and theory. If one is not satisfied with the current level of public-sector performance, some kinds of innovations (or at least organizational changes) will be required to improve performance, though of course this does not mean that any proposed innovation automatically should be supported as a source of performance improvement. So the association between concern with public-sector performance and concern with innovation is a natural one.

There is, similarly, a natural connection between concern with innovation and interest in the political role of nonelected public managers. It is when innovations are being proposed that would rejigger an organizational status quo that the political role of public managers in gaining support for such changes comes out clearly, whereas during everyday organizational business as usual, managers' political role may be obscured.

Because of their pioneering nature, the best-known products of Kennedy School school innovation research are quite well known within the world of academic public administration and public management (even if the Kennedy School school has not returned the compliment by linking to others). The citation count in Google Scholar for the two most-cited works in the field of innovative government, those by Moore (1997) and Barzelay (2002), is very high:

3. Multiple responses were allowed for this question, so the total for Borins's various categories was greater than 100 percent.

4. This section is based on Kelman (2007a).

390 and 334, respectively; the third most-cited work, Bardach (1998), also has a large number of citations, 158. To be sure, these works are not mainly cited as works about innovation or in research about innovation or organizational change (even in research on the public sector, and not at all in work on innovation or change in the larger world of organization studies), but they have received considerable scholarly attention nonetheless.

But the Kennedy School school literature also has important weaknesses that limit its usefulness, especially in an era when it is time to continue to move forward along the paths the school first pioneered. Perhaps the best way to think of the contribution of this literature is as having opened up new lines of inquiry and thought and having generated many interesting hypotheses. But now, the Kennedy School school has stagnated. It needs to face up to its limitations—limitations that were always present but were less important, or perhaps less obvious, when it was breaking new intellectual paths—if it is to continue to contribute to better public management research and practice.

A first thing to note about the Kennedy School school literature is that it is remarkably self-referential. The two lead essays in the Altshuler and Behn (1997) collection, *Innovation in American Government,* are Altshuler's "Bureaucratic Innovation, Democratic Accountability, and Political Incentives" and Altshuler and Mark Zegans's "Innovation and Public Management" (1997). The former contains thirty-eight scholarly references (not counting government reports, articles in the general press, and nonacademic books), of which twelve are by Kennedy School faculty, four are by other Harvard faculty, and two are by the scholar who sponsored the innovations program at the Ford Foundation, so that the total of one-half the references comes from a very narrow circle.[5] Six of seven Altshuler and Zegans references are from these categories of source. Of fifty-four scholarly references in Borins (1998), twenty-four are by Kennedy School faculty (including innovations awards program–sponsored research) and four are by other Harvard faculty. The Kennedy School school is quite disconnected both from other literature in public administration and from mainstream literature in organization studies, much of which is by scholars trained in social psychology or sociology who are working at business schools.

Furthermore, most of the Kennedy School school research literature is distant from the frontiers of contemporary social science methodology. One particularly serious problem that is particularly prevalent in this literature is so-called best practices research using only successful innovations (in particular, innova-

---

5. This includes one book by non–Kennedy School faculty but sponsored by the Innovations in American Government Program.

tion award winners) as the empirical material for the research.[6] This creates a problem with "selection on the dependent variable" (Lynn 1996). This is a fancy name, but the intuition about the nature of the problem is straightforward. If you choose only successes and find that they did a, b, and c, you really can't conclude from this that a, b, and c caused the innovation to succeed, because for all you know, failed innovations did a, b, and c as well.

It is remarkable how little the Kennedy School school literature is connected to the academic literature on organizational change or on diffusion of innovation—two areas that, unfortunately, also are insufficiently connected (Kelman 2007a). A striking example is the Paul Berman and Beryl Nelson paper (1997) on replicating innovations in the Altshuler and Behn collection (1997), which cites none of the voluminous literature on diffusion of innovation in organization theory or political science. "Groping along" from Behn and Golden has long intellectual antecedents in the work of Charles Lindblom (1959, 1965) and in Karl Weick's work on "small wins" (1984).

The isolation of the Kennedy School school from larger debates in mainstream organization studies, or even in the specific field of public administration, is partly the intellectual equivalent of bad manners. Even if other literature hypothetically added nothing to the findings coming from the Kennedy School, it seems intellectually arrogant to assume in effect that others have little to teach one, that every wheel one invents has never been invented before. Beyond the bad manners, locating the Kennedy School school contribution in a larger context of a "performance turn" in public-sector management practice and scholarly work serves actually to amplify its importance.

Furthermore, at the time the first generation of Kennedy School research was being written in the 1990s, the scholarly quality of much work done by those identifying themselves with the public administration tradition had been rather poor, but a younger generation of public administration scholars has become much more sophisticated methodologically (see, for example, Heinrich 2000; Brown and Potoski 2003, 2006; Heinrich and Fournier 2004; Hill 2006; Bertelli 2006; Bertelli and Feldman 2007), as have the leading journals in the field such as the *Journal of Public Administration Research and Theory*. Kennedy School research has mostly failed to keep up with these methodological improvements, which is embarrassing and suggests that Harvard is now falling behind evolving research standards in the field.

Finally, locating the work of the Kennedy School school in the broader context of other scholarly research, especially in organization studies, provides both

6. This problem is noted by Borins in his introduction (chapter 1 of this volume).

additional insights on issues this work raises and additional questions for research on innovation.

The Kennedy School Literature and the "Performance Turn" in Government

A starting point for the performance turn is a view that government underperforms because, compared with business firms, it pays less attention to performance in the first place. All organizations have both *goals* and *constraints* (Wilson 1989, chapter 7; Simons 1995).[7] Goals are *results* an organization seeks—for firms, profit, market share, or customer satisfaction. For the Environmental Protection Agency a goal is improved air quality; for the National Cancer Institute, a better understanding of cancer. Constraints are *limits* on the acceptable behavior of organizations or their members, even behavior meant to contribute toward meeting goals.[8] For firms, constraints include respecting accounting rules, not dumping toxic wastes, and not kidnapping competitors. For agencies, constraints include that officials not take bribes or lie to the public, that citizens be treated fairly and due process be respected, and that there be accountability to the public for agency actions.

Since constraints often embody important ethical values such as respect for persons, honesty, and integrity, they should not be seen as unimportant for any organization. At the same time, organizations (or individuals) about which it can be said only that they have respected constraints would typically not be judged successful. Imagine a journalist who during a long career never revealed a source or fabricated evidence—but who had never uncovered a good story. Or imagine a company that had never cooked its books, but also had never succeeded in making a sale. Furthermore, organizations (or individuals) that need to focus significant energy on ensuring that constraints are respected are not normally considered successful, because that energy is unavailable for goal attainment. Instead, a healthy organization (or individual) is one where constraints are taken for granted. If an individual needs to spend hours each day worrying about how he or she will avoid murdering others, that individual is unlikely to be successful at achieving substantive goals. We seldom think of "don't kidnap your competitors" as a constraint for firms, because we take the constraint for granted. (But consider Russia in the early 1990s—a place where this couldn't be taken for granted, with society consequently in bad shape.)

---

7. James Q. Wilson uses the term tasks to describe what I call goals, and Robert Simons uses the phrase boundary systems to describe what I call constraints.

8. In linear programming or economics one often speaks of maximizing goals subject to constraints.

In the world of practice, firms almost always focus in the first instance on achieving their goals: a business that doesn't do this won't stay in business. However, a central fact about the practice of government, in most times and places, is that in the environment in which government operates, closer to the opposite is true—governments must in the first instance focus on paying attention to constraints; a failure to do so often inflicts the same pain that failing to attend to goals inflicts on a firm (Wilson 1989, p. 115). This is so for several reasons. First, in government, goals are often controversial (Should affirmative action be required? Should free trade be pursued?), but "everybody can agree" that it's wrong to lie or show favoritism. This makes constraint violation an easier story for the media or opposition politicians to tell. Second, goal achievement is not fully under agency control and occurs over time, whereas constraint violation is immediate. Third, pursuing goals is about "maximizing good government," whereas respecting constraints is about "minimizing misgovernment" (Gregory 2003, p. 564, quoting Uhr); many have such limited aspirations for government that reducing misgovernment is all they ask—a standard for success that firms would find incomprehensible.[9] Fourth, agency accountability is a central value in a democracy. This focus is a constraint, since it is only about process and says nothing about results.

All organizations should seek to maximize attainment of goals while respecting constraints. For firms, goal focus increases the probability that they will perform well, but also the risk that they will ignore constraints—the Enron problem (Schweitzer, Ordóñez, and Douma 2004). For government, the problem is less that constraints are violated (although the way the media cover government may produce the misimpression of common misbehavior) than that government performs poorly—the Katrina problem. Traditionally in government, the tail wags the dog—constraints loom larger than goals, inhibiting good performance.

The importance of constraints is tied to dominance of bureaucratic organizational forms in government, since rules and hierarchy are important control tools. As Herbert Kaufman (1977, p. 4) famously noted, "One person's 'red tape' may be another's treasured procedural safeguard." Hierarchy, combined with rules developed at the top so that those lower down are merely executing directives, also fits into the desire to subordinate unelected officials to political control

---

9. More broadly, greater attention is paid in government to mistakes than to achievements. Even in the 1920s, Leonard D. White (1926, pp. 243–44) observed that public officials perceive that "whenever we make a mistake, some one jumps on us for it, but whenever we do something well nobody pays any attention to us. We never get any recognition except when we get 'bawled out.'" A half century later, Derek Rayner, the CEO of the British department store Marks & Spencer, brought into the British government under Margaret Thatcher, noted that in government (quoted in Hennessy 1989, p. 595) "Failure is always noted and success is forgotten."

(Warwick 1975). If one cares about minimizing misgovernment rather than maximizing good government, one will be disinclined to grant officials discretion. As Theodore Roosevelt stated a century ago (quoted in White 1926, p. 144), "You cannot give an official power to do right without at the same time giving him power to do wrong."

Over the past twenty years, what Donald Kettl (2005, p. 1) calls "a remarkable movement to reform public management" has "swept the globe." Christopher Hood (1991) labeled this the "New Public Management"; in the United States it came to be known as "reinventing government." The movement originated with practitioners, initially most in the United Kingdom, New Zealand, and Australia. It has sought public-sector self-renewal, a break from the preoccupation with constraints in favor of a drive to improve performance. In the United Kingdom, management reforms came from Margaret Thatcher and were part of an anti-government conservative ideology, though Tony Blair continued and deepened reform after Labour came to power in 1997. In New Zealand and Australia, reforms were introduced by left-of-center governments. In the United States, reform grew out of the Clinton-Gore effort to reposition Democrats away from their traditional role as standard bearers of "big government," while simultaneously endorsing a positive government role. Just as the Kennedy School literature has been critical of the impact of bureaucracy on government, so, too, has one central theme in public management reform efforts been debureaucratization.

Some public administration scholars have aligned themselves with the performance turn. However, a disturbing proportion, likely a majority, of the field, particularly in the United Kingdom, has reacted with cranky skepticism or downright hostility, often displaying nostalgia for good old days of a public sector that did not need to concern itself with pesky performance demands. The three editors of the journal *Public Administration Review,* serving when New Public Management emerged, all took a negative view of it. The field's two most recent handbooks (Peters and Pierre 2003; Ferlie, Lynn, and Pollitt 2005) have been predominantly critical.

In the public administration literature criticizing the performance turn, a conscious defense of the primacy of constraints over goals emerged in close association with what frequently was referred to as "traditional" public administration values. Donald Savoie (1994, p. 283) worried about "rejecting traditional public-administration concerns with accountability and control, and giving way to the business-management emphasis on productivity, performance, and service to clients." Thus, the bane of government is presented as a virtue, and "performance" itself is presented as a negative word. Beryl Radin boldly titled a recent (2006) book *Challenging the Performance Movement.*

Embracing constraints, the critics reject reformers' attacks on bureaucracy. Peter Du Gay, in *In Praise of Bureaucracy* (2000), lauds bureaucracy for promoting constraints while demeaning the significance of performance goals that bureaucracy might hinder. Du Gay extols bureaucracy for being "ordered, cautious," and terms such as "probity" and "reliability" abound. By contrast, New Public Management advocates judge agencies for "failure to achieve objectives which enterprise alone has set for it" (p. 87), presumably performance and cost consciousness. "If the rule of law is to be upheld and there is to be a system of accountability within government the hierarchy becomes the crucial link between ministers and the decisions taken in their name by their numerous subordinates in the field" (Peters and Wright 1996, p. 632). Guy Peters (2001, p. 200) muses about "a return to the bureaucratic Garden of Eden."

Sometimes the tone of the anti-performance literature is lackadaisical, displaying the opposite of the urgency about performance that reformers seek, evoking the atmosphere of a gentleman's club. Du Gay (2000, pp. 92–93) belittles "a 'can do' approach to the business of government," and derides the "dangers that the demand for enthusiasm pose" to the traditional role of civil servants as advisers who, without displaying commitment, present ministers with options and emphasize pitfalls of proposals. The Kennedy School literature argues that commitment to agency mission is an important source of motivation for innovation in government. But du Gay (p. 129) mocks the effort of one senior civil servant "to ensure that her staff were infused with a discernible sense of 'mission.'"

The sad result has been that, "unlike in the transition to the twentieth century," when public-sector reform was "led by the Progressives and orthodox public administration," current transformation efforts have proceeded "largely without intellectual or moral support from academia" (Kettl 2002, p. 21). Perhaps the most important contribution of the Kennedy School school of innovation research is as an important participant in that movement. But this has been largely self-unacknowledged. It is interesting, and troubling, that Kettl doesn't notice the contributions of the Kennedy School literature. Scholarly supporters of the performance turn needed, and need, help.

The Kennedy School Literature and the Politics versus Administration Dichotomy

Here the problem is basically what I earlier called intellectual bad manners, rather than anything more serious. Mark Moore's *Creating Public Value* especially may fairly be criticized for presenting a cartoon version of a public administration embracing the 150-year-old Wilsonian dichotomy between "politics" (the job of the elected official) and "administration" (the job of the nonelected manager). The criticism of public administration scholarship in *Creating Public Value* is misplaced: the field deserves to be criticized for its lack of focus on performance, but not for its unwillingness to see public managers engaged in the political process.

In fact, attacking the politics-administration dichotomy became a major theme in public administration following World War II. Participation of unelected officials in the political process was a major element in P. H. Appleby (1949) and in a widely noted essay by John Gaus (1950) called "Trends in the Theory of Public Administration," in the tenth-anniversary edition of *Public Administration Review,* which concluded with the flourish, "A theory of public administration means in our time a theory of politics also." Most important, a version of this theme—increasing democratic participation in administration— was central to Dwight Waldo's influential attack on the founders of public administration in *The Administrative State* (1948).[10] The so-called "Blacksburg Manifesto" scholars of the 1980s expressed strong support for an active political role for career officials, albeit using language that sounds, perhaps intentionally, dated and stilted:

> The popular will does not reside solely in elected officials but in a constitutional order that envisions a remarkable variety of legitimate titles to participate in governance. The Public Administration, created by statutes based on this constitutional order, holds one of these titles. Its role, therefore, is not to cower before a sovereign legislative assembly or a sovereign elected executive [but rather] to share in governing wisely and well the constitutional order [Wamsley 1990, p. 47].

The fretting about applying business metaphors to public management on the part of critics of the performance turn has occasioned resurrection of the politics-administration dichotomy in the context of concern about the idea that public managers should behave like "entrepreneurs." Larry Terry (1993; see also Terry 1990) titled a *Public Administration Review* article "Why We Should Abandon the Misconceived Quest to Reconcile Public Entrepreneurship with Democracy." Savoie (1994, p. 330) states, "Bureaucracy is designed to administer the laws and policies set by elected politicians, and as a result, authority delegated to career officials must be handled bureaucratically in order to accept direction." In an unfortunate passage, Peters (2001, p. 113) maintains, "It is not clear that in systems of democratic accountability we really want civil servants to be extremely creative."

10. Somewhat later this became a theme in political science as well (see, for example, Lowi 1969; Aberbach, Putnam, and Rockman 1981; Gruber 1987).

The Kennedy School School and Mainstream Organization Studies

In this section a number of the research questions raised by the Kennedy School school literature will be discussed in the context of research in mainstream organization studies and public administration.

Innovation, Organizational Change, and Performance

From the beginning of the program there has been some discussion and even tension regarding the Innovations in American Government Awards about just how new and novel a change needed to be to become an award winner. The award criteria have always required novelty. A program that successfully executed a change within an organization that could not be considered novel—say, achieving a customer-orientation focus in an organization traditionally lacking one—would not be eligible for an award, even if achieving the change both was difficult and made a large difference in improving the value the agency provided the public.

If one sees innovation and noninnovative organizational improvement as simply additive, this criterion is not a problem: innovation, encouraged by the awards program, makes its contribution to government performance improvement, and general organizational improvement makes its additional contribution. There is, however, an influential strand in contemporary organization theory, associated originally with James March (1999, chapter 7), that suggests that these two sources of performance improvement may be in conflict. March contrasts "exploitative" and "exploratory" learning in organizations. Exploitative learning involves getting better at one's current activities; March associates exploitative learning with words such as *refinement, implementation,* and *execution.* Exploratory learning involves looking for new possibilities; he associates it with such words as *search, risk taking, experimentation, discovery,* and (notably) *innovation.*

The dilemma arises because it is hard for organizations to be good at both kinds of learning. Both March and the authors of a good deal of the follow-on literature to March's original paper seem above all to be afraid that exploitative learning will drive out exploratory learning. As March notes, the payoff to exploratory learning is more uncertain than to exploitative learning because so many innovations fail, and in the short term, while the organization is transitioning to new ways of behaving, performance will often actually decline. In a business context, existing products are typically more profitable, initially, than most new products; furthermore, new products may cannibalize existing ones (as online newspapers have cannibalized print), leading to internal organizational opposition to investing in them. In this case, one would need to look for ways to protect the space in government organizations for innovations, for reasons over and above the list of obstacles to innovation in government the Kennedy School literature enumerates. But March notes that one may also imagine the opposite danger, an organization innovating so often that it never stabilizes production long enough to gain the benefits of exploitative learning. In a public-sector context, one could argue that because innovation is so difficult and requires such extraordinary organizational energy, managers might typically be advised to concentrate on exploitative learning and not even try for exploratory learning.

To cope with the exploitation-exploration trade-off, Michael Tushman and Charles O'Reilly (see, for example, 2002) have introduced into the organization-theory literature the concept of "ambidexterity." They suggest that ambidexterity be created through separate units within an organization, one promoting exploitation of existing products, the other exploration for breakthrough new products. Senior managers would be in charge of overseeing both kinds of operations. (This could also be done with temporary teams.) But it is hard to see how this kind of organization could readily be pursued in a typical government context—one can hardly, say, keep an existing social services organization to provide children's services and develop a parallel organization to provide a new form of the same services. (Although having said that, it is common in government to assign new missions to new organizations rather than counting on an existing organization effectively to produce the new mission; the practice goes back to the New Deal. Arthur M. Schlesinger [1959, p. 534] writes that "Roosevelt felt that the old departments, even with new chiefs, simply could not generate the energy and daring the crisis required. . . . The new agencies simplified the problem of reversing direction and correcting error." However, this is different from using a new organization to provide, say, innovative ways to deliver an existing service.) Another possibility is for organizations to pursue a kind of "punctuated equilibrium" approach (Romanelli and Tushman 1986; Gersick 1991),[11] where long periods of organizational constancy characterized by exploitative learning are punctuated by short bursts of revolutionary change, characterized by exploratory learning.

One possible relationship between innovation and overall organizational performance would be a contingency view, a variant of the argument, going back as far as Tom Burns and G. M. Stalker (1961; see also Lawrence and Lorsch 1967), that organizations in stable environments do better with hierarchical structures, and those in changing environments with flat ones. In this view, innovation is likely to be more associated with good overall performance in firms than in government, on the assumption that given competition among

---

11. By analogy to theories in evolutionary biology.

firms, change in the environments in which most firms operate is likely in general to be greater than what is typical for government organizations.

Rules, Bureaucracy, and Performance

I share the worries in the Kennedy School school literature concerning government's being excessively rulebound. In fact, though, scholarship on the connection between rules and organizational performance is considerably more ambiguous than the Kennedy School school literature, which is influenced more by pop management gurus than by academic research.

It is true that many scholars studying organization design, going back to the classic work by Robert Merton (1968) on rules and goal displacement, have been worried about the impact of rules on organizational performance. Henry Mintzberg (1979) notes that rules, which express a minimum standard of performance, in reality tend to come to represent a maximum performance standard. Connie Gersick and Richard Hackman (1990, p. 73) worry that, "because behaviors in the group are being executed mostly by rote [in a rulebound environment], there are diminished opportunities for members . . . to grow in competence, skill, and/or perspective."

However, there is also an important strand of organization theory literature (for example, March and Simon 1958; and especially Nelson and Winter 1982) that regards routines—rules or standard operating procedures—as key elements of an organization's capabilities. This is partly because procedures often embody accumulated wisdom about how to perform a task that allows avoidance of a constant reinvention of the wheel and an ability for ordinary people to perform extraordinary tasks—think how the Air Force entrusts the maintenance of incredibly expensive aircraft assets to people with only a high school education, thanks to the detailed maintenance procedures the Air Force has developed. Arthur L. Stinchcombe (2001) argues that rules are helpful when they are both "accurate" and "cognitively economical." In addition, the very mindlessness, to use Langer's (1989) term, with which routines are applied is itself a source of an organization's capabilities (Gersick and Hackman 1990), because they economize on time and energy: "A group need not spend time creating and choosing the behavioral strategy that will guide the work" (p. 71).

Within public administration there is a body of theoretical and empirical work on the nature and consequences of "red tape" (Rainey, Pandey, and Bozeman 1995; Bozeman and Scott 1996; Bozeman 2000; Pandey and Scott 2002; Pandey, Coursey, and Moynihan 2007). Something of a consensus has developed in this literature to distinguish "red tape" from the older organization theory concept of "formalization," where the latter simply reflects the extent to which rules determine the content of a job and the former refers to a subset of rules that "entail a compliance burden but have no efficacy for the rules' functional object" (Rainey, Pandey, and Bozeman 1995, p. 567). In factor analyses (Pandey and Scott 2002), the two dimensions are distinct. One study (Pandey, Coursey, and Moynihan 2007) found that respondent perceptions of a high volume of "red tape" (conceptualized as worthless personnel rules) correlated with perceived poor organizational effectiveness.[12] There is no corresponding study of the impact of formalization on organizational effectiveness, but Leisha DeHart-Davis and Sanjay Pandey (2005) do find that high perceived formalization at the organization level is associated with increased job satisfaction, organizational commitment, and job involvement at the employee level.

This suggests a distinction between situations where rules are a source of organizational capability (presumably because of the nature of the work or the organization's environment) and those where they aren't (probably where the rules embody constraints rather than goals).

The connection between rules, and especially hierarchy, and *innovation* is less controversial in the broader literature than the bigger question of the connection between rules and overall organizational performance. In the economics of organization literature, Raaj Kumar Sah and Joseph Stiglitz (1986) present in formal terms the intuition that if there are agents with the ability to decide to go ahead with a project (what they call "polyarchy"), more projects—both good and bad—will be approved than if agents must get their projects authorized by a higher level of review (what they call hierarchy). Edward Lazear (1998, chapter 16) makes a similar point, noting that the choice between these two forms "depends on the costs of rejecting good projects relative to the costs of accepting poor ones. . . . Fewer bad projects are accepted by the hierarchical firm, but more good projects are rejected" (pp. 453, 455). This is a useful, more formalized way of thinking both about why government tends to be more hierarchical than firms (avoiding the bad is considered more important than achieving the good) and also about the consequences of the choice for innovation; indeed, these arguments express in formal terms the gist of Theodore Roosevelt's words, noted earlier in this chapter.

This is also the conclusion of the organization-theory literature. Merton, in his essay on goal displacement, argues that people can gradually come to see following a rule as a goal in itself rather than a means to a goal, and thus resist rule change. Mintzberg (1979) notes, "An organization cannot put blinders on its personnel and then expect peripheral vision" (p. 346); Mintzberg's observation

---

12. This finding is not meaningless, in that it is certainly in principle possible that red tape might conceivably be annoying but not reduce organizational effectiveness, though the study is potentially marred by problems of common method variance since information about both the dependent and predictor variables came from the same respondents. However, the authors are admirably sensitive to this issue and took steps to try to deal with it.

about rules coming to embody a maximum level of performance would also suggest they hurt innovation, since innovating involves going beyond minimum job requirements. The organization ecology school, founded by Michael Hannan and Steven Freeman (1984), argues that "structural inertia" coming from rules makes it very difficult for existing organizations to adapt to environmental change; change, these authors argue, comes from organizational turnover (old organizations go out of business when environments change) rather than organizational renewal.

Engaging in innovation may be seen as an example of what in the organizational behavior literature (for example, Organ and others 2006) is called "organization citizenship behavior," that is, employee efforts going beyond job requirements (for an application of this construct to innovation behavior, see Kelman 2006). The empirical literature on what job features are associated with organizational citizenship behavior (Organ and others 2006, chapter 5) suggests that greater task autonomy increases organizational citizenship behavior, so that, inversely, a rulebound environment discourages it.

One classic view in the literature (Burns and Stalker 1961; Lawrence and Lorsch 1967) takes a contingency approach: organizations with clear technology and little-changing environments are well served by rules, whereas those with an unpredictable and rapidly changing environment, where innovation is more important, are more poorly served by rules. One may also argue that just as there is a trade-off between exploitative and exploratory learning, there is also a trade-off between the ability of rules and routines to create static capabilities and the resistance to innovation that they engender.[13] In the case of the exploitation-exploration conflict, and to the extent that rules create organizational capabilities, there may exist a trade-off between promotion of the good performance of the organization's ongoing work and innovation.

There is some limited empirical evidence on the question of the relationship between innovativeness and overall performance in a public-sector context, mostly coming out of the research group centered at Cardiff University and Warwick University in the United Kingdom. Both Rhys Andrews and others (2005) and Kenneth Meier and others (2007) examine the impact of different strategic orientations by top management on organizational performance. The first paper compares English local government organizations that they describe as "prospectors" (local authorities identifying themselves as being "at

---

13. Even here, however, James March, Schulz, and Zhou (2000) argue, and provide empirical evidence for, the proposition that rules evolve over time in response to organizational learning. Martha Feldman (2000; see also Feldman and Pentland 2003; Stinchcombe 2001) argues both that routines give agents more freedom to pick and choose about how they are actually performed than often seen, and also that purposive, mindful agents (though she doesn't use the latter word) engage in a dialogue with existing routines, producing modifications in them over time.

the forefront of innovative approaches") and "reactors" (those identifying themselves as primarily responding to pressure from outside auditors and evaluators). The authors find that prospectors have better average performance than reactors, as measured by U.K. Audit Commission ratings of overall local authority performance.[14] By contrast, in the second study, which used Texas school standardized test scores as the dependent variable, superintendents classified as "defenders" (operationalized as those who concentrated on improving test scores as a priority) did better than prospectors (operationalized with a slightly different question than in the Andrews study, agreeing with the statement, "A superintendent should advocate major changes in school policies"). The authors use this to conclude that when what is at stake is reliable delivery of a basic technology, a defender strategy may produce better performance than an innovator strategy.[15] One way of interpreting the results of Erin Withers and Jean Hartley (2007) is that they suggest that more innovative local governments in the United Kingdom generally show greater performance improvement over time than less innovative ones (although these results need to be interpreted with caution because of a number of methodological issues).

Public Service Motivation, Creativity, and Organizational Performance Improvement

As noted earlier, the Kennedy School school literature often presents a sense of commitment to an organization's mission as an important motivator for innovative behavior that can counteract disincentives for innovation in the public sector. This commitment is generally referred to in the public administration literature as "public service motivation" (for example, Perry and Wise 1990; Crewson 1997); it is a subset of what in the psychology and organization studies literature is referred to as "intrinsic motivation" (see Deci and Ryan 1985; Deci and others 1999; Frey and Oberholzer-Gee 1997). In addition to the effect of public service motivation postulated in the Kennedy School school literature, one may imagine other effects: on overall individual performance in public organizations, and on creativity, independent of its role in counteracting innovation disincentives specific to a government context.

14. These results may be partly endogenous—organizations that perform well may develop the self-confidence to innovate.

15. Here as well there are grounds for caution about these conclusions. Partly, there again may be issues of endogeneity (people whose schools are performing well on the standardized tests may more likely emphasize them, since they are performing well on that dimension; high scores on the "prospector" measure in this study—"advocating changes" rather than "being at the forefront," in the earlier study—may occur because poor performance on the tests causes a superintendent to "advocate" policy changes. Also, it perhaps should not be surprising that those who report focusing on school test scores obtain better test scores for their schools than those who don't.

There is very limited empirical research on the connection between an individual's public service motivation and the individual's overall performance. In regression analyses with a number of control variables, both Katherine Naff and John Crum (1999) and Pablo Alonso and Gregory Lewis (2001), using the same dataset, found that high public service motivation was associated with an employee receiving a higher performance evaluation, although endogeneity might be a problem for these results (people develop a greater public service motivation when they get good performance appraisals).[16] Gene Brewer and Sally Selden (1998) found that public employees with high "regard for the public interest" were more likely to report wasteful or illegal activities they observed than those with low regard, but the measure of "regard for the public interest" was so closely tied to the specifics of motivation to report wasteful or illegal activities (rather than a broader construct) that the value of the findings is reduced. By far the most interesting paper on this issue—partly because its experimental design precludes concerns about endogeneity and partly because of how dramatic the results are—is by Adam Grant (2008, forthcoming), which finds that modest manipulations in a field experimental situation (involving over-the-telephone fundraisers for a university scholarship) of the salience of how one's work helps others produced very dramatic performance improvements.

However, there is more evidence, though not specifically in a public-sector context, about the relationship between intrinsic motivation and creativity. Particularly relevant here is Teresa Amabile's work on creativity in the work environment (1996), finding that intrinsic motivation encourages creativity, whereas many, though not all, uses of extrinsic rewards may discourage it—although, in the manner of exploitative versus exploratory learning (terms Amabile does not use), extrinsic rewards encourage better performance at existing tasks. The empirical literature (Organ and others 2006) also suggests that the more that job tasks are intrinsically significant or intrinsically satisfying, the higher the organization citizenship behavior. Kelman (2006) found that the "change vanguard"—the earliest supporters of organizational change in government organizations—were more likely to characterize themselves as idealists than other respondents. Following Amabile, the benefits of public service motivation would not simply be that they encourage public officials to slog on despite the incentives against innovation in the system (which is how one might characterize the perspective in the Kennedy School literature), but also that it promotes creativity directly.

If public service motivation is an important spur to innovativeness, especially in an environment with many disincentives to innovation, then the role

16. Also, Alonso and Lewis did not find this effect using a different dataset, with somewhat different and arguably inferior questions used to measure public service motivation.

of public managers and leaders in encouraging and nurturing such motivation becomes an important tool for increasing innovation in government. This suggestion ties in to a strand in leadership studies originating with Philip Selznick (1957). Selznick argued that one of a leader's main roles was to articulate an appealing organizational vision. Leaders should "state, in the language of uplift and idealism, what is distinctive about the aims and methods of the enterprise. Successful institutions are usually able to fill in the formula, 'What we are proud of around here is . . .'" (p. 151). A rekindling of interest in a value-infusion role for leaders occurred during the 1980s and 1990s. John Kotter (1990; see also Burns 1978) refers to one of a leader's roles as "motivating and inspiring": leaders should work to satisfy "very basic human needs for achievement, belonging, recognition, self-esteem, a sense of control over one's life, living up to one's ideals, etc." Kotter even distinguishes "leaders" from "managers" significantly on this basis. Weick (quoted in Pfeffer 1992, p. 284) suggested that "the appropriate role for the manager may be evangelist rather than accountant."

Crisis, "Burning Platforms," and Organizational Improvement

The Kennedy School literature contains a number of fairly casual suggestions that organizational crisis promotes innovation (or, more broadly, organizational change). This is also a common proposition in pop-management business literature on organizational change (Kotter 1996; Hammer and Stanton 1995). Since change is painful, the argument goes, leaders and employees must understand there is no alternative. As often expressed in consultants' slide shows, getting people to accept change requires a "burning platform"—from a story about what it took to rouse workers on a North Sea oil rig from complacency.

This argument receives a scholarly formulation in Richard Cyert and James March's theory of problemistic search, presented in *A Behavioral Theory of the Firm* (1963, pp. 120–22). Cyert and March argue that search is "problemistic": absent problems, little motivation to change exists. People look for new solutions when current ones aren't working.

This view is controversial, however; in the scholarly literature on corporate downsizing—a form of organizational crisis—many (for example, Ocasio 1995) maintain that crisis *inhibits* organizational change. The most important argument for this counterassertion grows out of the theory of "threat rigidity" (Staw and others 1981), according to which people faced with crisis tend to fall back on familiar behavioral responses rather than seeking out new ones. Barry Staw and others base their argument on psychological research suggesting that "when placed in a threat situation, an individual's most well-learned or dominant response may be emitted" (p. 502). This is advantageous in situations where heightened energy in applying traditional methods is the appropriate response.

But where crisis requires changed behavior, threat rigidity decreases the likelihood of an appropriate response. In this view, necessity serves not as the mother of invention but as the mother of rigidity (Mone and others 1998). A related argument is that time and workload pressures, which grow in crisis situations, inhibit creativity by reducing freedom and exploration (Amabile 1996; Amabile and others 1996).

Kelman (2006) examined this question empirically in a government context, looking at the impact of two kinds of crises in the procurement system in the 1990s (workforce downsizing and the advent of competition for organizations previously enjoying a customer monopoly) on the degree of organizational change at the individual employee level. He found that a problemistic-search response dominated a threat-rigidity response, but in the specific case of downsizing as an organization crisis, this response was canceled out by the negative effects on behavioral change of employee resentment of a perceived violation of a "social contract at work" between employee and employer.

Future Research Directions

What might be fruitful research directions, both substantively and methodologically, in this area? Substantively, for most of the topics discussed in this chapter, we need more and better evidence than we have. Specifically, we need to know more about the impacts, in different kinds of task situations, of different organizational design and leadership practices on performance and innovation, such as different ruleboundedness, hierarchy, and accountability regimes. Because of the growing importance of cross-boundary work across government organizations, and between government organizations and private and nonprofit ones—itself an innovation in government, as Borins's discussion of award winners notes—we need to know much more than we do about the conditions under which such innovations can be made to work. More broadly, we need to know more about what specific management and leadership practices are associated with the success of different categories of innovations.

Methodologically, public management research in general and public-sector innovation research in particular should begin to make much greater use of laboratory studies, with civil servants rather than college sophomores as subjects, if possible. This is one of the most important research methodologies in mainstream organization studies research, but has been essentially absent from the public management field. One frequently used method for inducing variation among subjects in a lab setting is to prime subjects to think about different kinds of situations they face (Aronson and others 1990; for an example, see Galinsky, Gruenfeld, and Magee 2003). One can imagine this method being applied to many performance and innovation research questions. One could, for example, use lab methods to test the impacts of different ruleboundedness, hierarchy, and accountability regimes. I know of only one study that attempts to do anything like this, Patrick G. Scott and Sanjay K. Pandey (2000). The results of the manipulation were fairly predictable: the more forms a person had to fill out to grant a potential welfare client assistance, the less assistance he or she granted (though there was an interesting interaction effect where the effect of the forms was much less for "worthy" clients). One might also use experimental methods to examine the impacts of public service motivation on performance and innovation, either field experiments such as the Grant paper (2008, forthcoming) discussed earlier or lab experiments that induce variations in public service motivation.

Regarding methodology, too, public management research needs to go beyond the first generation of quantitative studies—which have now, happily, come to play a greater role in the field's research output—to quantitative work that is more sophisticated methodologically. Too much regression-based work on public management has used survey respondent self-reports of some aspect of the organization's performance as the dependent variable, while gathering information about predictor variables using self-reports from the same survey, creating the problem of common-method bias that exaggerates relationships because of response-set problems (Salancik and Pfeffer 1978; Boyne and others 2005). Furthermore, much regression-based research in public management, based on cross-sectional analysis of data, suffers from potential endogeneity problems: the direction of causation is unclear—did the hypothesized cause produce the state of the world we are trying to explain, or did the state of the world produce the hypothesized cause? (An example: If we find, using cross-sectional data, that organizations where employees are treated well perform better than those whose employees are not treated well, is this because good treatment leads to better performance or because well-performing organizations can afford to treat employees well?) There are ways to use cross-sectional data to try to deal with such problems, but they have seldom been used in public management research. One should also look for opportunities to do quantitative research involving innovation and performance in specific public service areas where there are large numbers of units producing the public service in question and where there are good performance data, most obviously schools, police forces, and job-creation programs; the strongest research on public organization performance tends to be of this type (for example, Levin 1998; Heinrich 2000).

Additionally, as noted from the beginning of this chapter, studies of what causes innovations to succeed, whether they be large-N quantitative studies or even smaller-sample thicker cases, must include innovation failures as well as successes. As tempting as research based only on award winners is (and, to be sure, it is also so much easier in terms of locating examples), it has inevitable, and nearly fatal, methodological limitations. Finally, the field might explore the utility of computer simulations for testing hypotheses about organizational performance and innovation (Davis, Eisenhardt, and Bingham 2007), though this is a domain I know less well.

It would be nice if, during the next twenty years, the Kennedy School, having pioneered an important turn in scholarly thinking about public management, could be in the forefront of emerging efforts to put public management research on a sounder footing of evidence and method, and thus be better able to serve the public sector with results that might further the aims this tradition so boldly announced.

4

Citizen Participation in Government Innovations

ARCHON FUNG

This book is about innovations in *government*. The Innovations in American Government Awards Program was conceived in large measure to renew respect for and trust in the public sector by recognizing the creativity and accomplishments of officials in government. In order to be eligible for an innovations award, programs must be administered by government. Consistent with the vision of the awards program and indeed the perspectives of much scholarship in public management and administration, most of the chapters of this book focus on various aspects of public agencies and their programs such as performance, organization, coordination, and replication. It is somewhat surprising, then, that many of the winners of innovations awards have created programs that build bridges between governments and the citizens they serve. Indeed, in his review of the first ten years of the innovations program, Sandford Borins writes, "Fully a third of the applicants (34 percent) . . . claimed that empowering citizens, individually or as communities, is a characteristic of their programs" (Borins 1998).

A surprisingly large number of programs that have received Innovations in American Government Awards do not simply seek to improve the operations and services of government by improving organizational structures, management

I thank Sandford Borins, Gowher Rizvi, Jonathan Walters, Eugene Bardach, and Marta Farah for very helpful comments and suggestions on a previous version of this chapter.

techniques, or productive methods. They reach beyond the boundaries of public agencies to incorporate the views of citizens and to enlist their energies to the production of, in Mark Moore's felicitous phrase, "public value" (Moore 1995). In this chapter, I survey some of the initiatives in citizen and community engagement that have been recognized by the innovations program, in order to understand how public managers are incorporating citizens into their activities, assess the kinds of contributions that citizens make, and, finally, to explore the tensions and conflicts over mission, priorities, and prerogatives that can arise. At several points, I also juxtapose initiatives recognized by the innovations awards program with several others that have been widely recognized in order to suggest some horizons of citizen participation that the program may want to explore in the future.

Throughout, I use the term *citizen participation* broadly to denote not just instances in which participatory mechanisms are endowed with decisionmaking authority, but also cases in which individuals are organized to contribute their advice or their energies to a public project or toward solving some social problem. The primary aims of this chapter are modest: to illuminate the wide range of governmental innovations that encourage some kind of public participation and to understand the purposes and potential contributions of these innovations to advancing governance. I do not aim to assess whether they accomplished these purposes well and sustainably, much less to understand the sources of their success and failure. Those important questions are best left for another occasion.

We often imagine government agencies as operating somewhat independently from both the political processes that set their purposes and the citizens—or clients—whom they seek to benefit. The story often goes like this: Political and legislative processes instruct governments to produce certain goods and services or social outcomes, such as education or public safety. Citizens then receive and consume these goods and services much as they enjoy the products that they buy in the private marketplace. In this common view, the public-sector manager in government works at some remove from both politics and citizens. Innovations occur within the four walls of public agencies. For example, managers invent ways to use their financial or human resources more efficiently or they develop more effective techniques to produce desired outcomes.

This image of government, of its relationship to politics and the public, and therefore of the appropriate nature of public-sector innovation cannot explain why so many of those who have applied for innovations awards (and presumably many public officials who have not applied) have created programs that reach beyond the boundaries of government to enlist private citizens to advance the public interest. These innovators have discovered that they often cannot do their various jobs well unless they secure the cooperation and contribution of citizens and community organizations. Unfortunately, they frequently lack the methods, techniques, and skills to interact effectively; these are not the sorts of things that we teach, or they learn, in schools of public administration or management. That is why successful civic engagement with government requires innovation.

Social Cooperation

Many public policies require citizens and clients to cooperate—sometimes in ways that substantially change their behavior—with public edicts and public officials. In order to secure and maintain that cooperation, public officials must sometimes educate their clients and the larger public, instill in them a greater sense of public responsibility, and even alter their deeper values and priorities. The programs operate in a sociopolitical reality in which many citizens are unwilling or unable to comply and cooperate according to legal and social norms and regulations. In such cases, one job for government is to induce or capacitate cooperation (or else society may be forced to adopt different, less demanding, norms and regulations). Many might complain that public officials who act didactically in these ways intrude paternalistically on the private choices of citizens and do so without political warrant. Without engaging in such moral questions, it is notable that several programs have been recognized as government innovations because they invented new ways of fostering social cooperation.

In 1987, for example, the city of Seattle set out to dramatically increase the rate of recycling in its solid waste stream. The city launched a marketing campaign that included billboards and radio spots to encourage its 300,000 residents to participate in curbside recycling and other waste management programs. Additionally, the city began to charge residents for picking up additional nonrecycled waste at the rate of $108 per year per additional weekly can. As a result of these admonishments and incentives, the city nearly doubled its recycling rate from 1987 to 1990 to encompass 44 percent of the waste stream (Borins 1998, pp. 76, 88, 204). After only one year of operation, 78 percent of eligible households were participating in the program. In 2005 the city imposed a requirement to recycle paper, metals, and glass. Beginning in 2006, the city began to enforce the requirement by refusing to collect garbage cans containing more than 10 percent recyclables (Seattle Public Utilities 2006). At minimum, local officials created opportunities for residents to manifest their environmental commitments in their daily decisions about how they create and dispose of waste. They may also have used their public authority and resources to bring many residents to embrace enhanced environmental responsibility. The innovations awards program recognized the Seattle effort with an award in 1990.

Given the rising profile and urgency of environmental problems such as global climate change, whose causes reside in the uncoordinated behaviors of billions of individuals around the world, public innovators would do well to reexamine this and similar initiatives.

Several innovations awards finalists and winners have created programs that enlisted the cooperation of citizens and clients in the course of delivering public services to them. In these cases, the ultimate value depends not just on the quality of some public service, but on the character of the interaction between client and provider. Paradigm examples come from health care. Effective treatment and management of chronic diseases often depend not just on quality medical care but also on patients who are responsive to doctors' suggestions, take their medications responsibly, and engage in appropriate diets and lifestyles.

Consequently, several innovations in the field of public health have sought to alter the relationship between officials and clients in ways that involve patients more deeply in caring for themselves or those who are close to them. The Baltimore Project sought to reduce infant mortality and low birthweight in several of the city's poor urban neighborhoods. In addition to making Medicare, family planning, preventive care, and emergency medical services more accessible, the program used a peer-to-peer outreach model. Neighborhood residents were trained as lay public-health workers and then were hired to enroll pregnant women in the program, which offered case management, education, counseling, and support groups. In its first several years of operation, the Baltimore Project enrolled 85 percent of the pregnant women from its area of operation. In 1993, in the course of Baltimore's Healthy Start initiative, the project was expanded to cover more neighborhoods.

Beginning in 1987, the New York City Bureau of Child Health expanded the mission of its fifty-five child-care clinics from infant care alone to health care from infancy through adolescence (Borins 1998, pp. 11, 49, 159–60). A central component of this reform was to improve the relationship between children in disadvantaged families and their physicians. Families were assigned to particular doctors, and as a result the percentage of children seeing the same doctor consistently increased from 44 to 88 percent between 1989 and 1993. As the mission expanded, program staff required greater levels of cooperation and contribution from children and their families. To take one small indicator, the percentage of kept appointments increased from 54 to 65 percent between 1989 and 1993. When the city embarked on asthma treatment through these clinics, they moved from simply distributing inhalers and other medications to enlisting parents in more proactive efforts to help their asthmatic children through preventative and environmental interventions.

Several innovations embark on the more daunting challenge of securing cooperation from recalcitrants. The hard hand of the police, courts, and prisons are appropriate for many lawbreakers. Often, however, the criminal-justice system operates in ways that fail to protect the most vulnerable; there simply are not enough resources for policing and prosecution. Sometimes, less coercive and more persuasive methods can moderate antisocial behavior. When available and effective, such methods are often better for the individuals, those close to them, and their communities.

The Quincy Model Domestic Abuse Program, under the umbrella of the First Justice of the Quincy Court in Massachusetts, combined criminal penalties with a range of treatment programs that empower abused women to protect themselves and rehabilitate those who abuse them. The program began by making legal instruments and protective services such as filing complaints, providing court advocacy, obtaining restraining orders, and providing shelter more accessible to victims of domestic abuse. The court tied these instruments to both stricter enforcement and more vigorous treatment for abusers. The court confiscates weapons, monitors compliance with substance abuse regimens, and sends wife batterers to a variety of treatment, therapy, and rehabilitation programs. As a result of these initiatives, many more women obtain restraining orders and file formal complaints, and more abusers are enrolled in court-supervised monitoring programs. Most important, the number of deaths from domestic violence has declined substantially since the program's initiation. The Quincy Model Domestic Abuse Program won an innovations award in 1992.

Noncustodial fathers who fail to make child-support payments to the mothers of their children and to fulfill other child-rearing responsibilities—deadbeat dads, for short—receive little more sympathy in the public eye than those who batter their spouses. Punitive measures such as imprisoning or fining noncompliant parents may do more harm than good by further diminishing the support that those parents provide to their children and families. But designers of the 1994 innovations award–winning Minnesota Parents' Fair Share Program realized that the failures of many noncustodial parents stem in part from their lack of individual capacity and opportunity. The initiative joins a set of supportive social services to improve the situation and capacities of noncustodial parents through peer support, mediation sessions, and child-care classes with employment and training programs to boost their incomes and so enable them to make support payments. After less than two years, the program more than doubled participants' support payments, from an average of $51 per month to $110.

Perhaps the minimum level of social cooperation that we expect from all citizens is that they refrain from violence. In 2004 the San Francisco Sheriff's Department won an innovations award for its tapestry of efforts to decrease violent attitudes and behavior in criminal offenders. In an era when the emphasis in many correctional agencies has shifted from rehabilitation to sanctions and incarceration to protect communities, the San Francisco Sheriff's Department expanded its mission by seeking to make violent criminals less likely to re-offend. Its Resolve to Stop the Violence Program (RSVP) uses both therapeutic and restorative-justice strategies to make offenders and ex-offenders less violent. Therapeutically, the program uses educational and group sessions to make inmates more aware of their own emotional and behavioral responses and triggers. The restorative-justice elements of the program seek to develop and improve relationships between victims and offenders through mediation and restitution, involve inmates in community service, and connect offenders with a range of education, substance abuse, and job-training services after their release.

Communication and Understanding

Before public agencies attempt to secure cooperation from clients and citizens, it is often important for officials to know the character of the people they serve. When local officials hail from the communities in which they work or from very similar ones, much of the relevant social knowledge is second nature to them. In a highly pluralistic society, however, wide sociological gulfs can separate officials from their publics. These gulfs are often exacerbated by social inequalities and group discrimination. When they face these social and cultural walls, even well-intentioned officials can have a difficult time discerning a community's needs and devising effective means to satisfy them. When officials recognize that their social understandings and methods of working do not fit well with some of the subgroups they seek to serve, some of them develop innovations that bridge the worlds of public agencies and insular communities.

Ignorance, misunderstanding, and distrust often separate law enforcement agencies from gay and lesbian communities. There is good reason to think that crimes against gays and lesbians are underreported and that police investigations of crimes that are reported are hampered by these problems of social distance. Since 1997 top leadership in the Police Department in Washington, D.C., has recognized these difficulties and sought to address them through a variety of outreach efforts and internal reforms. The department formed a Gay and Lesbian Liaison Unit, staffed by several full-time officers who develop relationships and investigate crimes that occur within the gay and lesbian community. Partially as a result of solving several homicides and other violent crimes, the Gay and Lesbian Liaison Unit has improved the reputation of the police, and so the trust in them, among gay and lesbian residents of the capital. In fact, officers in the unit view it as a success that the number of hate crime reports they receive has *increased* because they feel that they have overcome some of the distrust that results in underreporting. The Innovations in American Government Awards Program recognized the Gay and Lesbian Liaison Unit with an award in 2006.

Financial products and services, too, are developed to suit particular communities and types of individuals. People from different cultures and traditions can
have a difficult time obtaining credit and banking services. Among Native
American families, only half own their own home, as compared to three-quarters of non-Hispanic white families. Part of this differential stems from economic inequalities, but part of the difference also stems from the historical fact
that many generations of Native Americans were told where to live rather than
choosing where to live. Lacking such traditions and experience, bankable credit
records, and the skills and aspirations that make homeownership possible, it is
not surprising that many housing programs targeted to Native Americans meet
with failure. To overcome these challenges, the Chickasaw Nation created a
homeownership program called Chuka Chukmasi (literally "beautiful home"),
which sought to educate and reform both financial institutions and prospective
Native American homeowners. The program identified major barriers to Native
American homeownership such as limited credit histories or lack of funds to
make down payments and pay closing costs. Program leaders then negotiated
partnerships with mainstream financial institutions to develop programs that
utilized the strengths of Native American borrowers despite their failure to meet
these standard lending criteria. Chuka Chukmasi also developed an instruc-
tional program in home purchasing, mortgage lending, predatory lending,
home maintenance, and other aspects of financial literacy that it requires its
clients to understand. By 2003 the program was financially self-sustaining and
had facilitated $20 million in mortgage lending. The program bridged knowl-
edge gaps on the part of lenders who did not understand the risk characteristics
of Native American communities and on the part of Native Americans who
lacked the knowledge necessary to navigate modern financial institutions.

Civic Mobilization for Co-Production

In an era of limited public resources and increasingly demanding social problems, many government innovations seek to expand the capabilities of the public sector through mobilization and partnership with citizens' and civic
organizations. For their part, civic and other nonprofit organizations frequently
find partnership with government organizations beneficial because it allows
them to leverage authority and resources to advance their missions. Despite the
danger that the public-benefit purposes of partnerships can get lost in the deal
making that occurs between private and government entities, such partnerships
do have the potential to expand the power to find solutions to public problems
by mobilizing civic ideas, energies, and resources. The innovations awards program has not been remiss in recognizing the accomplishments of some of the
most imaginative and successful projects in this realm.

The insufficiency of government action and consequent necessity for civic collaboration come into sharp focus with conservation and wildlife protection issues. For a variety of political and practical reasons, state action alone frequently cannot accomplish these environmental objectives. For example, endangered wildlife frequently reside on private lands where the reach of environmental regulators is limited by legal and political obstacles. Furthermore, many environmental challenges are sufficiently complex that devising effective solutions requires deliberation that draws on a wide range of knowledge and expertise that is both local and global, lay and professional. Finally, many of the solutions that emerge from such processes require complex and coordinated actions from many parties, including federal officials, local regulators, nonprofit organizations, and private landowners.

The Grassroots Conservation Program of the U.S. Fish and Wildlife Service won a 2006 innovations award for creating a collaborative conservation initiative that brought together government, civic, and private energies to conserve Montana's Blackfoot River watershed. Decades of mining, timber harvesting, and grazing had so degraded the ecosystem that the Blackfoot River was listed as one of the nation's ten most endangered rivers in 1992. In response, the Fish and Wildlife Service began working with conservationists, landowners, and other agencies to restore the local ecosystem and to protect threatened species such as bull trout, grizzly bears, and lynx. Regulators in the conservation program developed durable relationships with civic partners, especially the Blackfoot Challenge, a nonprofit conservation organization led by landowners. In subsequent years, this and other civic partnerships of the Grassroots Conservation Program made substantial gains in protecting endangered species such as the bull trout, in restoring natural habitat through measures such as easements, grizzly bear fences, and the removal of fish barriers, and in promoting sustainable forestry. These collaborative conservation efforts have involved more than 500 community members and seem to have diminished the polarization and conflict among developers, landowners, environmentalists, and government that frequently characterize the politics of threatened ecosystems.

Moving from a rural setting to a densely urban one, New York City officials in the 1990s faced the challenge of revitalizing an enormous system of urban parks that were underfunded, dilapidated, and underutilized. Realizing that they lacked the resources and authority to repair this enormous system within the Parks and Recreation Department, officials began to reach out to community organizations and wealthy individuals for assistance.[1] Staff sought to create local groups to support and guide revitalization efforts around the city's parks. Cooperation with the Central Park Conservancy and the Prospect Park Alliance

---

1. See John F. Kennedy School of Government (2004).

led to early and visible successes for the New York City Partnership for the
Parks Program. These groups and individuals, together with a host of others
concerned with smaller parks, contributed more than $50 million and also pro-
vided volunteer labor to improve these neighborhood public goods. Perhaps
more important, however, they became the cutting edge of a mobilized political
constituency who pressed for greater investment and attention to the quality of
all the public parks in the city. Parks and Recreation officials describe themselves as having moved from the role of professional stewards of park facilities
into a far more complicated, public, and political role that is "part ombudsman,
part community organizer, part consultant, and part agency liaison."[2] As a result
of their efforts, the partnership has worked with civic groups and neighborhood
residents to restore the waterfront along the Bronx River, mobilized thousands
of volunteers to clean and maintain city parks, and hosted or attended more
than 6,000 community events in and about New York City's parks.

Public Consultation

Several important areas of public-sector experimentation and invention have
received minimal attention from the innovations awards program. One of these
is public consultation. It may be that the selection criteria of the awards program deemphasize procedural innovations in favor of those that aim directly at
substantive policy outcomes or that procedural innovators are less inclined to
apply for innovations awards. Yet public consultation can play an important
role in helping agencies to better understand their constituents' needs and
adjust their programs accordingly. Many of the innovations just described show
the importance of adjusting agency priorities and actions according to the views
and needs of various constituencies. Yet the methods for obtaining the views of
citizens and clients, such as the traditional public hearing and notice and comment procedures, exhibit deep and well-known flaws. For one thing, participants tend to be unrepresentative of the general public in that they are often
more deeply interested in the particular issues under discussion, have more
extreme views, and are more educated and wealthy than the average member of
the public (Fiorina 1999). Furthermore, the way in which discussion and decisionmaking are organized in many public hearings frequently produces polarization or alienation rather than constructive engagement (Kemmis 1992).
Fortunately, a variety of public and civic actors—sometimes jointly and sometimes in parallel—are working to improve the methods of pubic consultation.
Although these innovations focus on the quality of the democratic political

2. Partnership for Parks, application to Innovations in American Government Awards Program, 2000.

process rather than on concrete outcomes, the innovations awards program may consider expanding its ambit in the future to include them.

In the aftermath of the September 11, 2001, attacks that destroyed the World Trade Center towers, planning and development officials charged with the redevelopment of Lower Manhattan faced contending priorities and constituencies such as residents, business owners, victims' families, and the area's leaseholder. By the middle of 2002, journalists and activists were bombarding the preliminary plans produced by the two agencies leading the reconstruction effort—the Port Authority and the Lower Manhattan Development Corporation—with vocal criticism. In the face of these conflicts, the agencies agreed to solicit public input to guide the planning process. The process culminated in a large-scale "twenty-first-century town meeting"—a process designed and organized by a nongovernmental organization called AmericaSpeaks—at New York City's Jacob K. Javits Convention Center that was attended by about 5,000 people.

Event organizers used community-organizing methods, group facilitation techniques, and collaborative communication technologies to make this large-scale event possible and to overcome the main deficits of typical public meetings (Fung and Rosegrant 2006). To address the problem of unbalanced representation of the public at-large because of self-selection, community organizers publicized the event in communities and among individuals who would be less likely to participate on their own initiative, such as socially isolated minorities and low-income groups. At the event itself, participants were organized into small groups of ten or twelve so that all would be able to express themselves and actively engage in the day's discussions. In order to integrate and aggregate dozens of separate discussions on any one theme, scribes recorded conversations at each table on laptop computers and relayed dozens of streams to a centralized "theme team," which picked out common themes and relayed them back to the table groups. Through this layered process of small-group discussion and large-group aggregation, participants discussed an array of questions about the visions and values that ought to guide planning and reconstruction. The event received substantial coverage in local and national media and compelled public officials to fundamentally revise both their planning parameters and their procedures.

Another example of consultative innovation comes from James Fishkin and his colleagues at the Center for Deliberative Democracy at Stanford University. As stated earlier, almost all public participation mechanisms invite individuals to select themselves to participate and so produce a mix of participants that is skewed toward those who are wealthier, more educated, more directly interested, and more opinionated. To get around this problem, since the late 1980s Fishkin has been conducting a new form of public consultation called Deliberative Polling, which overcomes these "selection biases" by attempting to bring together a statistically representative group to consider some public issue.

Fishkin's central innovation is to select participants randomly, using the same methods as a well-conducted public opinion poll. The group is constructed by randomly selecting individuals in some area—a city, state, or even the whole country—inviting them to participate in a focused public discussion, and compensating them for their time and effort. Individuals who accept the invitation are sent briefing materials and then come together at a central location, usually for a weekend, where they meet with one another and with experts to deliberate about various public issues. Fishkin and his group have worked with public-sector leaders to organize deliberative polls in the United States and abroad around issues such as energy policy, foreign affairs, crime, aboriginal issues, and others.[3] Research on these events shows that participants gain issue knowledge and shift their views in systematic ways as a result of the deliberating they do. Deliberative Polling is thus a promising innovation in the public consultation realm that should be utilized more often by leaders in the public sector.

Twenty-first-century town meetings and deliberative polling concentrate the energy of participation into a short period—one or a few days. For many issues, though—especially at the local level—it is both feasible and desirable for individuals to meet with one another in a more sustained way to foster relationships and more thoughtful deliberation. Dozens of local governments in the United States have worked with the Study Circles Resource Center to create venues for deliberative public consultation that bring together public officials, stakeholders, and citizens to address concerns such as education, safety, racial and ethnic conflict, poverty, and economic development.[4] Under the Study Circles method, organizers begin the process by inviting a diverse set of participants—usually including public officials and citizens drawn from diverse groups in a given community—to form a study circle. These participants typically use printed issue booklets—often prepared by the Study Circles organization but sometimes produced in local communities—to guide their deliberations over several "rounds," often spanning several weeks. Through this process, participants work to frame their understanding of some community problem, set priorities, generate ideas about how to solve that problem, and pool their individual and organizational resources. Study circles frequently culminate in "action forums" in which participants ratify concrete plans and next steps to take that grow out of their deliberations. The Study Circles method has been used successfully to translate community polarization into greater understanding and agreement and to integrate socially isolated minority groups.

---

3. See "Deliberative Polling: Toward a Better-Informed Democracy," http://cdd.stanford.edu/ polls/docs/summary [accessed October 9, 2007].
4. See Study Circles Resource Center homepage at www.studycircles.org [accessed October 9, 2007].

The public hearing—though its flaws are glaring to academic critics, public officials who run them, and citizens who participate—is by default still the predominant method of organizing citizen consultation in democratic governments across the globe. Fortunately, there exists a menu of innovations—not just twenty-first-century town meetings, deliberative polling, and study circles but also methods such as consensus conferences and citizen juries—that promise to improve the quality of representation and deliberation in public consultation. Doing so, however, requires that public officials know about these innovations and have motives to use them to improve the quality of public consultation.

Accountability

The accountability of politicians and government agencies to the publics they serve remains a critical challenge in the United States and in other countries. Fortunately, several recent innovations show how direct citizen participation can be used to increase government accountability. It is notable, however, that innovations that increase the accountability of government to citizens' views and interests have not figured prominently in the innovations awards program. This may be because public-sector entrepreneurs—except, perhaps, for up-and-coming district attorneys—would like to stress government's positive accomplishments rather than its tendencies toward corruption and self-dealing. Or it may be because the most ambitious and successful of these innovations for greater accountability have occurred outside the United States. Consider two illuminating examples.

When legislators are faced with changing the rules of their electoral systems—perhaps modifying the boundaries of electoral districts or choosing majority rule or proportional representation systems—many are tempted to make decisions that protect their own electoral prospects rather than advancing democratic objectives such as electoral competitiveness, voter choice, or community representation. For example, in the United States, redistricting questions are most commonly decided by legislative committees. The process of carefully drawing district lines to maximize the probability of the incumbent party's maintaining a majority has risen to a computer-assisted science. Partially as a result, incumbents have been reelected at rates of more than 90 percent in U.S. federal elections.

In the Canadian province of British Columbia, public leaders recently invented a novel process called the Citizens' Assembly to decide whether the province should move from a system of majority rule to proportional representation (British Columbia Citizens' Assembly on Electoral Reform 2004; Lang 2007). The Citizens' Assembly was composed of 160 citizens who had been randomly selected from provincial voting lists. In order to ensure a degree of descriptive representativeness, selection was stratified by region and gender. The assembly convened every other weekend for day-and-a-half-long meetings over the course of one year. Over this time, members learned about various electoral designs, attended open meetings to gather public opinions, and deliberated about the merits of various voting systems. Attendance was very high—around 94 percent.

Members decided that British Columbia's electoral system ought to serve three fundamental values: fairness, understood as proportionality in the allocation of legislative seats; local representation, understood as the connection between an elected representative and his or her geographic constituency; and voter choice, understood as the number of candidates and parties. To analyze the merits of alternatives, assembly members simulated the operation of various voting systems. Eventually, they settled on two alternatives—a mixed-member proportional (MMP) system and a version of the single transferable vote (STV). The STV option defeated MMP by 123 to 31 in a vote of Citizens' Assembly members. Bypassing the legislature, the citizens of British Columbia considered this recommendation in a provincial referendum in May 2005. The requirement for passage was a "double majority": more than 60 percent of the total ballots cast and more than 50 percent of the ballots cast in forty-eight of the province's seventy-nine electoral districts called ridings. In other words, a simple majority in more than 60 percent of the constituencies was required for passage. The measure won a majority in all but two of the constituencies, but it garnered only 57.4 percent of the total vote. Although the result fell just short of the required supermajority threshold, it appears that many voters did consider the Citizens' Assembly process legitimate. As of the fall of 2007, the Liberal Party government had announced that it would hold a second referendum on the Citizens' Assembly proposal in 2008 to allow time for greater public debate. The situation also creates a certain awkwardness; the government holds power by virtue of an electoral system that a majority has voted against. Ultimately, the Citizens' Assembly may provide a more democratic and accountable method of deciding questions of political structure than the conventional methods of legislative committee and independent commission.

Despite the recent invention of the process, two other Canadian provinces have copied the British Columbia process, and several other jurisdictions in other countries have adapted it as a device for electoral system reform. The social and political circumstance of British Columbia might be especially favorable for such a process. For example, major political parties on all sides were dissatisfied with the first-past-the-post system in British Columbia. Without such precipitating conditions, it is unclear whether any effort to replicate this innovation will meet with similar enthusiasm.

In many urban areas of developing countries, and in some developed ones, public decisions are distorted by the politics of patronage. Politicians make decisions about public investments in clinics, schools, houses, roads, and other basic infrastructure by selecting contractors and employers who advance their political fortunes rather than selecting projects to improve public welfare. Politicians in the Brazilian city of Porto Alegre developed an innovative method of making decisions about public investments that has substantially reduced the frequency and effects of patronage. "Participatory budgeting" (*orçamento participativo*, or OP) shifts decisions about the infrastructural portion of the municipal budget from the city council and line agencies to a system of popular neighborhood assemblies. Every year, residents in every neighborhood meet to determine their public investment priorities, and actual allocations of the city's budget follow from them. Since the OP process was initiated, in 1989, the percentage of Porto Alegre's neighborhoods with running water has increased from 75 to 98 percent, sewer coverage has expanded from 45 to 98 percent, and the number of families offered housing assistance has grown sixteenfold. Furthermore, surveys show that the reforms seem to have suppressed patron-client relationships: 18 percent of long-time neighborhood association leaders admit to engaging in patron-client exchanges of benefits for political support, whereas only 2 percent of leaders who became active after the initiation of the OP process did so (Baiocchi 2005). Another study found that prior to the OP, 41 percent of neighborhood associations secured public funds and other governmental benefits by contacting politicians directly, whereas after OP, none relied on such unmediated channels (Avritzer 2002).

The British Columbia Citizens' Assembly and the participatory budget in Porto Alegre successfully confront the problem of unaccountable government by moving the locus of the relevant decision away from officials and putting that authority in the hands of carefully convened citizens. In both cases, those citizens enjoy a certain moral advantage—they are tempted neither by the promise of reelection nor by the benefits of clientelism. In both cases, the innovations also have made it possible for participants to acquire the knowledge and expertise necessary to make reasonable decisions. Members of the Citizens' Assembly met with political scientists and other voting-rules specialists over four months to learn the merits and problems of various electoral arrangements. Porto Alegre's neighborhood residents receive instruction on project planning and implementation that they combine with their own knowledge of local needs and priorities. The more general lesson of these two innovations, then, is that direct citizen participation in decisionmaking can work as a powerful corrective to conventional representative structures where the normal checks and balances on representatives and agency officials fail to direct their energies to the public's interests.

Such accountability-enhancing innovations are not common because they require special political conditions to thrive. Public officials are often loath to cede their authority and prerogatives, but there are exceptions. The British Columbia Citizens' Assembly would not have occurred without the sustained personal commitment and political capital of Gordon Campbell, the leader of the Liberal Party and British Columbia's premier. In Porto Alegre, the Workers' Party championed participatory budgeting, not just for ideological reasons but also for electoral motives. They promised that the reform would deliver greater public investment to their constituents and allow them to shape the content of those investments. Participatory budgeting was not just a policy reform; it was also a political innovation that garnered the Workers' Party many successive victories in races for the municipal executive. Understanding the genesis and success or failure of all innovations always requires grasping their political logic and context, and this political dimension is especially crucial and problematic for innovations that aim to enhance the accountability of government.

The Problem of Public Ends

Despite the accomplishments of these various participatory innovations in the areas of social cooperation, communication and understanding, civic co-production, consultation, and accountability, the very reasons that make direct public engagement appealing can also threaten the integrity of public policies and state actions.

Often, the portion of the public that engages itself will expect or demand a voice over the determination of public ends and the public good in exchange for its involvement. Such voice can be a powerful and democratically legitimate corrective, especially when—as the problems of electoral reform and municipal clientelism illustrate—public officials are corrupt or overly self-interested. But activist citizens, especially when they are unrepresentative or are organized into special-interest groups, can also distort the mission of public agencies. For example, in the New York City Partnership for the Parks, officials of the city's Parks and Recreation Department naturally courted wealthy patrons to provide material support and civic leadership. The personal backgrounds and values of these private individuals who serve on governing boards, select programs and projects, and plan renovations and expansions will inevitably color their decisions. Their priorities may be skewed and unrepresentative of the broader public interest.

Of course, public officials themselves have no monopoly on clear-eyed insight into what constitutes the public good. At the U.S. Fish and Wildlife Service, the collaborative Grassroots Conservation Program exemplifies a range of ecosystem management initiatives—including habitat conservation plans and watershed councils—that shift the development and implementation of environmental policy away from regulatory agencies and toward clusters of local stakeholders (Fung and Wright 2003; Brick, Snow, and Van der Weterling 2000). Despite its many advantages, one danger of this approach is that the negotiated settlements of those stakeholders will fail to respond to important public interests and priorities. For example, there is strong reason to suspect that many habitat conservation plans are dominated by landowners and give economic development higher priority than, say, habitat conservation favored by environmentalists (Thomas 2003). In order to respond to this danger of lopsided interest groups, public officials must not simply devolve control of policy to local stakeholders but must see to it that the stakeholders use public powers and resources in ways that are consistent with broader public purposes. Too often, however, public officials have regarded successful stakeholder negotiations as sufficiently expressing the public interest. But devolution of decisionmaking is not enough; public officials must also ensure that those settlements and agreements advance public purposes by developing the capacities for exacting review and monitoring (see Fung 2004).

This potential for citizens or stakeholders to use mechanisms of civic engagement to hijack public power has led some skeptics to be suspicious of the full range of participatory innovations. Perhaps, following the conventional model of the representative policy process, the determination of public ends should be insulated from direct citizen participation and left to elected officials and public administrators. No doubt this solution can sometimes be the best course, democratically speaking. But, as the innovations described show, it fails as a general prescription for two reasons. First, and most important, elected officials and public servants can themselves make decisions in very self-interested ways that disregard public priorities. Second, ordinary citizens often possess valuable insight that ought to be included in the determination of public ends. The appropriate extent of direct citizen involvement in the determination of public ends often depends on both social and political context; it is a matter for situated democratic judgment.

The Problem of Public Means

Citizen participation may also hamper the development and implementation of effective strategies and methods. When parents engage with school staff, they may, for superficial reasons, favor an inferior classroom teacher, curriculum, or principal. With urban planning and infrastructure investment, residents may pick projects and plans that answer short-term instead of long-term needs, that favor neighborhood priorities but do not make sense for the city as a whole, or that are technically unsound. When complex questions such as voting rules arise—as with the British Columbia Citizens' Assembly—citizens may lack the expertise to judge the consequences of various choices and so make mistakes in this crucial area. Generally, citizens may lack the knowledge and competence to make wise choices about the means to achieve valued public goods. Even when they formulate sound strategies, they will often be less reliable in executing those strategies than public-sector professionals because their efforts are usually voluntary and not compensated.

These dangers are real. However, the risks they pose to competence may be offset by two competing considerations. First, the need for innovations that engage citizens often arises *because* the methods available to government alone are incapable of accomplishing some public task. As we have seen, governments need social cooperation, cultural knowledge, civic resources, and public input to develop effective public policies and strategies in areas such as waste management, human services, domestic abuse, neighborhood planning, and ecosystem management. In these areas and others, civic engagement is a necessary component of many effective strategies. Second, therefore, public leaders and managers should not regard the skills, competence, and knowledge of citizens as a fixed constraint. The public capabilities of citizens can be enhanced through education, assistance, and other support. In the Baltimore Project, neighborhood residents were trained to become lay public-health workers. Participants in the British Columbia Citizens' Assembly learned the details of alternative voting schemes through academic lectures and educational materials. Porto Alegre's participatory budgeting process includes a didactic component in which residents engage with urban planners to learn about the feasibility of various infrastructure projects. Initiatives that rely on public engagement often risk faltering because of citizens' lack of competence, so it is crucial that public leaders seek to improve the relevant capabilities of citizens rather than take them for granted.

The Problem of Too Many Evenings

Many initiatives that aim to elicit civic engagement founder on the shoals of tepid participation from an apathetic public. Perhaps the most common worry about civic engagement initiatives is that they will require too many evenings of citizens who are properly concerned with their own personal, economic, or political affairs.[5] It is notable that the innovations discussed in this chapter did not fail for want of participation, so it is instructive to see how they succeeded in getting people to participate, where other innovations have not met the challenge of citizen nonparticipation.

---

5. Oscar Wilde is said to have quipped, "The problem with socialism is that it takes too many evenings." This remark has also been attributed to George Bernard Shaw.

First, the initiatives discussed here require varying levels of participation, in terms of both group size and time commitment. It is tempting to think that the ideal level of participation is the entire adult population of some jurisdiction or catchment area. But this ideal is neither appropriate nor feasible for most initiatives. The Seattle solid waste program aimed to alter the behavior of all Seattle residents and had to touch many of them in order to be successful, but the Montana collaborative conservation effort required a small number of key landowners, conservationists, and residents to participate intensively. Thus, the desired extent of participation should follow from the purposes of an initiative or the character of the problem that it seeks to solve. Successful collaborative conservation requires engaging directly interested parties such as landowners, developers, and environmentalists and then also a range of others who may be less manifestly concerned with a local ecosystem but who can take action to help conserve it. The accountability-reinforcing deliberations in Porto Alegre and British Columbia do not require everyone, or even most eligible citizens, to participate. Rather, they require enough citizens to produce decisions that incorporate a range of interests and that are democratically legitimate.

Second, most of these initiatives elicit substantial participation because they grapple with problems that are urgently and acutely felt by the groups they target: domestic abuse, homeownership, development and control rights over land, and neighborhood infrastructure. Third, some of these programs establish the reasonable expectation that individuals who engage will be able to influence public decisions and actions. These two features together combine to create forms of empowered participation that provide people with strong reasons to devote at least some of their evenings to solving public problems, as opposed to merely consultative or placatory varieties of engagement (Arnstein 1969; Fung 2004).

Fourth, public authority can be used to compel citizens to contribute their time and energy. At the extreme, citizens are required by law to serve on juries when called. In San Francisco, participation in Resolve to Stop Violence was not strictly required, but it was addressed to an audience that was literally captive. In Montana, the threat of time-consuming and costly litigation as well as strict environmental protection regulation created background conditions that made negotiated and collaborative approaches to conservation appealing to both environmental and landowning interests. These experiences illustrate some of the ways in which successful innovations in civic engagement can use state authority to compel or induce participation.

Conclusion

We have considered just a few of the many initiatives that have been recognized by the Innovations in American Government Awards Program and a handful that lie outside of that scope. Several conclusions emerge from this limited overview. First, innovations that attempt to solve pressing public problems— the target of the awards program—must frequently reach beyond the four walls of public agencies to engage citizens. Second, citizen participation in public problem solving takes many forms. Sometimes it takes the form of community discussions following the model of the town meeting, and sometimes it arises from social marketing and education, intensive individual development through counseling and casework, or focused teamwork. Third, citizens make different kinds of contributions to public problem solving. Some innovations improve on the methods through which citizens articulate their interests and views and use their local knowledge to inform public action. But the innovations surveyed above also illustrate a range of less well-understood citizen contributions such as cooperation, ingenuity, financial resources, and political accountability. The specific responses to the general challenge of harnessing citizens' desires and energies in order to deal with urgent public issues are properly called innovations because they have resulted from the ingenuity and creativity of public leaders in government and civil society. The finest tribute to these innovators and the programs that they have created would be to incorporate successful practices of deeper citizen engagement into a wide range of public-sector activities and so deepen democracy by bringing citizens into more regular and fruitful association with their government.

5

Subnational Government Innovation in a Comparative Perspective: Brazil

MARTA FERREIRA SANTOS FARAH AND PETER SPINK

After launching the Innovations in American Government Awards Program in 1985 as a counter to declining public confidence in government, the Ford Foundation went on to discuss similar activities in other countries that were also facing moments of transition and challenge. In the Philippines, Galing Pook was conceived by a group of local governance advocates who shared a vision of sustainable development through the empowerment of local communities. They were responding to the challenges of the Local Government Code of 1991, which granted substantial autonomy to local government. Administered through the Asian Institute of Management, the award was officially launched in October 1993. Brazil was the next, in 1996. Here, too, a new constitution had provided much clearer guidelines for subnational government and posed a considerable challenge for service provision. Other countries followed: South Africa, with Impumelelo, a program created by local nongovernmental organizations; the United States, with a program for Native American tribes also based at the Kennedy School; Chile, with a program initially based at the National Foundation for Poverty Reduction; Mexico, at the Center for Economic Research and Teaching (CIDE); China, at the China Center for Comparative Politics and Economics; Peru, at the interuniversity Network for the Development of Social Sciences; and, most recently, East Africa (Kenya, Tanzania, and Uganda), in conjunction with UN-Habitat. In all these cases use of the open access approach to awards was not seen as an end in itself—after all there is nothing new about giving awards for performance—but as an important instrument to focus debate on the possibilities of action and to provide an independent answer to the question, "How is government meeting today's challenges?" In this chapter, we consider this question through the experience of the Brazilian innovations awards program, Public Management and Citizenship. We begin with a discussion of the study of *innovations* awards as a research method (what we term the "innovations approach") and comment on the place it occupies in relation to best-practices and action research. We then describe the Brazilian program and provide a general overview of its results, before looking more closely at how innovation is seen by those involved as well as at the very important issue of diffusion. Finally, we examine our findings in the light of some of the comparative conclusions raised by Sandford Borins (2001) and also in relation to the arguments in favor of or against "groping along" (Behn 1988).

Innovations: Between Best-Practices and Action Research

In orthodox research terms, the innovations approach aims to provide empirical evidence to inform specific debates on government and governance. The argument in favor of increasing the effectiveness of public organizations and governance seems self-evident, but discussion of the means by which such increase should be sought has generated considerable conflict over the last thirty years. During this period, the pendulum of "good government" first swung way out toward the position that "good government means less government and long live the market." It then tracked its way back through "good government means business-style government and management," with an emphasis on "governance and accountability," to swing out again on the other side under the banner of "good government means citizenship, social inclusion, and rights." These different generations of reform (Abrúcio 1998) have each had their champions, and their arguments and counterarguments have been both technical and ideological in character (Bresser Pereira and Spink 1999; Schneider and Heredia 2003).

The different innovations programs have sought to contribute to this debate through focusing on the capacity of governments, usually subnational, to solve the many problems of everyday life. They start from the assumption that government is important and test this by seeing how capable it is of facing current challenges (Barzelay 2002). In doing so, they position themselves along the pro-government axis—they do not seek innovative examples of less government—but they do so in a relatively open way. They seek to find out what is happening at the leading edge of day-to-day government activity: in regulatory agencies, in street- and field-level services, in different areas of action, in both the big urban centers and the tiny towns and villages. In doing so, they are as open to the conclusion that *nothing interesting* is happening as they are to the conclusion that *a lot of interesting* things are happening. In each of the different Ford Foundation–supported innovations programs, the general question was posed in a specific way, relating to the here and now of each country.

In Brazil, we linked the question about public management to citizenship, because we wanted to know not just whether government was capable of innovative service provision but also whether it was capable of effecting it in a way that had a positive impact on the construction of citizenship in a country characterized by marked social inequality (Spink 2007). Even in 2007, more than ten years after the first awards cycle began in January 1996, we can still remember the anxiety of the countdown to the first entry deadline. Would subnational jurisdictions think that the challenge to discuss innovation was a valid one? Was there really anything happening apart from a few showcase experiences? Our anxiety was made worse by the Brazilian tradition of leaving everything to the last minute: we received more than 600 entries in the last twenty-four hours.

There are many approaches to discovering innovations. Placing the search for innovation within an awards framework is merely a question of method. It is, however, a methodological choice with certain advantages. By emphasizing open access and self-nomination and by spreading news of the awards to as wide a population of public-sector actors as possible, entries are encouraged from places that are beyond the horizon of the usual urban observatories, entries relating to issues that might never be nominated through a more orthodox approach. What is more, highlighting the importance of the practices being submitted (in Brazil, for example, all valid entries are included in the innovations program database, which currently includes more than 8,000 cases) and showcasing the finalists, the awards approach provides an important mechanism for positive and public recognition of those involved in the day-to-day workings of public service.

One of the important and at times undervalued features of the innovations awards approach is the surprise factor. The cutting edge of problem solving, and consequently of innovation, is not easily defined. It can often emerge in areas where it is not expected and in places of which people have never heard. It is this surprise factor that can cause tension between innovation-focused researchers and their mainstream colleagues, who are more used to formal sampling models and who often forget Kurt Lewin's earlier (1935) criticism of the Aristotelian assumption of repetition in claims of knowledge validity. As Lewin argued, if we accept the scientific assumption of the possibility of laws, and if we assume that laws provide explanations and predictions about things happening, then when something happens—even once—there will have to be laws. We might not recognize them. We might miss the important feature. But if they happen, then so do the laws. So when a small and very ordinary municipality finds a breakthrough way of stimulating local development, it is not a question of saying, "Yes, but so what? It is only one municipality." On the contrary, the necessity is to find out how and why and to consider the transferability of the phenomenon—in other words, to recognize that knowledge is present. For example, just as individual swallows have insisted on announcing summer, so single innovations have provided us with important practices such as federalism, party-based democracies, civil disobedience, and social cooperatives, to name but a few. At the level of policy implementation and public-service management, the list is even longer.

Research adopting the innovations approach often raises the question of its similarity to (and difference from) best-practices methodology. Clearly, in the search for underlying concepts and formulations that can help to guide policy-makers and those interested in better and more effective government and in strengthening democracy, examining practical experiences that seem to be working or looking at situations where everything appears to be going wrong are both valid investigative choices. Similarly, there are those who prefer to start from a deductively derived theory and those for whom the inductive type of grounded theory is preferable (Strauss 1987). Both the best-practices and the innovations approaches to public service improvement clearly favor what is working over what is not working, but they tend to divide over their stance on theory. In general, best practices tend toward detailed criteria and extensive descriptions in order to consider an activity as valid, whereas innovations approaches tend to be more open. The danger here is that detailed expectations can reflect underlying judgments about what is appropriate and can run the risk of creating a self-fulfilling hypothesis, in which only those experiences that fit the template are considered and the outliers remain outside. The more open approach of the innovations programs, with very few restrictions on entry (for example, time and public-sector leadership) and an emphasis on analysis and debate among panel members, provides a firmer guarantee that the outlier will be considered. If on one side the innovations approach shares a common boundary with best-practices approaches, on the other it shares a common boundary with the broad tradition of action research. The dangers of relying on conventional wisdom will always be present, even among the most broad-minded of academics and public-sector specialists or the most enthusiastic of open-minded students, but if the different innovations programs were to have a shared motto, it would probably be, "If you think what you are doing is innovative, we are at least prepared to listen."

In the 1997 cycle of the Brazilian innovations program, one of the finalists was a maternity hospital in the northeast of the country. Faced with the challenge of premature births among a population of mothers, many of whom were very young, the hospital had adopted a technique initially developed in Colombia in the 1970s: using the warmth of the mother's chest to maintain the newborn baby at a safe temperature in a natural incubator. Many adaptations were made to the original procedure, and the result became a small but important social project. Not only were the babies safe, but the bonding process between the juvenile mother and her child was not interrupted by the mechanical barrier of the traditional incubator, a physical separation that had often led to psychological separation and to babies being given away for adoption. Taking advantage of the mothers being together with their babies, the program was able to make advances in the area of child health, to address other aspects of the mothers' emotional, social, and work worlds, and to provide a role for the fathers (it was quickly discovered that the natural warmth of the human chest is not a gendered characteristic). The project was not selected for a major award, but it was one of twenty finalists. In the audience for the announcement were members of the Social Directorate of the National Bank for Economic and Social Development (Banco Nacional de Desenvolvimento Econômico e Social, BNDES). After the event, funds were provided to systematize the initiative and consolidate the procedures involved, including some more detailed research evaluation. (It later emerged, for example, that the area of the chest between the breasts has an amazingly quick temperature-adjustment cycle.) Several years later, the "kangaroo mother" technique was formally adopted as a program for the whole of the Brazilian public-health system in a ceremony in which the minister of health announced that the procedure had been ratified and that major funding was available for its use within the system. The members of the evaluation panel were indeed prepared to listen and not write off the experience as a local strategy for dealing with young mothers in low-income groups or as something to be used only in hospitals where mechanical incubators were not available.

In the different countries where the innovations approach has been adopted, the individual awards programs have made considerable contributions to public policy through this very pragmatic approach to knowledge and action. The emphasis in each country has differed, reflecting particular action research orientations and guiding the debate to questions of effectiveness, citizenship, relations with civil society, and local identities. In each, innovations have been identified, debates about change stimulated, and practical solutions disseminated. In some cases, the experiences that have emerged have shared common features—for demands on subnational governments in different countries can be quite similar at times—and in others have differed significantly, being responses to very specific local agendas. In a number of joint seminars involving both practitioners and researchers from different countries, we have noticed how often public managers, mayors, and service providers will nod their head in agreement, despite difficult language barriers. They might not adopt the same solution, and different institutional incentives and constraints may be present, but they recognize the problem and, more important, the process. What they have in common as either elected officials or service managers is a commitment to improving the human and social condition, to increasing the public good. In doing so, they intuitively make the forms of connection that Ivan Illich described as *learning webs* in his discussion of new educational institutions and the deschooling society. As he phrased it, "The planning of new educational institutions . . . must not start with the question, 'What should someone learn?' but with the question, 'What kinds of things and people might learners want to be in contact with in order to learn?'" (Illich 1973, p. 80).

Introducing Brazil and the Brazil Innovations Program

Brazil's federal structure is divided into three levels: the federal government, located in the Federal District of Brasilia, twenty-six states, and more than 5,500 municipalities. Twelve municipalities have over a million inhabitants each, including São Paulo, with 10 million in the city and nearly 20 million in the greater metropolitan area. At the other end of the scale are more than 4,000 municipalities (73 percent of the total) with fewer than 20,000 inhabitants, many with populations of fewer than 5,000.

For most of the twentieth century, through alternating periods of authoritarian government and attempts at building democracy, the dominant model of public administration in the country was based on the concentration of decisionmaking power and execution of services in the executive branch of the federal government, with residual powers and competences ceded to the state level and a few areas of local interest assigned to the municipalities. Fiscal powers followed similar lines, leaving states and municipalities in a dependent relationship. The 1988 constitution sought to provide a clearer framework for the different components of the federal system, laying down rules for the distribution of taxes, fiscal decentralization, and transfer mechanisms for redistribution. It also introduced the idea of a more active citizenship. Various instruments for direct democracy and consultation were detailed, broadening the public space and responding to the pressure of social movements that had grown in strength toward the end of the military period. The new constitution also increased social rights. These were dependent on the development of effective public policies and public investment, however, and could only be introduced in a gradual way. The democratic constitutional agenda defended decentralization and popular participation, affirming that democracy and decentralization should go hand in hand. The result was the slow strengthening of Brazilian municipalities, turning the country into a federal triad; it is one of only a few of the world's federal countries where municipalities are considered federal entities along with the states and the union itself.

At the same time that the constitution was pushing for decentralization, Brazil's hectic high-inflation economy began to show signs of coming under control, with considerable implications for fiscal adjustment and state spending. There was much debate about the need to move away from a development strategy oriented excessively to the public sector. A new wave of public-sector reforms began to take place, including a search for new forms of interaction with civil society. New forms of management of state agencies were introduced in an effort to provide the agencies with greater agility and effectiveness and thus reduce the bureaucratic rigidity and the excessively hierarchical structure of decisionmaking. But the tight economic controls had a severe impact on the labor market: unemployment rates rose, creating even further demands for social services and programs for alternative income generation. And it was often the municipalities that had to come up with the answers.

This was the environment in which the Public Management and Citizenship Program was set up at the Center for Public Administration and Government of the Getulio Vargas Foundation's São Paulo School of Business Administration (Escola de Administração de Empresas de São Paulo, EAESP-FGV) with an initial grant from the Ford Foundation and later support from the BNDES. Its aim is to identify, debate, and disseminate innovative practices among subnational Brazilian governments (states, municipalities, and indigenous peoples' tribal governments) that have had a positive impact on citizenship and quality of life. It focuses on experiences—policies, programs, projects, or activities—that are innovative in service provision, can be reproduced in other localities, use resources and opportunities in a responsible manner, and extend the dialogue between civil society and public agents. During ten years of awards cycles from 1996 to 2005, the program identified and registered some 8,000 innovative "experiences" based in 890 municipalities of different population sizes and varied socioeconomic levels, as well as in all the Brazilian states, among a number of the indigenous peoples, and among the executive, legislative, and judiciary branches of government. The initiatives registered cover many areas of government action and provide important evidence of what is taking place, in the more advanced areas of subnational government, at least. After ten years of successive awards cycles and having achieved its initial goal of raising the level of debate about public-sector capacity in the country (to the extent that a number of other awards have been developed by other agencies for specific areas of public service), the innovations program team decided to use its remaining funds to follow up on many of the experiences identified in order to learn more about the processes of innovation and diffusion. Since the data we use in this chapter were drawn from the annual awards cycles, we begin by describing the typical cycle, to clarify the methodological assumptions on which our discussion is based.

The awards cycle took place over the entire calendar year. It began with the generation of a folder containing information about the program and its activities, the regulations for application to the awards program, and an application form posing a number of questions, such as "What are the goals of the initiative?" and "Which public does it benefit, how does it work, why should it be considered innovative, and what are its main results?" The folder also contained a list of areas of governmental action. To guarantee that there was no mistake about cross-cutting themes, the choice of identifying the sector of activity was left to the entrants themselves. Applicants had to satisfy a few very general and minimal criteria: they had to be coordinated by a subnational public-sector organization and to have been running for at least a year; the initiative had to represent substantial change, qualitative or quantitative, in relation to former practices; it had to be potentially replicable in whole or in part or at least had to permit dialogue with other themes and areas of work as well as be transferable to other regions and jurisdictions; it had to broaden or consolidate forms of access and dialogue between society and its public agencies; and it had to use resources in a responsible manner.

The program's selection process was divided into three phases, very similar to that of the Innovations in American Government Awards Program. In the first phase, 100 applicants were chosen as semifinalists. Participating in the selection process were members of the program's advisory board, university professors and researchers, postgraduate students, specialists in public management, and members of nongovernmental organizations. All selection participants received a number of application forms beforehand to assess individually. Over the two days of the semifinalist meeting, these were discussed in groups along with similar assessments made by other evaluators. This was followed by an open discussion by all the evaluators of the proposed lists of semifinalists, a debate that usually involved around forty to forty-five people. After selection, the semifinalists chosen received a list of more detailed and specific questions calling for more information in a number of areas. A similar process was used in the next stage of evaluation, this time with the additional information. Thirty programs were selected as prefinalists, and these received a technical site visit to verify that the program was what it claimed to be. The visits were carried out by an independent team of thirty researchers from different universities, research centers, and nongovernmental organizations and were supervised by senior researchers. In the final stage, the advisory board, aided by a number of specialists, discussed the different reports and the previous material supplied by the applicants themselves and selected twenty finalists. At the awards ceremony, following further presentations and discussions, five were selected as "outstanding" by an independent panel drawn from civil society organizations, the press, and international organizations.

At each step in the process, the underlying approach was always the same. The list was never considered final until everyone present felt satisfied with the choices made. When doubts were raised, as often happened, the debate was always steered back to the program's theme: public management and citizenship. It may be easier to apply a template, add up the numbers, and rank applications in order, but open and honest discussion makes better sense and, we would suggest, better science.

Results

Since there are many more municipalities than states, it is not surprising that municipal governments submitted the majority of applications. But their presence also reflects the broadening of municipal responsibilities that stems from both the constitution of 1988 and a number of years in which federal economic policies placed considerable restraint on national government spending, thus implicitly passing other responsibilities downward. Today, for example, it is not unusual to find municipal governments grappling with local economic development; racial, gender, and ethnic inequality; agricultural policies; infrastructure; and policing—issues traditionally handled by Brazil's state and federal powers. Overall, 17 percent of all entries came from state-level organizations and institutions, 82 percent from the municipal level, and 1 percent from indigenous peoples' own governments (see Eller and others 2005 for all data). The presence of the indigenous peoples' own tribal organizations was particularly significant in the Brazilian context, an important political statement of jurisdictional authority over tribal lands that has played a notable role in inverting a number of stereotypes about Brazil's original peoples.

During the ten years of our study, participation by region remained relatively stable. The south and the southeast of the country maintained a strong presence, with 78 percent of entries; together they also accounted for seven states, 51 percent of Brazilian municipalities, and approximately 62 percent of the country's population. By the tenth cycle, some 890 municipalities had participated at one time or other. The spread of municipalities tended to follow that of the states, with slightly more municipalities taking part from the south and southeast and fewer from the north and midwest.

Table 5-1 shows the distribution of the 890 municipalities that participated in the awards cycles of Public Management and Citizenship between 1996 and 2005, by their population size. As the table indicates, there was high turnout over the years from the larger municipalities. Around 90 percent of municipalities with more than 500,000 inhabitants sent applications to at least one of the award cycles, and every one of the twelve major Brazilian cities with more than 1 million inhabitants also made its presence felt. But the smaller municipalities

Table 5-1. *Municipalities Participating in Brazil's Awards Program,*
by Population Size, 1996–2005[a]

| | All municipalities | | Municipalities participating | | Participants as a percent of all municipalities in |
Number of inhabitants	Number	Percent	Number	Percent	the size group
Total	5,506	100.0	890	100.0	. . .
Up to 20,000	4,019	73.0	358	40.2	8.9
20,001–50,000	964	17.5	211	23.7	21.9
50,001–100,000	301	5.5	135	15.2	44.8
100,001–200,000	117	2.1	92	10.3	78.6
200,001–500,000	76	1.4	66	7.4	86.8
500,001–1,000.000	18	0.3	16	1.8	88.9
1,000,001 +	12	0.2	12	1.4	100.0

Source: 2000 Census; Eller and others (2005).

a. Of all entries received from 1996 to 2005, 82 percent were from municipal jurisdictions, 17 percent from states, and 1 percent from tribal governments.

were also represented and, despite a lower relative turnout, provided nearly two-thirds of all initiatives that we registered. This suggests that, despite the difference in size and in resources (which are generally distributed unequally throughout the country), there may be much more capability and competence in small municipalities than is often imagined.

Almost half (46.6 percent) of the applicant programs in the ten awards cycles fell within the broad area of public services, which includes themes common to local government agendas such as education, health, housing, and social assistance, among others. Other areas with a large number of entries were citizenship and human rights (24.5 percent), which includes policies aimed at children and adolescents, the elderly, and women, and economic and social development (10.3 percent), which includes job creation and income generation. Table 5-2 shows the distribution of entries in the more significant categories.

The fact that the overwhelming majority of applications came from the executive branch is certainly thought-provoking. Brazil's government at the subnational level follows the executive orientation of the federal model. Local municipal government is based on a separately elected executive mayor and has none of the variety found in the United States. At the same time, the major emphasis on innovation in government in most parts of the world tends to fall toward service delivery rather than to specific activities of the judicial (almost by definition conservative in most countries) or the legislative branches. This does not mean that innovations do not occur in these areas or that, when they do occur, they are less important. In the case of Brazil, a significant number of the

Table 5-2. *Entries to Brazil's Awards Program, by Main Areas of Public Action, 1996–2005*[a]

Subject	Percent	Subject	Percent
Education	16.9	Women and gender	1.6
Children and adolescents	14.2	Housing	1.6
Health	11.7	Public security and policing	1.6
Social assistance	6.3	Sanitation (water and sewage)	1.5
Cultural, historical, artistic, and heritage	4.7	Minorities	1.2
Professional training and income generation	4.1	Traffic, roads, and public transport	1.2
Regional and local sustainable development	3.5	Urban planning, land use, pollution control	1.1
Management and planning	3.5	Information systems	1.1
The disabled and people with special needs	2.7	Staff training and administration	0.8
Leisure and sports	2.5	Judiciary	0.7
Senior citizens	2.4	Industry, commerce, science, and technology	0.7
Popular participation	2.4	Prevention in landslip and other risk areas	0.6
Solid waste collection and treatment	2.3	Young people	0.5
Preservation of ecosystems and water resources	1.8	Legislative	0.5
Farming, fishing, and food supply	1.8	Improvements in working conditions	0.4
General citizenship issues	1.7		

Source: Eller and others (2005).

a. For comparison, 1 percent represents eighty-two experiences.

relatively few applications received from these institutional areas have been very important. Let us cite three examples: a program for education and back-to-work activities for first-time offenders with prison sentences, which was developed by local judges and later supported by a state secretary of justice and spread to neighboring states; the work undertaken by the municipal chamber in a small rural community to restore confidence in local government after the ousting of a corrupt mayor, which involved, among other activities, holding the ordinary sessions of the chamber on different days in different parts of the rural zone so that the population could follow the chamber's work; and the work of one of the state accounting tribunals in teaching the population how to read and follow the accounts of their municipalities and how to report signs of possible misuse of public funds. In this last case, the information strategy included the use of a far-from-austere equivalent of bluegrass and country music songs.

Within the wide variety of areas of public action reported in table 5-2, seven account for some 76 percent of all entries. These are, in order, education; children and adolescents; health; social assistance; culture, historical preservation, and the arts; job training and income creation; and regional and local sustainable development.

All seven areas fit many of the expectations about what local government should be doing, but each has its own story to tell. Education has mainly involved basic schooling, which in the Brazilian model corresponds to grades one through eight. Basic education has traditionally been the responsibility of states and municipalities, with the federal government providing financial support for basic services and determining the minimum curriculum. If there has been any change at all, it has been in the relation between the states and the municipalities in the area of what is called the "municipalization" of school places. This trend has seen the transfer of buildings and organizational responsibility for education at the local level from the state to the municipality, along with budgetary requirements for states and municipalities to invest at least 25 percent of their tax-based income in the maintenance and development of educational programs.

In the case of children and adolescents, as well as other issues of social welfare, arguments can be made for the importance of the 1988 constitution, which provided a route map of municipal responsibilities in these areas, contributing to the political processes of decentralization taking place in Brazil and elsewhere in Latin America (Arretche 2000; Campbell 2003). The preponderance of health initiatives, too, is no surprise, given implementation of the Single Health System (Sistema Único de Saúde, SUS) following the 1988 constitution. The prevalence of job-training and income-generation initiatives may reflect successive government economic policies and an overall shift in the labor market from "formal" to "informal" work contracts and to high levels of unemployment, thus making income generation and employment very much part of the many day-to-day demands placed on local government. These phenomena may also be reflected in programs of regional and local development. Culture, preservation, and the arts are also very much local affairs, with municipalities increasingly linking their local heritage to tourism and job creation and being supported in this in different ways by state governments.

One oft-noted feature of Brazil's democratic system is its wide range of political parties, which run across the whole political spectrum. Even though, as could be expected, governments of the more progressive parties tended to register more innovations, the range is by no means restricted. No single party was involved in more than 8 percent of entries, and eleven parties each were involved in at least 3 percent of entries. (Political affiliation was not included on the entry form, and the data for this observation were taken from the Federal Electoral Tribunal's public access database.)

Perhaps one of the most striking features of the various applications submitted was the constant involvement of various types of organizations from the public, private, and third sectors. Of the programs, projects, and activities submitted, 66 percent reported having working links with other governmental agencies at the local or other level, and 60 percent reported links with what can be broadly termed local community-based organizations, business, and other associations. In 46 percent of the cases, these overlapped, and links were reported with both other governmental agencies and community and local organizations and associations. In only 20 percent of the cases was there no mention of alliances or partnerships at all. In policy terms, this suggests that in only 20 percent of the cases were actions being undertaken using the model still commonly assumed and taught of the hierarchical public-sector agency working alone in its own patch, developing and implementing new practices in accordance with its own perspective. In the remaining 80 percent of cases, other organizations were involved, either creating arenas for interagency cooperation or spanning the public sector and civil society or, more significantly, doing both. Management in Brazil is far from vertical and often involves more horizontal and negotiated working relationships (a characteristic also noted by Borins 2001).

Why Innovate?

In a previous study (Spink 2006a), we took a closer look at the reasons given for these actions. We analyzed a cross section of replies from semifinalist programs to the question posed in the first and second phases of the selection process: "Why is your policy, program, project, or experience innovative?" As the question was open-ended, the answers were subjected to qualitative analysis.

Seven distinct themes emerged from the analysis of the replies, and only a quarter of the replies fell into two or more thematic categories (see table 5-3). Among the seven there were three major themes. The first of these, present in some 58 percent of the replies, referred to "assuming the initiative in the search for new solutions to existing problems." The solutions could be technical, administrative, or organizational, but running throughout was the idea of actively reaching out to the population in focus. The second and third themes together accounted for a further 40 percent of the replies and referred to significant changes in the approach toward action. The second expressed the importance of "changing the frame for thinking about action"—for example, moving to an interdisciplinary approach or introducing broader ideas of sustainable development or collective health. The third related to a change in the relationship between government service providers and society, where service providers actively sought to include focal populations in a collective manner through participation and co-management of actions and policies.

What is interesting about these three major themes is that they seem to sum up what happens once it is assumed that the role of public managers is to resolve

Table 5-3. *Reasons Given by the Applicant for Why a Cross Section of Experiences Is Innovative*

Reason	Percent giving the reason
Assuming the initiative in the search for new solutions for existing problems	58
Changing or broadening the frame for thinking about action	21
Actively involving the community in the search for and the co-management of solutions	19
Creating new inter-organizational arrangements and linking the solutions with other bodies	11
Changing priorities and making services more receptive and "human"	10
Transferring solutions from one area to another, adapting existing technology	2
Pioneering, the first time this was done in the region	1
Total (multiple classifications possible)	122

Source: Spink (2006a).

the serious problems of the increasingly democratic society within and for which they were elected. Perhaps most of us would assume this to be at least the theoretical tenor of modern service delivery and indeed the institutional design of the democratic state. Yet how many of us could say that it is effectively taking place in our own country?

The fourth theme was far less common and referred to forms of linkage and the creation of new inter-organizational arrangements. At first glance, this may seem strange, given the widespread presence of such relationships among the entrants described above. Perhaps the explanation is that, for many, this is something taken for granted that may also be present when people talk about participation or that involves bringing together resources that are necessary in order to produce results. This was often an extra item in a multitheme answer.

The fifth, sixth, and seventh themes were also less frequent, but again point to important conclusions. The fifth referred to making services more "human" or reaching the "excluded," probably a belated acknowledgment of values overlooked in the push to democracy that many would assume to be self-evident. The sixth and seventh, present in less than 3 percent of the replies, referred to themes that are normally identified by business leaders and scientific policymakers as the key aspects of innovation. The sixth referred to the transfer of technical or administrative technology from one area to another and was usually part of a multitheme reply. The seventh and most infrequent of all (present in only 1 percent of replies) mentioned the novelty aspect of innovation that normally fills the advertising pages of car and information technology magazines: "The first time in the area. The first of its type. Pioneering."

Table 5-4. *Continuity of Finalist Awardees from the First Seven Years of the Program (1996–2002) in 2004*

Percent

Characteristic	Number of cases	Continuity	No continuity
Municipal	102	94	5
State	30	77	20
Tribal	8	64	36
With change in political party[a]	95	87	11
Same party in power[a]	37	92	8

Source: Farah (2004).

a. Does not include tribal awardees.

One of the constant features of the "government is inefficient" movement is unfavorable comparison of government with the business sector. Leaving aside the obvious reply that organizing the production and delivery of tangible goods is very different from the co-production and co-definition of social goods such as health and happiness—a debate that would require at least another Festschrift—it is interesting to return to the leading theme that those who have been practically involved in producing solutions presented in justifying their actions. How to "assume the initiative in the search for new solutions to existing problems" is precisely the question on which business leaders dispense fortunes in the form of motivational seminars, consultants, and books—all in the search for "know-how." The answer from the public sector seems to be, "Get on with it. Go out and solve the problems people have."

What Happens to Innovations? Continuity and Diffusion

In 2004 we carried out a major evaluation of the impact of the Brazilian awards program, concentrating on the finalists from the first seven years and covering 140 initiatives from municipalities, states, and indigenous groups (Farah 2004). This included follow-up conversations and telephone interviews with each program and focused on the continuity and diffusion of the different activities. Some of the key results from this study are shown in table 5-4.

In terms of continuity, nearly all of the municipal-level programs were still in place (94 percent), as were three-quarters of the state-level programs and more than two-thirds of the indigenous programs. Of the sixteen that had been discontinued, four had changed location from the public to the nongovernmental sector, and seven had been discontinued for political reasons. But political reasons, such as a change in party, were not overall a significant factor. In the forty-five cases in which there had been a significant change in party, most of the programs (87 percent) were continued. There was no difference in level of continuity between the northeast and the southeast of the country or by the size of municipality. It is also interesting that of the sixteen programs that were interrupted, more than half had been taken up elsewhere. Take one example, the *bolsa-escola,* or school grant scheme. This program provided financial support to poor families on the condition that they keep their children in school, thus combating both child labor and the problem of petty street crime. The scheme was created in the Federal District of Brasilia during Cristovam Buarque's administration and won an award in the first cycle in 1996. It was stopped for explicitly political reasons by his opponent and successor, Joaquim Roriz, yet later became a core component of what is now one of Brazil's key social security programs, the family grant. It has been replicated in other parts of Latin America and Africa.

Taken together, the results suggest that continuity rather than discontinuity is a characteristic of effective local innovation, despite political changes. Activities are being continued because they are making a contribution and have become part of the local service arena. It is likely, too, that the presence of alliances and partnerships plays a part. It is far less easy to stop a multidimensional network of actors from different organizations, or an activity that has reached out in a significant manner to local communities, than it is to order a subordinate to stop an in-house service.

Overall there is clear evidence that 56 percent of the award-winning initiatives had been diffused or transferred either directly or indirectly. In only 13 percent were staff involved in the individual program or project convinced that no diffusion had taken place, and in the remaining 31 percent, staff were unsure. Diffusion is not a magical process, and, as Bruno Latour has pointed out (1987), ideas do not float around by themselves. For ideas and practices to travel and be transferred, there have to be links and interests, arguments into which they can fit and to which they contribute—that is, they must be part of the governmental agenda at the point of reception (Farah 2006a). Such formal or informal linkages can involve the exchange of information and the insertion of the experience in a network of institutions and social and political actors (Rogers 1995; Sugiyama 2004). Information exchange can sometimes lead to the view that there is nothing to be learned, especially when characteristics that may be "specific to the way they do it there" (Donahue 2005) become overemphasized as the news travels. Although this can happen, our evidence suggests that this is much less present in Brazil, at least at the seemingly pragmatic level of subnational government innovation (Farah 2006b).

Natasha Sugiyama has followed up the process of diffusion involving the school grant program, which was later merged with a second and similar program that also started at the municipal level and aimed to provide a minimum wage for very low-income households. She argues that social networks do not by themselves explain the diffusion of public policies and governmental programs. Nevertheless, "they have important functions that contribute to policy diffusion: they help explain how learning occurs and the geographic spread of information. At the most basic level, associations and networks provide information on the latest policy initiatives, distribute information, and maintain professional norms" (Sugiyama 2004, p. 19).

In another recent study (Farah 2006b) we looked at different patterns of diffusion. We found that the rapidity with which ideas spread can sometimes create an impression of simultaneity. One such experience in Brazil is the "one-stop-shop" approach to public services such as identity cards, driving licenses, housing loans, job offers, savings banks, municipal taxes, and many other paper-and-pencil activities that often plague the daily lives of citizens forced to go from one side of town to the other in search of their "documents." The same idea seems to have emerged virtually at the same time in very different parts of the country—the north, the northeast, and the south. Another factor in its quick dissemination is that it coincided with a push to public responsibility and the widespread use of information technology by the public sector.

Where we have specific information about dissemination and diffusion, the results are quite impressive. The 2004 study showed that 34 percent of initiatives had been reproduced in more than ten jurisdictions, 14 percent in six to ten jurisdictions, 33 percent in two to five jurisdictions, and 13 percent in just one other jurisdiction. The 2006 study showed that horizontal diffusion between jurisdictions at the same level is a dominant pattern, counting for 81 percent of examples of diffusion. Vertical diffusion from the federal level to states and municipalities, or from states to municipalities, is less frequent (16 percent), but can play an important role, especially when serving as a disseminator of practices that have emerged from state or municipal levels, as in the "kangaroo mother" program described above.

A good example of vertical diffusion is the Permanent Commission for the Investigation and Control of Labor Conditions in Mato Grosso do Sul (Comissão Permanente de Investigação e Fiscalização das Condições de Trabalho em Mato Grosso do Sul). This was a state initiative that involved the judiciary, business leaders, and nongovernmental organizations, developed originally to focus on the plight of the largely informal workforce (which included children and indigenous people) in the traditional charcoal production enterprises in rural areas of the municipality of Três Lagoas. The program has since been broadened by the state to include other municipalities. The commission was a pioneer in the fight against child labor in Brazil, and its multi-actor alliance served as an example in different parts of the world and subsequently motivated the formulation of a Brazilian federal policy against child labor, the Eradication of Child Labor Program (Programa de Erradicação do Trabalho Infantil, or PETI), which now exists all over the country. In the case of the permanent commission, there was a double process of dissemination: one downwardly vertical, from the state to the municipalities, and a second, upwardly vertical, through which the federal government offered incentives for other states and municipalities to adopt a similar program.

The use of the terms *horizontal dissemination* and *vertical dissemination* has some affinity with the distinction established between the voluntary transfer and the coercive transfer of public policies (Dolowitz and Marsh 2006; Conde Martinez 2005). What we have found is that there is usually negotiation between the voluntary and coercive dimensions, since the local actors almost always play an active role in the decision about which policies and programs to adopt, and at the same time upper levels of government and multilateral agencies influence local governments' actions through guidelines, incentives, and sanctions. The federal government in Brazil can offer strong incentives and can withdraw funds in a number of circumstances, yet the resultant push-pull generally stops short of compulsory introduction. Policy is neither a solely top-down nor a solely bottom-up affair.

The institutional or jurisdictional "neighborhood" is an important element in the horizontal dissemination of municipal and indigenous programs. The three indigenous programs that have been disseminated followed a horizontal pattern of diffusion, and all of them diffused regionally, obeying a spatial pattern. Key to this seems to be the similarity of problems faced by neighboring localities. In the case of the municipal programs that reported horizontal dissemination and diffusion, 57 percent of cases evidenced the "neighbor effect." One clear example of the local neighborhood agenda is the water conservation program A Drop of Water (Pingo d'Água), which began in the municipality of Quixeramobim in the state of Ceará, located in a semiarid region of Brazil. The program reportedly was reproduced in at least eighty-seven of the neighboring 100 municipalities in Ceará most affected by drought and also in other municipalities and states of the region.

In the remaining 43 percent of cases of horizontal diffusion, other factors came into play: political party networks, professional networks and associations, nongovernmental organizations, conferences and other sponsored forums of discussion, as well as information published by the Public Management and Citizenship Program and similar awards. Information on programs was also transmitted through the press and media (Mattos 2005). Another important dimension of the dissemination-process analysis is related to the role assumed by social and political actors from the localities that "receive" the innovation. Contrary to the models of wholesale imitation prominent in the institutional literature, the absorption of the innovation is not an automatic process but is the result of an active process of choosing, a search for alternatives that can be adapted to the specific locality (Melo 2004).

What these results show is that the process of dissemination or diffusion is quite distinct from the replication of a template, which supports our initial perspective on the subtle differences between innovations and best practices. What seems to travel is the inspiration, representing an alternative taken from a repertoire of possible answers to a social problem common to different localities— that is, the conception behind the specific solution, rather than the solution itself. The practical example is important because it points to the possibility of change and also provides the opportunity for dialogue. But unless it can find a place or be absorbed within an existing set of concerns, or within the priorities of an agenda for action (Kingdon 1995), all the prizes and praises in the world will have no effect (Farah 2006a).

Comparing Conclusions

In his 2001 article comparing public management innovation in economically advanced and developing countries, Sandford Borins pointed to the important counterintuitive contrasts provided by the United States, which, despite its developed economy, does not follow the trend evident in other economically advanced countries, where innovations tend to be directed at the general population. Instead, with an emphasis on the poor, the young, and those at risk, it tends to follow the pattern of the developing world. As Borins put it (2001, p. 717),

> The USA has a much less secure social safety net than the economically advanced countries of the Commonwealth, a larger underclass, and greater inequities in income distribution. As a consequence, many of its innovative programs aim to provide health care for the uninsured, improve safety and public services in urban ghettos, protect young people at risk of joining gangs and taking drugs, and improve the life chances of children born into poverty. This finding suggests opportunities for dialogue between innovators in the USA and in developing countries.

This is certainly the case with the results from Brazil and from other innovations programs. In two recent texts (Grafilo 2006; Spink 2006b) the Innovations Programs Liaison Group for the first time brought together experiences from all the different programs in one language, English. The result is quite remarkable, and the experiences and underlying ideas connect with very little difficulty.

Our data suggest conclusions that differ slightly from, yet also confirm, a number of the results from Borins's study (2001), which emphasized "holism, the introduction of new technology, process improvement, the involvement of organizations or individuals outside the public sector to achieve public purposes, and the empowerment of communities, citizens, or staff" (p. 729). As we have commented, partnerships and other forms of inter-organizational arrangements emphasized in the programs Borins studied were possibly taken for granted by our informants. Cultural factors may be operating here, as well as the particular ways in which individual federalist models deal with territorial questions. In relation to what he described as a holistic and more system-wide analysis, we certainly found some evidence of these factors among the reasons given for why activities were innovative. We found little evidence that the use of new technology was the primary reason for innovation, yet we did find evidence that subnational governments reached out to forge links with communities for decisionmaking, policymaking, and co-management. They may not have used the word *empowering,* but the result is very similar. At the same time, our informants did tend to emphasize a very simple yet often forgotten feature of innovation: "assuming the initiative in the search for new solutions to existing problems."

This pragmatic approach to problem solving and to the situational knowledge that action creates is what distinguishes another feature of many of the experiences that we were able to study. Very few of them followed the guidelines issued by the international development community for project management. And they certainly did not follow any manual on strategic planning. Here we follow Robert Behn's observations (1988). "Management by groping along" may not be the most elegant formulation, and there may be a better one somewhere, but the conjunction Behn seeks to convey of possessing a sense of objectives yet lacking clarity as to how to achieve them—of seeing the top of the other side of the valley but not knowing quite how to get there—is very much the sense we get, though still with a difference. Our respondents tend not to be worried about what is over the top of the next hill until they get to it; in that sense, they are also incremental: "One horizon at a time" seems to be the motto. Most initiatives started life as local public challenges that resulted in local public practices, raising questions, gathering other resources, and making alliances along the way. Participatory budgeting, which has spread around the globe from its humble beginnings, is a case in point. It may have evolved into a major policy, but that was not the initial intention. Initiatives may have started life in the community and been adopted by local government, or they may have started through the actions of public servants who are in direct contact with the day-to-day workings of communities in poverty settings. Often it is a mix of both, and, within the Latin American context, this blending together of public policy and social action in the local setting, of public officials, activists, and civic leaders working together to solve problems, is being increasingly referred to as the space of *public action* (Cabrera Mendoza 2005).

Consider the following: ten years ago one of our finalists was Tupandi, a poor rural municipality (population 3,000) in the south of Brazil. The municipality was in decline. Youngsters were no longer showing interest in farming, preferring instead to move to the larger cities in search of unskilled factory work, and given the widespread informality of the rural economy, the local administration had very little income for action. One contributing factor identified was the difficulty small farmers had in marketing their produce (chicken, pigs, milk, and fruit) in the more formal economy, due to the absence of an effective infrastructure for guaranteeing quality. Meeting together in the village church, members of the community and the local government decided to create a municipal development fund from which they could make small nonrepayable grants to each farmer of approximately $1,000, to be used in constructing sheds and barns. The conditions of the grant were that, in exchange, the farmers would introduce up-to-date technology, respect the environment, and only sell their produce with a formal receipt that would include the Brazilian sales tax. A proportion of this tax is automatically returned to the municipality, and the idea was that somehow this would compensate for the initial subsidy. (How the municipal government managed to create this fund is a story in its own right. The law it created in effect saw the municipal government give public money to people in exchange for an agreement to abide by the law. In practice, what mattered was not the law itself but the moral agreement made in public discussion—an example of public action.)

When we first made contact with the initiative it was already in its third year, and the gain in production and in the related tax base was already offsetting the original investment. Youngsters were growing enthusiastic about the commercial possibilities and were returning to the area. We recently returned to see what had happened since that first visit, and the results were astounding. Nearly all the farmers had benefited from the fund, and as a result of the moral agreement, the per capita internal product of the municipality went from $2,514 in 1993 to $16,007 in 2004, an increase of more than 600 percent. The local government's own income had risen tenfold as a result of the increase in the tax base, and wise investment and the effective use of other available subsidies had led to paved roads, guaranteed electricity for all rural properties, piped water for 99 percent of the properties, and twenty-four-hour public-health and hospital service. Housing had been improved, and the municipality now had a thriving network of community associations and sports and cultural clubs. As well as encouraging youngsters to stay in the area as a result of the economic development, the municipality also could provide them with tuition grants and subsidies for

50 percent of the travel costs for university attendance, enabling them to remain at home while studying. In 1993 there were no banks in the town. In 2004 there were four, a very good indicator of the growth in commercial and small-scale food-processing activities. The town was still the same size, and the same families were still there.

Nobody would have predicted in Tupandi in 1996 where the municipality would be ten years later. What they had to do was to assume the initiative in the search for new solutions to existing problems—they had to get to the first hill-top. Now the Tupandi experience is spreading around neighboring small municipalities and has already crossed state lines. It may not be the sort of experience that has the glamorous appeal of the great urban renewal programs, of the strategic cities, or of the major breakthroughs in state–civil society relations. But if it works for Tupandi and neighboring municipalities, that is what is important in terms of a pragmatic approach to knowledge. A contrasting point of view was expressed to one of our colleagues who recently discussed this and other somewhat idiosyncratic experiences with a senior member of a Washington-based development bank. In essence, the response was that if it was not possible to guarantee that an innovation could be broadly applied in many different places, and quickly, the innovation was not worth anything. Aristotle would be pleased at the way his views continue to inform the technical opinions of the staff of these institutions.

Clearly, diffusion of ideas does take place, but recognizing this is a very different theoretical position than requiring it in order to accept the validity of a practice. One of the great contributions of the different innovations programs has been to validate the value of local collective action. Innovative experiences are rarely the product of a single mind; on the contrary, they are the product of much discussion, concern, trial, and error. They are learning processes that may be organizational, social, communal, or collectively based, and the knowledge they produce is not elegant. But when push comes to shove, they are basically about people getting out there and trying to solve problems. Congratulations to the Kennedy School, the Ford Foundation, and the Ash Institute. Thanks for taking the lead.

6

The Unaccustomed Inventiveness of the Labor Department

JOHN D. DONAHUE

For most of its first decade the awards program launched by the Ford Foundation and Harvard's John F. Kennedy School of Government to promote and celebrate public-sector innovation looked everywhere but Washington for evidence of inventiveness. It was not until 1995 that the Innovations in State and Local Government Awards Program opened eligibility to federal agencies and changed its name to the Innovations in *American* Government Awards Program.

That first year there was a flood of federal applications, and ten federal programs advanced to the finalist stage. Once the judges had met and pronounced their judgment, there were six federal winners. Two of the six were from the Department of Defense—then and now the biggest federal organization. Interior and Justice each had one winner. The other two winning programs were from the Department of Labor—among the smallest and, at least by tradition, stodgiest of federal organizations. The next year Labor won another award. During the first Clinton administration, under the leadership of Secretary of Labor Robert B. Reich, Labor accounted for a sharply disproportionate share of innovations awards semifinalists, finalists, and (especially) winners.

This chapter searches for factors that might cast light on the Labor Department's proclivity to inventiveness during those years. Unlike the other chapters in this book—and unlike most of my own writing—this is not an arm's-length scholarly inquiry. I am by no means an authority on the determinants of organizational innovation. My familiarity with the relevant literature is relatively slight. And since I worked at the Labor Department, in reasonably senior positions, for much of this period, I cannot claim to be a dispassionate observer. Consider this a set of personal reflections that may inform analysis—as a modest deposit into the bank account of real-world examples on which my research has always depended—rather than as a piece of completed analysis.

Profile of the Department

The U.S. Department of Labor was founded in 1913, after decades of pleas from workers' organizations for a voice in the cabinet, with two main duties: integrating the flood of new immigrants from southern and eastern Europe into the American workforce and tracking economic and labor data through the pre-existing Bureau of Labor Statistics (MacLaury 1998). With World War I came a spike in additional responsibilities—mobilizing labor and industry for war production; mediating industrial conflicts lest they undercut production—but with the end of the Wilson administration Labor lapsed into a decade of somnolence. It was under Franklin Delano Roosevelt's long presidency that the modern Labor Department took shape. Under the energetic leadership of Frances Perkins, America's first female cabinet officer, Labor built, adapted, or assimilated organizations to implement the new mandates for promoting employment (the Civilian Conservation Corps), buffering the shock of job loss (the Wagner-Peyser Act and the unemployment insurance provisions of the Social Security Act), and setting a floor under wages and a ceiling on work hours (the Fair Labor Standards Act) that were part of the New Deal.

What would become a major new mission, workforce development, started with the Kennedy administration and grew under Lyndon Baines Johnson. Over roughly the same period, the legislative and cultural revolution of the civil rights movement left Labor with a new layer of responsibilities for combating discrimination in the workplace. The improbably activist Nixon and Ford administrations brought a surge of additional duties, including a massive expansion of training and job-creation programs, the introduction of complex new occupational safety and health rules, and (with the 1975 passage of the vast and complicated Employee Retirement Income Security Act) challenging new responsibilities for the oversight of pensions and other employee benefits. The Carter, Reagan, and George H. W. Bush administrations saw ebbs and flows in funding and shifts in the priority accorded different Labor missions. But from the late 1970s to the early 1990s Labor reverted to its accustomed role as a decidedly low-profile department, tending to a tangle of worthy but dull programs.

Many observers were thus surprised when President-elect Bill Clinton announced that he would nominate Robert B. Reich as secretary of labor. Reich was an articulate, prolific, and occasionally controversial academic who had known Clinton since their years as Rhodes scholars, in the late 1960s. A *New York Times* profile by Stephen Greenhouse reported that Reich, who had seven books to his credit, had "shaped Democratic thinking on the economy more than any other academic over the past decade."[1] Reich had taken a leave from his teaching job at Harvard's Kennedy School of Government to play a central policy role in Clinton's campaign. After Clinton's victory, Reich—whom Clinton called "one of my most trusted advisers and closest friends"—was put in charge of the economic-policy transition team. The betting was that he would end up heading the Department of Commerce, the Council of Economic Advisers, or the new National Economic Council. Instead, he was named to what Steven Mufson, in an article in the *Washington Post,* termed "a job that for most of the past two decades has been a political and bureaucratic backwater."[2]

Washington insiders speculated that Reich had encountered resistance to his bid for a central economic-policy role or that the ivory-tower academic simply didn't know that Labor wasn't considered an A-list job. In fact, Reich had requested the Labor post. His thinking on the causes of lagging living standards and rising inequality had evolved to highlight the policy issues in Labor's portfolio. A decade earlier Reich had focused on high-level economic institutions and policies, but he had come to see the circumstances and capacity of the workforce—its education and training, its voice in the workplace, its claim on government's attention and enforcement powers—as central determinants of middle-class prosperity. Though he by no means intended to restrict himself to the labor secretary's traditional domain, and would weigh in vigorously on policy debates over taxes, trade, and fiscal policy from this unconventional perch, Reich embraced the role at Labor with enthusiasm and eagerly set to work.

Labor's Innovation Awards in Clinton I

The Labor Department submitted thirty-six applications to the Innovations in American Government Awards Program from 1995 to 1997.[3] Three of these

1. Stephen Greenhouse, "Nominee Devoted Years to Rehearsing for Role," *New York Times,* January 9, 1993.
2. Steven Mufson, "Reich Hopes to Revitalize, 'Expand the Vision,' of the Labor Department," *Washington Post,* December 11, 1992.
3. This section draws on Donahue (1999, chs. 4, 10, and 15). The OSHA and Pension Benefit Guarantee Corporation chapters were researched and drafted by Dalit Toledano (Toledano 1999); the chapter on the Early Warning Program, by Laura Ziff and John Trattner (Trattner and Ziff 1999). Unless otherwise indicated, all quotes and figures in this section came from Donahue (1999), which draws on internal agency documents, Innovations in American Government Awards Program materials, and press reports.

were eventually selected as award winners (the department also had one finalist and one semifinalist).

Maine Top 200 Targeting Program

The Occupational Safety and Health Administration (OSHA) was one of Labor's least-loved and most-troubled agencies. Employers denounced it as intrusive and unreasonable, while unions viewed it as timid and overmatched. OSHA's scant roster of supporters meant that there was continued downward pressure on its budget and workforce. By the mid-1990s OSHA and its state affiliates had fewer than 2,000 inspectors to enforce job safety and health regulations at more than 6 million workplaces.

Frustration was endemic at OSHA. One particularly galling instance of this general theme was the agency's Maine office, which had won awards for its tough enforcement record but without much improvement in the state's unenviable job-safety record. Bill Freeman, the head of the OSHA office in Maine, gradually became convinced that the cooperation of a firm's management was an essential concomitant to safety improvement. He and his associates improvised a set of procedural changes, within the confines of existing law, to motivate managerial cooperation. The strategy centered on 200 firms that accounted for a third of Maine's workforce and half of its workplace injuries.

Targeted companies were given a choice. One option was for management— in consultation with OSHA and with the engagement of its workers—to develop its own comprehensive safety plan. OSHA would minimize fines and other penalties for companies working in good faith toward a solid safety regimen. The other option was a conventional OSHA inspection, with the near certainty that violations would be discovered and penalties levied. This "choose your OSHA" strategy involved some bluffing; unless most firms opted for cooperation it would take years for OSHA to inspect the holdouts. In the event, 184 of the 200 firms chose to develop their own safety plans. Spending to reduce hazards surged, frequently in areas that OSHA would not have been equipped or authorized to insist upon. Most participating companies saw reductions in workplace injuries and illness. The invitation to "choose your OSHA" appears to have altered patterns of influence and authority *within* regulated firms, empowering corporate safety experts and undercutting those who viewed safety rules as unwarranted distractions.

This experiment in Maine had started in the prior administration, but Joe Dear, the Clinton administration's OSHA chief, embraced, celebrated, and sought to promulgate the model. By the mid-1990s reforms inspired by Maine

200 were under way in fifteen states, and the national office was developing a plan to make "choose your OSHA" the core enforcement strategy nationwide.[4]

The Early Warning Program

The Pension Benefit Guarantee Corporation (PBGC)—a separate agency overseen by both the Labor and Treasury departments—regulates corporate pension plans, setting standards for financial soundness. It also insures and, where necessary, takes over the assets and obligations of pension plans that troubled corporations can no longer maintain. Economic turbulence in the late 1980s and early 1990s led to a surge of plan failures and a sharp increase in the PBGC's burdens. The annual sum of corporate retirement payments covered by the government more than doubled between 1987 and 1993. Even more troubling was the steep increase in "underfunding" among private plans that were still in operation. (A pension plan is underfunded to the extent that its assets fall short of the present value of its expected obligations.) Underfunding had nearly doubled to $53 billion, raising the risk of more and bigger failures of private plans and potential insolvency for the PBGC itself.

The PBGC possessed tools to discourage underfunding, including the right to hold up corporate restructuring until its concerns were addressed. But without detailed and timely data on the operations, intentions, and financial status of insured firms, the PBGC was ill-equipped to use those tools. The Bush I administration PBGC director, James Lockhart, launched an effort to identify troubled plans before their failure was a fait accompli and to develop capacity for intervening. When Martin Slate took over in 1993 he sharply stepped up these initiatives. Slate equipped the PBGC to monitor the same financial data that Wall Street tracked, as well as submissions to the Internal Revenue Service, the Securities and Exchange Commission, and other financial regulators, in order to stay abreast of factors affecting pension funding. And he built up a twenty-person team of experienced, financially sophisticated negotiators to take the PBGC's side as deals were structured. Another idea that originated with Lockhart was retained and intensified under Slate, the "Iffy Fifty" list of the fifty companies with the shakiest pension plans. The annual release of the list became a much-anticipated event among the national business press, and companies scrambled to avoid appearing on it.

Convinced that the PBGC's existing authority did not suffice to motivate adequate funding, though, Slate and other officials at Labor and Treasury took

---

4. The effort to nationalize the Maine 200 strategy was derailed when an industry association successfully challenged it in court.

the lead on drafting the Retirement Protection Act of 1994 and driving it
through Congress. The act required firms with underfunded plans to provide
far more detailed financial information to the PBGC, to pay higher premiums
for PBGC pension insurance, and to inform workers and retirees about financial shortfalls. The new legislation amplified firms' incentives to fund their
retirement plans realistically.

Eradicating Sweatshops

In spite of laws limiting work hours and mandating minimum wages, the American economy still harbored workplaces with conditions so dire that they mer-
ited the antique-sounding label of *sweatshops.* Some of the worst abuses, and a
highly disproportionate share of the scofflaw workplaces, were in the frag-
mented, low-margin apparel industry. A raid in El Monte, California, in 1994
uncovered dozens of young immigrants chained behind barbed wire, sewing for
sixteen hours a day or more for as little as 70 cents an hour. Official probes and
exposés by the press suggested that such conditions were pervasive among some
20,000 small operations that did cutting and sewing work under contract to
major apparel firms.

Enforcing wage and hour laws in such settings was hampered by low visibility (most shops were small and located in rural backwaters or low-end industrial
parks), rapid change (a sweatshop shut down by regulators could reopen under a
new name within hours), and anonymity (customers never knew who actually
made the garments bearing high-profile labels). These barriers to enforcement
and the paucity of Labor Department inspectors meant that sweatshops had little reason to fear legal sanctions.

Discussions among frustrated field inspectors with the Department of
Labor's Wage and Hour Division produced one promising tactic. A long-
neglected law barred the interstate shipment of goods made in violation of the
Fair Labor Standards Act, administered by the Wage and Hour Division.
Exploiting this latent enforcement tool, Labor officials seized inventories from
several manufacturers and retailers that had come into possession of sweatshop-
made apparel. Each seizure had a multiplier effect, as larger firms, facing the
prospect that theirs would be the next shipment scooped up by Wage and Hour
Division inspectors, suddenly had more of a motive to check into the production practices of their suppliers.

Reich heartily approved of the legal tool that field inspectors were employing to
get the attention of the apparel industry's heavy hitters. But he suspected that the
financial pain of a lost shipment was a minor matter compared to the damage a
firm's reputation could suffer if the public learned it bought from sweatshops.
Reich was acutely aware of the power of public opinion and the leverage that a

coherent, well-framed message could exercise. He was highly effective both in print and on screen—and rather enjoyed being in front of the television camera—and had hired sophisticated public-affairs experts to staff the Labor Department's press office. Reich and his team reasoned that companies in the fashion industry were uncommonly concerned about their image. The prospect of contaminating a brand's carefully nurtured aura of glamour should spark top managers' anxieties. Motivating brand-name manufacturers and retailers—who were better positioned than the Labor Department to identify the bad actors in the diffuse cut-and-sew business—to shun sweatshops could reshape the industry's ecology.

When Wage and Hour Division inspectors identified an abusive workplace stitching garments with a well-known label, they soon began to send word to the department's front office, and Labor's message mavens went to work. Reporters and television producers, they had learned, loved the mélange of glitz and squalor in a story about some glamorous brand's dependence on illegal, exploitative subcontractors. It did not take many prime-time sweatshop stories to galvanize the fashion industry's attention. Industry leaders seized the initiative to set and enforce codes of conduct for apparel subcontractors. In 1996, at a White House event, the "No Sweat" label was unveiled, along with a set of industry-developed codes for monitoring labor conditions throughout the apparel industry's production chain.

In the second Clinton administration, under Alexis Herman's leadership, the Labor Department had three innovations awards program semifinalists and one finalist, but no winners. In the first seven years of the George W. Bush administration, under Secretary Elaine Cho, Labor had two semifinalists. The Reich years account for all of the Labor Department's innovations awards to date.

Is There Anything Unusual to Explain?

Before speculating as to factors that might account for Labor's uptick in inventiveness during the first Clinton administration, it is prudent to consider the possibility that there is nothing very unusual to explain. It could be that scoring three innovations awards for an organization the size of the Labor Department over the four years when Reich was at the helm is no better than par. This notion is readily tested. The department submitted thirty-six applications from 1995 (the first year of federal eligibility) to 1997 (the last year of Reich's watch). Having three winners works out to a success rate of more than 8 percent. For

5. All references to Innovations in American Government Awards Program applications, semi-finalists, finalists, and winners come from awards program data supplied by Christina Marchand and Emily Kaplan, whose assistance is gratefully acknowledged.

Innovations in American Government Awards Program applications in general, the odds of winning an award are less than half of 1 percent.[5]

The all-application average might not be the best reference point, of course, since the federal government was excluded from competition until 1995 and might reasonably be expected to have had a backlog of strong contenders. Indeed, there were thirteen Labor Department applications in the first year, and all of the first-term award winners built to some degree on pre-1995 antecedents. But whereas an initial surge and subsequent fall in applications did mark the federal government as a whole, it did not characterize the Labor Department, which submitted about as many applications in 1996 and 1997 as it had in the first year of eligibility. There *is* some evidence that the whole federal government, not just Labor, started out with a backlog of promising candidates for innovations awards. Federal entities other than Labor submitted 880 applications, and won seven awards, between 1995 and 1997. This success rate, about 0.8 percent, is appreciably higher than the overall rate—but just a tenth of Labor's.

It is worth noting that Labor is one of the smallest cabinet agencies. In terms of personnel it is smaller than all but three other departments and indeed is smaller than several non-cabinet agencies, including the National Aeronautics and Space Administration and the Environmental Protection Agency. Labor's share of federal spending is comparably modest, usually less than 2 percent (Office of Management and Budget 2007). Yet it accounted for *30 percent* of innovations awards in the first Clinton administration. The department with the second highest number of awards (Defense, with two) outweighs Labor by an order of magnitude in financial terms and by even more in terms of personnel.

To be sure, winning an unusual number of Innovations awards does not conclusively prove unusual inventiveness. Skeptics might note that not just Reich but several other Labor officials (including me) had links to the Kennedy School, which runs the Innovations in American Government Awards Program. The deputy secretary, Tom Glynn, was an old friend of Alan Altshuler's, the Harvard professor who had built up the innovations awards program and chaired it throughout the Reich years. Might subtle or not-so-subtle gamesmanship, rather than real merit, explain why Labor won those awards in the first Clinton administration?

The possibility needs to be taken seriously, since the Reich team was both well positioned to wield influence and acutely aware of the message value of an Innovations win. Nobody would claim that the innovations program ran a perfect selection process impervious to bias (by the same token, nobody who knows Alan Altshuler would dare to suggest that it lacked integrity). Several considerations, however, work against the claim that the Reich team was not so much good at innovating as good at gaming the innovations awards program. Labor produced a long list of novel procedural or policy initiatives during those years that were never submitted as innovations candidates, including (to name only a few of which I had direct experience) a distinctive model for setting state funding priorities under the School-to-Work Opportunities Act of 1994, major reforms to the Targeted Jobs Tax Credit, and the introduction of tax advantages for higher-education spending, indicating an innovative bent that went well beyond initiatives appropriate to the awards competition. Another indicator is personal: Had there been some campaign to influence the judges or put a thumb on the scale of the process, it is all but certain that I would have been aware, if not involved, since during this whole period I had either recently left Harvard or recently returned from the Labor Department.

A final consideration is not so obvious but, to me, quite convincing: the pattern of awards, across the various areas of Labor Department activity, argues against manipulation. Well over half of the Labor Department applications from 1995 to 1997 were for the workforce-development programs that were closest to the hearts of Reich and his inner circle. But none of those applications won an award or even advanced to semifinalist status. All three of the winning applications represented the regulatory branch of Labor's agenda, which most of the Reich team were less passionate about and for which they submitted fewer applications. If Reich or anyone close to him had been inclined to risk reputation and conscience to improve the odds of winning an innovations award, the most likely motive would have been to nudge along a workforce-development contender.

A determined skeptic might still insist that it is far from proven that the Reich Labor Department was anything out of the ordinary. But consider, for the sake of argument, that this department, during those years, displayed an unusual proclivity to develop and deploy new approaches. If we accept, at least provisionally, that this pattern is real, what might account for it?

Accounting for Innovation: Potential External Factors

John F. Kennedy, when asked how he had become a war hero, famously explained, "It was involuntary. They sank my boat." Exogenous factors might similarly account for all or part of any unusual proclivity to innovation at the U.S. Department of Labor in the mid-1990s.

Urgency

Management theorists are fond of invoking the "burning platform" metaphor to explain receptivity to change (Kotter 1996). When the status quo becomes intolerable, the urgent need for some sort of alternative can stimulate inventiveness. (In the supposedly factual story behind the metaphor, there was a fire on a North

Sea oil rig; the adaptive behavior actually chosen—leaping off the burning platform—seems rather obvious.) Could the dire state of the Labor Department's
policy portfolio explain the surge of innovation? This was certainly a factor.
Across policy arenas—occupational health and safety, pension security, workplace conditions, job security, earning power—conditions were worse and
prospects grimmer than the Reich team was willing to accept. The White
House's determination to reduce the deficit, moreover, meant that scaled-up
conventional approaches were not an option. An inability or unwillingness to
tolerate the status quo, a long and ambitious set of obligations stemming from
promises made during the presidential campaign, and a sense from the start that
political capital was a perishable commodity contributed to Labor's openness to
new approaches. But neither the Labor Department nor the first Clinton term
had a monopoly on urgent pressures to innovate, so this can only offer a partial
explanation for the clustering of innovations at that agency during those years.

Intellectual Progress

James Madison and the other framers of the U.S. Constitution, as they accomplished their dazzling and durable institutional innovations, stood on the shoul-
ders of earlier thinkers, notably David Hume. Thomas Edison could not invent
the light bulb until a long list of predecessors, some famous and many obscure,
had accomplished antecedent innovations in electricity generation, transmission, and storage, materials development, and so on. It may be, similarly, that
Labor's burst of innovation depended on underlying intellectual enablers that
had only recently matured to the point where their experience could inform
concrete action.

One bit of evidence in support of this notion is the fact that all three Labor
winners had something to do with recognizing and responding appropriately to
heterogeneity among regulated firms. There is, at one level, a common game-
theoretic structure to the "choose your OSHA" proposition at the heart of
Maine 200, Reich's efforts to make it pay to be a fashion-industry good guy,
and the PBGC's multifaceted campaign to differentiate government's treatment
of well-funded and underfunded pensions. Relatively recent theoretical work,
such as Robert Axelrod's *The Evolution of Cooperation*, was both familiar to
some people on the Reich team and quite germane to the award-winning innovations (Axelrod 1984). Ideas "in the air" no doubt had something to do with
innovations at Labor, whether the projects were entered as award contenders
or not. Other considerations, though, argue against putting too much weight
on freshly developed conceptual tools to explain the spike in new approaches
at Labor. First, to the extent that ideas were the drivers, one would expect innovations to be distributed across agencies with related missions, rather than

concentrated on one agency. The Environmental Protection Agency, the Security and Exchange Commission, the Food and Drug Administration, and many other federal entities are at least as subject to inspiration from Axelrod and other game theorists as the Labor Department. It is hard to posit a rising intellectual tide that lifted Labor but left the rest of the government aground. Second, as the thumbnail descriptions suggest, each of the winning innovations originated, at least to some degree, with quite pragmatic improvisation in the field, rather than with front-office theorizing. It is unlikely that Bill Freeman of OSHA Maine relied on recent trends in game theory as he struggled to get his mission accomplished. Finally, any actual innovation depends to a great extent on empirical matters—the clear-eyed recognition of many mundane specifics about the state of the world—and to a great extent on conceptual considerations that were old hat to Jeremy Bentham and John Stuart Mill, if not Plato, if not Adam. It is rare, even when academics are among those sitting around the table trying to solve a real-world problem, that some truly new idea turns out to be more than a minor part of the answer.

Mandates

With rare exceptions, innovation is a matter of means rather than ends. Reducing occupational injuries, safeguarding pensions, and deterring abusive workplaces were established goals; what changed was the means for achieving them. Might new legislation or other changes in mandates have prodded Labor to improvise new means? In principle, yes, but in practice it cannot account for the three Labor winners. There was no new legislation or executive order related to OSHA or employment standards during this period, and the legislative shift at PBGC was a consequence, not a cause, of the reform campaign that Lockhart initiated and Slate brought to fruition. The major legislation that *did* reshape Labor's mandates in the Reich years—the Family and Medical Leave Act, the North American Free Trade Agreement, the School-to-Work Opportunities Act—left no legacy of innovations awards.

Another sort of mandate, this one broadly promoting change rather than requiring progress in any single policy area, was the National Performance Review, launched with much fanfare by Vice President Al Gore at the start of the administration. This high-profile campaign to "reinvent government" was by no means mere window dressing. It featured real pressure to do things differently and real White House empowerment for agencies and officials inclined to innovate. It surely explains part of the wave of experimentation at the Labor Department. The National Performance Review was a government-wide campaign, however, and so it does little to explain Labor's *differential* inventiveness.

Accounting for Innovation: Potential Internal Factors

If, in fact, distinctive features of the Reich Labor Department contributed importantly to a propensity to innovate, what might they have been? Enablers of inventiveness that are internal to an organization are likely to be the most interesting to both scholars and practitioners, particularly factors that are replicable rather than restricted to any one organization, team, or time. A standard frame for examining institutions—looking, in turn, to *people, systems, and culture*—provides a helpful device for speculating about salient features of the Department of Labor in the first Clinton administration.

People

The vast majority of the Labor Department's 18,000 employees were career civil servants who were there when Reich arrived and expected to be there still when he departed. Around 100 positions were "political appointees," hired (and potentially fired) either by the president or by the department secretary (U.S. Government Printing Office 1992). The Clinton administration had an extremely long list of office seekers who had been helpful in the campaign and who needed to be accommodated. Many freshly minted cabinet officers, in this as in all administrations, were chagrined to discover that their hiring discretion was sharply constrained by the White House personnel office.

The Reich Labor Department was to a great extent an exception to this rule, for several reasons. First, Reich was intensely focused on personnel matters. He was aware of his strengths and (more important) his limitations and was determined to surround himself with stellar staff members to leverage his advantages and shore up his weak suits. Second, Reich, who was also the head of the economic transition team, had a front-row seat for spotting talent—and for spotting trouble—among the campaign and transition staffers. Third, one of Reich's oldest and closest friends, John Isaacson, ran what was perhaps the best-regarded governmental and nonprofit executive search firm in the country and volunteered to help Reich find the best people. Fourth, and perhaps most important, Reich used his relationship with Clinton to parry pressure from the White House personnel staff. This relationship, in fact, was more one of long-standing mutual respect than close friendship. But Reich was happy to let stand the perception that Clinton would back him in any personnel dispute.

He was thus able to ensure that merit and commitment, rather than connections, determined who filled the roster of Labor Department political appointees. The first and most crucial hires were Tom Glynn as deputy secretary and Kitty Higgins as chief of staff. Glynn had been aptly described to Reich by his many admirers as "tough, cunning, disciplined, and doesn't suffer fools"

(Reich 1997). Gaunt and taciturn, Glynn seemed the opposite of the plump, gregarious, warmhearted Higgins. But they were friends of long standing, both of them shrewd Irish pols who had cut their teeth in the Carter White House, and both endowed with the reserves of Washington lore and well-practiced political and bureaucratic moves that Reich, for all his intellectual horsepower, knew that he lacked.

Other senior staffers were hired with an eye to their passion for the Labor Department's mission and their demonstrated ability to get things done. Larry Katz, for whom Reich created the post of chief economist, had been tenured at Harvard in his twenties and was universally considered among the best labor economists of his generation. Joe Dear's mix of affability and icy determination qualified him for the challenging post of assistant secretary for occupational safety and health. Doug Ross, who was tapped for the top job-training post, had a long list of accomplishments in politics and government, but perhaps his most important qualification for the position was his record of cheerful effectiveness as head of Michigan's Commerce Department during a rough stretch for autos and related industries. Karen Nussbaum, tapped to run the Women's Bureau, had cofounded 9to5, a pathbreaking voice for clerical workers. Olena Berg, unlike many others whose names the White House forwarded to Labor, was a California treasury official who had no interest in becoming assistant secretary for pension and welfare benefits. But after several pension experts who were asked to vet the White House's list compared even the best names on that list unfavorably to Berg, whose name was conspicuously missing, the Reich team cold-called her and persuaded her to join them.

Clinton had promised a government that "looked like America"—not too white, not too male—and Reich was happy to comply as he staffed his department. But in the event, ample representation of women and minorities entailed no sacrifice in qualifications. True, Reich got extra political credit for appointing Maria Echaveste, whose parents were Mexican migrant workers, to head the Wage and Hour Division—but Echaveste's energy, intelligence, and blue-ribbon credentials outmatched those of any other contender for the job. Tom Williamson, who was named solicitor of labor (the department's third most senior role, after secretary and deputy secretary) was African American. He was also a partner at Washington's premier law firm, an honors graduate of Harvard and Berkeley, a Rhodes scholar, and a trusted friend of the president.

Reich's obsession with staff quality, his relative freedom from White House interference, along with expert counsel from John Isaacson, meant that even when a slot was clearly earmarked for some particular constituency it was filled with a talented team player. The secretary, the deputy secretary, the solicitor of labor, and the chief of staff had spent little of their careers in national politics or the labor movement, yet they were part of the first Democratic administration in twelve years, after a campaign where unions had played a significant role in mobilizing voters. Reich clearly needed a senior staffer with connections to unions and to the inner circles of Democratic political operators. Steve Rosenthal, named associate deputy secretary, clearly filled the bill, with his address book that bulged with links to labor leaders and political street fighters and his wise-cracking, Joe Sixpack persona. But beneath that persona Rosenthal possessed astute judgment on substantive policy matters.

The Reich team had virtually no ability to hire or fire career staffers, of course, and only limited authority to move them around. But some long-term career employees were equal to the very best of the newcomers. John Fraser had distilled his experience with wage laws and regulations into flawless instincts about the practical and political effects of any initiative. Carolyn Golding combined a quick intelligence with deep familiarity with the institutions and history of job-training policy. Steve Wandner, whom Chief of Staff Higgins called a "brilliant geek from the bowels of the Labor Department," conjured from his knowledge of unemployment-insurance arcana the single most elegant policy innovation of the Reich years (Reich 1997).[6] There was occasional tension between the small cadre of political appointees—young, heavily female and minority, highly educated, eager to make the most of their moment in power— and the older, whiter, heavily male, and generally more tired career workers. But the political staff were encouraged to respect and exploit the expertise of the permanent workforce.

Several features of Labor's personnel situation in the first Clinton administration may have been particularly conducive to innovation. It surely helped that the political appointees tended to be exceptionally talented, but there were less obvious factors at work as well. Agency heads were chosen not just for their abilities, not just for their affinities with the Clinton agenda in general, but for their demonstrated commitment to the specific Labor mission with which they were entrusted—Berg, to secure benefits; Ross, to develop the workforce; Echaveste, to ensure fair workplaces; and so on. This intrinsic passion for the goals to be pursued and the consonance of the team's definition of each mission meant that Reich, Glynn, and Higgins could manage with a loose rein. Confidence that senior staffers were committed to the right ends meant that the departmental leadership could be broad-minded about means and open to novel approaches. If Reich had not trusted that his staff shared his values, he could not have granted them the level of discretion that invites innovation.

---

6. Wandner observed that simple statistical techniques could distinguish fairly reliably between laid-off workers likely to be recalled and those facing long-term unemployment, which permitted better targeting of reemployment services.

Reich's freedom to shop widely for his staff rather than choosing from White House short lists also let him recruit many key people from state and local government and from the private sector. Glynn, Berg, Dear, Ross, Katz, and many others (including Reich himself) all came to Labor from, and all eventually left Labor for, work beyond Washington. This external orientation made them less reluctant to shake things up than people anticipating a lifelong Washington career and more eager to accomplish successes dramatic enough to be comprehensible beyond the Beltway.

Systems

Reich was a charismatic thinker who had never managed an organization bigger than the thirty-person policy shop he had overseen at the Federal Trade Commission a decade earlier. Glynn was a meticulously organized professional manager whose stellar record included running the Massachusetts Department of Welfare and the Massachusetts Bay Transportation Authority. Their administrative instincts and habits differed rather sharply from each other, though each appreciated and respected the other's perspective. The systems that developed at Labor—inspired by Reich, crafted by Glynn, influenced by many others, and constrained by the long-established culture at the department—were an amalgam that exemplified what Thomas J. Peters and Robert H. Waterman famously termed a "loose-tight" management style (Peters and Waterman 1982).

Check-in Meetings

The secretary's formal meeting room, a dark-paneled chamber with a massive central table, mostly sat empty. But in a small glass-walled meeting area that had been carved out of the secretary's ceremonial anteroom there were frequent—*very* frequent—senior staff meetings that let Reich, Glynn, and Higgins keep tabs on initiatives in progress and that offered opportunities to share information and ideas. Scheduled gatherings bracketed the workday. The "huddle" took place around eight every morning, unless Reich was out of town. Reich, Glynn, Higgins, and Williamson always attended, as did the assistant secretaries responsible for public affairs, legislative relations, and policy, along with the chief economist, counselor, associate deputy secretary, Reich's scheduler, and a few others. Other assistant secretaries and equivalent staffers were welcome at any time, but were required to show up when one of their responsibilities was on the table. A parallel meeting, chaired by Glynn, was held around seven in the evening. This "dep sec's meeting" let Glynn track the progress of issues that had been flagged in the morning, share information on new developments during the day, and draft the agenda for the next morning's huddle.

The tone at both the morning and evening meetings was informal—first names and frequent wisecracks were the norm—but the pace was brisk. Most agenda items claimed only a few minutes. When a matter required more attention, Glynn would either route it to the appropriate specialized management system or ask a subset of the group to meet separately, process the issue, and report back. It was considered bad form to raise an issue that wasn't on the agenda, unless it had come up five minutes prior to the meeting, and *very* bad form to waste the group's time making speeches or making excuses. Some time in the morning huddle and the evening meeting was inevitably devoted to administration gossip and departmental firefighting. But Reich was convinced that urgent matters would always claim attention, while issues that were important but not particularly urgent frequently got short shrift. Hence the policy initiatives that Reich cared about most would almost always be on the agenda, even if nobody could have expected much progress to have been made since they were last discussed.

These meetings were hugely expensive in terms of senior staff time. Everyone, including Reich and Glynn, at times bemoaned the hours spent each week sitting around the table. But the certainty that the team would be checking in, every morning and every evening, had several beneficial effects for innovation. It provided regular, nearly constant, prods to keep things moving. It spared departmental leadership any anxiety that an initiative could head off in the wrong direction for more than a few hours, even in the worst-case scenario, making it easier to grant plenty of discretion to the staff. And it offered regular opportunities for reality-testing ideas and nipping in the bud problems that eventually might have derailed an initiative. (Without the constant check-in, for example, staff driving the Youth Apprenticeship Initiative might not have learned that labor unions felt very proprietary about the term *apprenticeship* early enough to switch the label to "School-to-Work" with no confusion or conflict.)

"Drivers"

The federal government is awash in titles, but one of the most important titles in the Reich Labor Department, particularly early on, was the informal one of "driver." Reich, Glynn, and Higgins insisted that each important initiative would have one person responsible for driving it toward closure. The driver may or may not have much formal authority in the relevant policy domain. If an assistant secretary chose to drive an initiative herself, fine. But she had to be ready to report on progress at any huddle or evening meeting when the initiative was on the agenda, take calls at any time, and accept responsibility for progress without invoking other duties as a shield. Most assistant secretaries learned the wisdom of delegating the role of driver to a talented and trusted subordinate. This tightly focused ownership of each initiative made drift less likely and made it easier to give, and to get, guidance on options and permission to change course. Clear assignments of responsibility enhanced flexibility.

Permeability

Loose structures and permeable boundaries were hallmarks of the Labor Department in the first Clinton administration. This was a marked departure from the bright-lined structural divisions more characteristic of earlier Labor Departments and an exaggerated version of the Clinton administration norm. Cross-agency task forces were routine. Officials were often lent to other units or moved from job to job within the department.

Reich had an instinctive aversion to institutional borders and often invoked the fecund chaos of the transition as a useful model to counterbalance any department's drift toward organizational sclerosis. In a concrete manifestation of this preference, he asked that the warren of offices occupied by the staff of the assistant secretary for policy, which took up precious second-floor real estate near the whole senior staff, be ripped out and replaced with a vast wall-less space filled with easily reconfigured modular cubicles.[7] This space, which Reich called the "skunkworks," was inspired by the low-rent D.C. building that had housed the economic transition team. Reich envisaged a rotating series of temporary task forces filling the space, and he wanted it next to his office so that he could drop in without announcement or ceremony, as he had during the transition, to see how things were progressing and to share ideas.

This organizational permeability was certainly overdone on occasion, generating wasted effort and confusion. One senior departmental manager was so noted for her exasperated cries of "Swim in your own lane!" that her staff made lapel pins emblazoned with the slogan. But costly as it may have been, it almost surely eased the sharing of ideas, devalued long-standing stakes in the organizational status quo, and lowered bureaucratic barriers to new approaches.

Culture

To the extent that Reich and his senior team were able to shape the workplace culture at the Labor Department—pervasively among the second-floor political appointees and to a much lesser degree among the career staff—it was emphatically and explicitly supportive of innovation.

---

7. I was the assistant secretary for policy at the time, and the career staff never forgave me for acquiescing in the loss of their private offices.

In his first weeks at the department, Reich would sometimes quite literally wander the building's cavernous halls, introducing himself to startled staffers and asking what was on their minds. As management systems matured and Reich conceded that he needed some shelter from the deluge of information and requests that would otherwise swamp him, he prepared a list of things he wanted to penetrate the "bubble" that was forming around him. High on the list: "Ideas, ideas, ideas: from department employees, from outside academics and researchers, from average citizens. Anything that even resembles a good idea about what we should do better or differently. Don't screen out the wacky ones" (Reich 1997).

Reich was convinced that a wealth of untapped inventiveness lay dormant within the career workforce. At a "town hall" meeting weeks after taking office, he solicited ideas from the assembled headquarters workforce, standing patiently on the stage until a few suggestions arose. He urged his assistant secretaries to mine their career staff for latent innovations. All three of the innovations awards winners, and countless other improvements undertaken at Labor, originated to some degree with frontline staff. Yet not every cubicle harbored a font of invention. While this openness to career-staff suggestions did yield some useful ideas, it eventually became clear that a large share of the most innovative workers had filtered away from Labor during its decades as a backwater. The exhortation to unleash career-staff inventiveness, however, itself underscored the importance the front office placed on fresh approaches. And it clarified that innovation was a matter not just of creativity at the top but of scanning for, cultivating, and scaling up good ideas originating elsewhere.

As Vice President Gore's National Performance Review geared up, it provided White House reinforcement and institutional structure for Labor's effort to motivate and validate fresh thinking. Labor agencies were encouraged to apply for the "Hammer Awards" that Gore's office handed out for breakthroughs in governmental performance, and every success was celebrated with high-visibility departmental hoopla. Even a minor process improvement or policy idea would be rewarded with a visit from Reich, an official photographer at hand to record the congratulatory handshake. Reich and Glynn made sure that any major innovation would earn a trip to the White House and a photo with the president or vice president (Reich 1997; Borins 2002).

Just as flexibility, creativity, and openness to new approaches were viewed as key virtues within the Reich Labor Department, inertia and its handmaiden, turf consciousness, were considered deadly vices. Glynn's mocking refrain "But we've always done it that way . . ." frequently capped the discussion of some questionably useful rule or process, and officials scrambled to get rid of outmoded approaches before they drew his attention. Reich scandalized career staff at the start of the administration when he insisted on sharing responsibility for the high-priority School-to-Work Opportunities Act initiative with the Education Department, rather than keeping the budget and bragging rights for his department.

Reich and Glynn formed something of a "good cop, bad cop" pair in shaping departmental culture. Reich was the affable cheerleader; Glynn was the stern taskmaster. Glynn was a demanding boss by nature, and the pressure he felt to keep the department on track made him even tougher than he had been in previous jobs. But although he came down hard on staffers who let key initiatives drift or who built their empires instead of advancing departmental goals, he could be remarkably tolerant of the honest errors that accompany experimentation. In setting after setting, the front office sent the message that mistakes were more forgivable than stasis.

Concluding Thoughts

This is not the place, and I am not the author, to generalize from these observations about a few years at a single department. As noted earlier, I cannot claim to be objective, both because I was involved in some aspects of this story and because I have long considered Reich a friend (though I have not consulted him or any other old Labor colleagues about this chapter). Nor do I bring to bear the mastery of relevant literatures or, more important, the kind of empirical references from *other* settings that could transform these Labor Department anecdotes into data. One motive for writing this chapter is the hope that others will be equipped and inclined to take those further steps toward extracting useful inferences.

It would be a stretch to describe the Clinton I Labor Department (borrowing Emerson's turn of phrase) as the extended shadow of one man. Attributing the department's spike of innovation wholly to Reich is implausible on its face, at odds with the record, and unfair to many other people who did their part. That said, it seems quite clear that Reich's motives, background, and character form an important part of the explanation for the unaccustomed inventiveness of the department during those four years.

Tom Glynn, Kitty Higgins, and the rest of the team played crucial roles in institutionalizing and implementing the campaign. But they would have been effective contributors to quite different management makeovers as well. Indeed, they probably would have been comfortable with a culture that gave a bit more weight to prudence and a bit less to creativity. Reich is a man of passionate convictions, a sense that opportunities to make things better are fleeting and precious, a remarkable tolerance for risk, and a philosophical response to setbacks. By temperament he would prefer a pattern of triumphs punctuated by crackups to a quiet life of respectable attainment. With so much wrong in the world to be set right, Reich views timidity as selfish and immoral. His admirers find these traits exhilarating; his detractors find them exasperating; all agree he is a rather unusual person.

To the extent that Reich's distinctive personality is part of the story, there may be limited implications from the Clinton I Labor Department for other organizations seeking to promote innovation. Not every leader can be a thick-skinned, softhearted, risk-tolerant, camera-loving intellectual. Yet there may be valuable, broad-spectrum, and thoroughly encouraging lessons to be drawn from the fact that a leader with those attributes, backed by a handful of supporters, was able, in a remarkably short period of time, to unleash a blizzard of change within the unlikeliest of institutions.

7

Developmental Processes:
A Conceptual Exploration

EUGENE BARDACH

Governmental innovation emerges from a months- or years-long developmental process, a process that accommodates many players and interests and typically involves many distinguishable subprocesses. But when we say "developmental process," what exactly do we mean? Certainly, the kind of process we have in mind is complex, with much occasion to feed back on itself. It is hard to model; indeed, I do not think that, in the long run, it can be done very well without the use of computer simulation tools. In this chapter, however, I attempt to do some conceptual spadework using the more primitive tools of words and diagrams.

I use as my text a particular subset of "innovations," those that stimulate inter-organizational collaboration or, more precisely, build "interagency collaborative capacity"—ICC for short. I also speak of an ICC when I discuss such a capacity as though it were a sort of virtual organization. (I discuss the reasons for using the "collaborative capacity" concept instead of something simpler.) Now in some sense, the act of creating such a thing is itself a sort of innovation, almost a minor miracle, a *creatio ex nihilo,* a making of something out of nothing. The process takes bits and pieces of existing organizations, somehow gets them to cohere, and creates a functioning ICC that is better than the sum of its parts. We are used to this in the physical world, where "a house" suddenly appears when only a few days earlier there was just lumber, plaster, cement, and a hole in the ground. Nevertheless, there is still a bit of a miracle, a miracle born of the nature of things, things that fit together and, in so doing, create other things of human interest and value. So it is with the joining of agencies' separate productive capacities and the recognition by those who worked on it that a new creation has come into the world.

Interestingly, the actors involved in such activities often think they have done not just a creative thing but an uncommonly difficult thing: "For the first time ever, we've got the agencies talking to one another" is a common refrain.

For the present purposes, though, probably the most important connection to government innovations is that innovation often requires people in different agencies to work cooperatively in some way. At least 29 percent of the 217 semifinalists (or better) in the Innovations in American Government Awards Program competition studied by Sandford Borins had the quality of "coordinate [coordinating] organizations" (Borins 1998, table 2-1, p. 20). Those who would innovate must often learn to cooperate across the tension-filled and occasionally hazardous borders between bureaucratic domains.

A Sample Scenario

To suggest the complex processes I aim to explore, consider the following scenario. A small group of middle managers from four land management agencies with overlapping jurisdictions gathers for lunch periodically to discuss their work. Eventually, they conclude that paying private landowners to cooperate in conservation work would be a promising, and innovative, strategy. It would require their agencies to work together, though, to create the payment fund and the rules for administering payments and monitoring the behavior of private landowners. As their ideas about the strategy evolve, so, too, do their ideas about their organizational relationships, which tentatively go beyond the payment project. As champions of both policy and organizational strategies, they seek adherents.

There is resistance initially, but it goes underground for a while, until it emerges in the form of sniping from the general counsel's office of one of the agencies. Older ideas, ideas with greater currency and better standing, ideas from the technical assistance traditions of two of the agencies, come to frame the newer ideas and put them in a better light. The problems to which the newer ideas are addressed suddenly look more interesting and more important, partly because someone seems to have a novel idea as to what to do about them. But novelty is suspect in powerful quarters, and the existing champions are obliged to look further afield for ways to neutralize or deflect the "old guard." Enough support finally accumulates to launch what is advertised as a pilot project. The pilot project works splendidly, and after two or three difficult budget cycles have passed, the model becomes routinized. Once it has secured an organizational beachhead, the innovators—and interagency collaborators—have greater legiti-macy to "go to scale." They apply for and win an Innovations in American Gov-ernment award, and their most excellent idea is all but unstoppable.

Unless, of course, two of the original champions depart their organizations in disgust after the first, and highly discouraging, early manifestation of resistance. Or unless the innovative (and collaborative) idea is put on hold while an even more all-embracing idea is allowed to compete for organizational attention and that larger idea bogs down in years of meetings and negotiations. Or unless the splendid success of the pilot project is widely ignored on the grounds that "well, that was just a pilot project and obviously the circumstances of its success are not replicable."

Other scenarios are also possible. Loss of the departing champions might prove to be a blessing in disguise, since the abrasive personality of one of them is keeping more potential adherents at bay than are being attracted to the cause and a new, more attractive, champion now has room to take over an operation previously destined to fail. Or the more all-embracing innovative (and collabo-rative) idea, languishing in endless meetings, receives a vivifying jolt from con-tact with the smaller and later but more potent idea, and so both the larger and the smaller now succeed. Or top leadership in the agency, having (realistically) foreseen the criticism that "the circumstances of its success are not replicable," avoids the pilot phase altogether and implements the innovation (or collabora-tion) rapidly and on a broad, though not quite universal, scale.

Thus might failure scenarios be deflected in favor of success scenarios. But is this too pretty a picture? The success scenarios may be vulnerable, unrealizable. The more attractive champion might be damped down by an organizational culture that distrusts any spark of seeming "egoism." Enthusiasm for the revivi-fied ensemble of innovative (and collaborative) ideas might be undercut by an unexpected budgetary crisis. An agency's top leader could lose political influ-ence overnight, when his sexual peccadilloes are revealed and his continuation in office is threatened.

I could take the reader on yet another round of successful coping with even these discouraging contingencies and the latent vulnerabilities in the innovative or collaborative process that make them possible. The "problems-solutions-problems-solutions" dialectic can proceed without end. It could, obviously, encompass many more actors, situations, and overall complexities than I have sketched. And it could have a very different initiation than the "idea-champion-resistance" framework that I postulated as the first layer of the process. But enough is enough. I hope the point is made that modeling how a drawn-out, back-and-forth, multiplayer, contingency-saturated, public-sector creative process works, whether producing innovation or collaboration or both, is bound to present a serious analytical challenge.

Nineteen Subsequent Histories

Although this chapter is primarily conceptual, underlying it is a great deal of empirical work. The primary sources of data and examples are seventeen of the nineteen cases that I studied firsthand in the early and mid-1990s for a book, *Getting Agencies to Work Together* (Bardach 1998), which was supported largely by the Innovations in American Government Awards Program.[1] Those cases covered a wide range: natural-resources management, at-risk children and families, depressed neighborhoods, environmental enforcement, military-base reuse and environmental cleanup, welfare-to-work programs, and contracts management. My understanding of those cases was based on several years of fieldwork, all of which, obviously, occurred before or during 1998. But I have also done a bit of updating. The editor of this volume encouraged me to learn what had become of the ICCs I reported on in my book in the ten to twelve years since I studied them. A research assistant and I were able to do about forty phone and two face-to-face interviews. We generally tried to track down people who had stayed in touch with developments over the past decade, who we thought would have a sophisticated overview of the process, and who were either relatively unbiased or whose biases we knew and could take into account. In several cases, websites contained much useful information. The results of our follow-up are shown in table 7-1. The designations of the cases in the table correspond to the designations in figure 3-1, p. 62, of *Getting Agencies to Work Together*.

The amount of work that went into learning about these cases, however, was much less than the first time around, in the 1990s. I am very aware of how easy it would be for some of my judgments to be completely mistaken. Hence, the reliability of my interpretations should be thought modest at best.

The first three rows represent, in descending order, varying degrees of success, which I explain later. That discussion also shows that success takes several forms, from straightforward production improvements (preventing fires, enforcing environmental laws, improving youth development) to disseminating models of good practice to other jurisdictions.

Thriving

A thriving ICC progresses more or less steadily toward a combination of structural stability and good cooperation. It might become institutionalized, with a

---

1. I omit here two cases I studied in the 1990s. One was a community organization in the Prescott neighborhood of Oakland, California, for it had already failed by the time I finished observing it in the 1990s. The second was military base reuse, which I deemed much too complex to learn about in a short spate of phone interviews. I did, however, retain the military base environmental cleanup case.

Table 7-1. *Estimated Current Status of Interagency Collaborative Capacity Projects Assessed in 1997*

Apparent trajectory since 1990s	Project	My 1997 assessment of relative success
Thriving	New Jersey School-Based Youth Services	High
	Hills Emergency Forum (preventing fires)	High
	Marin County Coordinated Youth Services Council (in reinvented form)	Low
	Elkhorn Slough watershed	High
Coping	Multimedia environmental enforcement	High
	Memorandum of Understanding on Biodiversity	Medium
	Welfare-to-work	
	Denver	Medium
	Oregon	High
	Riverside County	Medium
	Military-base environmental cleanup	High
	Antitobacco education	Medium
Lurching	Integrated children and family services	
	Maryland	High
	Oregon	High
	Tennessee	Medium
	Del Paso Heights Neighborhood Services Agency	Medium
	California Healthy Start	High
Dying	New York State contract administration	Medium

Source: Author.

budget of its own and some line items in partner agencies' budgets, or with its own legal identity and authority to hire employees of its own. School-Based Youth Services (SBYS) in New Jersey is a prime example of this, having gone from strength to strength in the twenty years of its existence (even though, owing to funding constraints, it still serves only about 20 percent of its potential constituency). This high degree of structural consolidation is not essential, however. The Hills Emergency Forum, an ICC established among a half dozen resource management agencies following the Oakland–Berkeley Hills fire of 1991, is a case in point. The agencies operate under rather informal and loosely drawn "letters of intent" but over time have increased their cooperative activities in fuel-load management and various aspects of training and preparedness.

These represent cases of success in the form of production improvements. SBYS also represents a case of success through dissemination of good practice (across school districts), as does the Elkhorn Slough watershed case. In the latter case we have an incorporated nonprofit consortium of many agencies and nonprofit partners near Santa Cruz that has, among other things, facilitated efforts to foster integrated watershed management through a combination of project activity and governmental regulation by a variety of agencies. Regulatory regimes, however, often discourage project activity by private partners. The district office of the U.S. Natural Resources Conservation Service, in combination with Sustainable Conservation, a San Francisco–based nonprofit, developed a creative permit coordination program, which they have managed to get replicated, to some degree, in another five or six areas in California.[2] As another example of dissemination, the California Environmental Protection Agency (Cal/EPA) was able to diffuse a task-force-based toxics discharger enforcement model across most California counties.

A special case of diffusion involves incorporating collaborative practices, originally mounted in the spirit of a demonstration project, into mainstream agency operations. When multimedia environmental enforcement was introduced at Cal/EPA (a case of "coping," however, rather than "thriving"; see the next section) in the mid-1990s on a project-by-project basis and organized by the secretary's office, the champion of the approach hoped that the Cal/EPA constituent agencies, such as the Water Board and Air Resources Board, would adopt the practice independently. My informants said that this hope may have been realized to a (very) modest degree, even while centrally organized multimedia enforcement has fallen to almost nothing. The Marin County, California, Coordinated Youth Services Council (CYSC) also represents a case of reinvention. It went out of business, was transformed into another entity with a similar mission but different approach, and was relieved of its original strategy of trying to coordinate the various service providers.[3]

Coping

Some partnerships reach a plateau and remain there, creating more value than would have been the case had the partners not joined forces but less than their full potential. Many scenarios might lead to this result, but the ones studied here have arisen when there is a formal or informal political mandate that more or less insists that they survive, in order to work out a problem that has been thrust upon them from on high. Following federal welfare reform legislation in 1996, it has been virtually impossible for welfare agencies, employment departments, adult schools, and job-training entities *not* to cooperate in some fashion.

---

2. See the Sustainable Conservation website at http://search.atomz.com/search/?sp-a= sp1002a7a4&sp-p=all&sp-f=ISO-8859-1&sp-q=permit&x=0&y=0 [accessed November 2007].

3. It is now called the Center for Restorative Practice. See www.restorativepractice.org/Whos Who.htm [accessed November 2007].

Antitobacco legislation passed by voter initiative in California in 1988. The public-health approach to the antismoking education part of the legislation conflicts with that of educators. There has been a lot of conflict between the agencies embodying these philosophies as well, especially at the state level, though less so at the local level. I do not believe there has been much change in the relationships since the mid-1990s.

Lurching

This trajectory involves being severely buffeted by external forces. Three of my cases involved attempts at the state and local levels to integrate services for children and families. These took place in Oregon, Maryland, and Tennessee. In all three states political leaders initiated formal reorganizations, and these were very disruptive.[4] In Oregon and Maryland, however, locally based collaboratives were able to operate to some extent independently of the state services-delivery systems. Some of these local ICCs flourished, whereas others did not. In California, a very large number, probably a majority, of school-based health programs started in the 1990s have died off altogether or substantially shrunk, mostly due to a withdrawal of state funds to support them. However, a great many of them have survived in some form with funding provided by local school districts from a variety of sources.

Dying

The New York State contract consolidation project involved what had been intended as a demonstration project run in New York State to consolidate aspects of the state's process for contracting nonprofit service providers. In 1990–91, staff from the New York State Council on Children and Families (CCF) were trying to reduce the burdens on nonprofit service providers. These were substantial, particularly on those agencies with multiple state contracts. The Door, a comprehensive youth-services provider in Lower Manhattan that in 1991 served some 6,000 adolescents, had seven contracts with three agencies for $1.4 million and filed eighty-four expenditure reports annually. CCF chose The Door as its experimental site to develop a master contract, and The Door was eager to be a guinea pig. One important result was that the seven contracts were folded into one, and the expenditure reports were reduced to four. The Door was able to let three to five professional accountancy and bookkeeping staff go and to return from the brink of insolvency. State contract evaluators

4. For the case of Tennessee, see Maloy (1997); Heflinger and Simpkins (1996).

monitoring contract compliance were able to have a more realistic understanding of how The Door actually did its programming and kept its books. Thus, the master contract with The Door was a smashing success, but the consolidated contracting model was picked up by only two other locales since my visits in the mid-1990s. One involved The Door's contracting relations with the City of New York. The second was Monroe County, New York (where Rochester is located), whose Public Health Department designed a master contract for many of its contractors.[5]

What Is to Be Explained or Understood?

I am interested in explaining, or understanding, the developmental processes underlying interagency collaboratives. But what exactly does this entail?

One obvious approach is to ask, about the cases in table 7-1, why some succeed better than others. In *Getting Agencies to Work Together* I offered a number of hypotheses, including the more technical nature of the task, the availability of good leadership, the conditions fostering trust, and so on. But hypotheses such as these relate to situational, or static, conditions. Given our aims of dynamic analysis, however, the comparisons across cases can be distracting unless one already has a conceptual model of the processes that occur over time within a case. That is why, in the discussion that follows, I do not make explicit comparisons of the cases but use the case materials to illustrate conceptual arguments.

Looking within single cases, then, what is to be explained? One possible candidate is changes in the relative performance (or, better, "capacity"; see the next section) of the aggregate of the partner agencies prior to the collaborative effort. If performance went from 50 to 60 on some scale, there is a 20 percent improvement. But another candidate is the proportion of the distance between actual past performance and the theoretical potential that the agencies could achieve by collaborating in some theoretically ideal, but nevertheless reasonable, fashion. If 120 is that ideal, say, then an increase of 10 from 50 to 60 represents an improvement of only $10/(120-50)$, or 15 percent.

I believe the latter benchmark leads to more interesting questions and, ultimately, to more interesting insights, though it does present a conceptual problem: to wit, where such a theoretical standard might come from. To address the problem, begin with the fact that interagency collaboration seeks to exploit a latent opportunity to create value. The opportunity typically arises from potential economies of scale or scope or from the potential to treat a problem—such as a troubled family on the books of several public agencies or a watershed span-

5. For an overview of the history, see Lepler, Uyeda, and Halfon (2006).

ning several jurisdictions—holistically.[6] The potential is elastically bounded on the upper end by the efficaciousness of the instruments available to the relevant agencies and by the legal authority under which they can operate. To be sure, the magnitude of any putative potential is not measurable in any precise way. Nevertheless, it is intuitively meaningful, as in, "Sure, the police and the fire departments work well together during emergencies, but not nearly as well as they could if they did more joint planning."

In some policy areas, the theoretical standard in any given locale might be indicated to a first approximation by empirical standards of "best practice" established by experience in other locales. But in cases where "innovation" is at stake, this may be impossible by definition. And in all cases, the definition of "potential" has a local component, its borders being defined by the local configuration of personalities, politics, resources, and so on. Hence, if achieving the fullest of the local potential is the standard, it can only be theoretical, or notional.

Capacity, Not Behavior

Turning from the ontological to the concrete, what entity should we think of as approaching excellence or receding from it? That is, what should we think of our process as aiming at? In management studies generally, we find three possibilities: outcomes, outputs, and capacity. Although outcomes are what we actually care about, they typically are produced by so many factors besides agency activity that they do not help us to focus on how managerial tasks should be carried out. Outputs are a very common, and very useful, focus, though in the case of ICCs, production processes are so varied (regulatory programs, subsidy programs, projects, and so forth) that a general model of ICC construction focusing on outputs would probably be too general. Capacity seems to me the right choice, partly by default and partly because it has other useful attributes. First, at a very general level, the nature of collaborative capacity is relatively homogeneous from one ICC to another. Second, capacity also has the opposite virtue of consolidating under one rubric rather varied components, such as individuals' psychological dispositions (to collaborate, engage in joint problem solving, contribute effort, mobilize others to collaborate, and so forth), organizations' contributions of tangible assets, important political figures' willingness to protect collaboratives from hostile forces, and an operating system designed to optimize joint efforts at the task level. In addition, it permits us to "give credit," so to speak, for collaborative success that may not look much like collaborative

6. Some of the greatest collaborative successes have occurred in natural-resources management. See Wondolleck and Yaffee (2000); Karkkainen (2002–03); Freeman and Farber (2005).

behavior on the surface, such as quarrels and threats that serve the purpose of clearing the air and preparing the way for more productive work. From a technical viewpoint, capacity also has the advantage of looking like a smoothly continuous variable. Finally, it is, somewhat counterintuitively, a more valid conception than behavior of what we as analysts probably care about in the general domain of interagency collaboration: actual behavior may be stifled or delayed by temporary and somewhat random events, even though the capacity exists and will soon enough be actualized.[7]

Explanation and "Understanding"

Our object, therefore, is to explain how, given some general value-creating mission and some approximate set of potential partner agencies, interagency collaborative capacity approaches or fails to approach some theoretical standard of excellence. And the critical role in the explanation is to be played by "developmental processes" or "dynamics."

That said, an urgent amendment is needed. The term *explain* carries misleading connotations here because of its close association with explaining variation. Consider an analogous explanation in the physical world, how a baseball leaving a bat ends up as close to (or as far away from) a benchmark as it does. Of course, the "variables" of bat speed, the angle of incidence, the location of the ball when struck, and so on, are part of the explanation. But what about the part of the explanation that tells us that the arc of the ball will be a parabola no matter where or how it is struck and that, in a sense, all the other facts of the case simply tell us along which of the infinite family of parabolas the ball will travel? Should our explanation of where the ball lands include something about the nature of parabolas and why a ball struck by a bat traces a parabola rather than some other curve?

It should do so. This fuller explanation I would call *understanding*.[8] I would like to understand the generic trajectory of ICC development as though it were the counterpart of the parabola and then understand how specific ICCs come to follow specific trajectories that are variants on the generic.

An even better analogy than to the world of baseballs and parabolas is to the biological world, with its teleological metaphors. To return to our categories

---

7. Capacity is a dispositional concept and may not be looked upon kindly by tough-minded empiricists. But it is like the capacity of sugar to dissolve if put in water or of a racing car to go 150 miles per hour if handled correctly. Capacity may be real, even if not always actual.

8. Lawrence B. Mohr may have been the first social scientist to write at length about two different "approaches to explanation," namely, *variance theory* and *process theory* (Mohr 1982). His ideas about the latter seem to have been unduly shaped by the pull of variance theory as the regnant form of the time.

from table 7-1, the "thriving" variant may in some sense express the successful maturation of some pseudo-organic entity, such as an ordinary organization or an unconventional virtual organization such as an ICC. Like any maturation process, it can be said to follow a stylized generic trajectory. And like any maturation process, it can succeed in different degrees and is susceptible to failure and various distortions, such as—as I named them in table 7-1—*coping, lurching,* and *dying.* There also could be many more such variants of the maturation process not yet identified or labeled.

A still better analogy is to a construction process. Construction proceeds, in part, according to an internal logic dictated by physical laws, the nature of materials, the connections of markets, the routines of contractors, the plans of architects, and the weather. From all these elements one can describe a generic process. But of course that generic process can have many variants, some of which even end in failure, such as the owner's bankruptcy or the collapse of the local real estate market or an earthquake.

Unlike throwing baseballs, growing plants, or building buildings, constructing an ICC takes place in a hostile environment in which failure is almost overdetermined. The relatively high success rate suggested by table 7-1 is illusory because the set of cases here represents the rather small universe in which collaboration is even attempted relative to the much larger universe in which it is not attempted or even contemplated because it seems so difficult.[9] These difficulties are of many sorts and emanate from various quarters. Even chance, as I shall show, is on the side of failure. To tilt the odds back in the other direction, an energetic counterforce, typically emanating from a cadre of skillful entrepreneurs, is required. The ensuing dialectic is at the heart of understanding the phenomenon and is what the rest of this chapter explores. I divide the discussion into two portions. First comes a sketch of the developmental challenges and opportunities. Following that is a discussion of the "smart practices" that may be able to deal with them.

Developmental Challenges and Opportunities

Before turning to the strictly developmental challenges and opportunities, I review the static challenges and opportunities, since these are, in effect, the raw materials for subsequent developments.

9. It is true that efforts at collaboration are much more prominent now than they have ever been and that the trend is strongly upward (Agranoff and McGuire 2003). The idea of delivering goods and services through networks is in very good standing these days (Goldsmith and Eggers 2004; Agranoff 2007), and in some policy areas it is normative and indeed inescapable.

Static Challenges and Opportunities

These come in two forms: technical issues and institutional and political challenges.

TECHNICAL ISSUES. Consider first that ICC construction, like building construction, is a technical process. As I argue in *Getting Agencies to Work Together,* a cadre of individuals or organizations setting out to create an ICC would have to think about how to perform four broad and essential functions: acquiring resources; designing and running an operating system (that is, a system for performing ground-level tasks); creating and maintaining a communications network and cultivating an atmosphere of (justified) trust; empowering and legitimizing a steering (or governance) process and a set of individuals to run it. Although there is obviously some latitude in how well these functions can be performed, they all need doing. And whatever structures are created to embody them must in turn embody some other functions—for example, the operating system must allocate responsibilities and resources, recruit and train competent personnel, incentivize and monitor performance, facilitate teamwork, and so on. Moreover, allowing here, too, that latitude is permissible, these functions must be reasonably well integrated, so that each supports the whole and at least does not greatly interfere with the others.

INSTITUTIONAL AND POLITICAL CHALLENGES. In the United States, as in most pluralistic democracies, large-scale institutional design templates make cross-boundary cooperation much more difficult in the public sector than in the private sector. These templates foster output-based controllability and input-based accountability, not high-quality performance or inventiveness. The spate of books about working in teams, continuous creation of knowledge, incremental versus discontinuous innovation, organizing for innovation, and so forth, so characteristic of the business marketplace, is inconceivable in its public-sector counterpart. This is obviously not to say that effective cross-boundary cooperation in the public sector is not possible (or that it is so easy in business organizations), only that it is a steeply uphill struggle against the odds. The behavioral manifestations are everywhere, and I mention only some of the highlights. Agencies can be recalcitrant, protect their turf, refuse to assign staff, refuse to provide funds, or make only token contributions. Individuals who are nominally supposed to help forward the collective effort might have difficult personalities, conflicting career objectives, or paranoid fears of exceeding their agency's tolerance for cooperating with "the other." Individuals who seek to play a (typically much-needed) leadership role may be consistently undercut by egalitarian suspicions among nominal partners of the whole idea of leadership.

However, because ICCs can genuinely add value to public-sector productive arrangements, and because many individuals working in and around the public sector wish to do exactly this, a lot of talent and effort are often available for trying to meet such challenges.

Emergent Threats and Opportunities

As the ICC construction process unfolds, new threats and opportunities emerge. They come from three main sources: momentum, sequencing, and life-cycle vulnerabilities. Depending on how these are managed (see the next major section), they can increase or decrease the odds of success.

MOMENTUM. Momentum effects depend on actors' perceptions of the emerging ICC itself and other actors' behavior vis-a-vis each other and the emerging ICC. They are of four principal kinds:

—*Bandwagon effects.* The more an ICC looks like it will succeed, the more resources it will attract. As with the strengths of a legislatively oriented coalition, the more influential individuals and organizations give verbal and practical support to the ICC, the more the ICC signals that it is likely to succeed, and the more supporters it is likely to attract (and opponents neutralize). Conversely, the less successful the prospects, and the fewer influentials who support it, the more actors shun an association with the enterprise.

—*Consensus effects.* Other things equal, the more people who certify an ICC as a good and valuable endeavor, the more reasonable its vision and method are likely to appear, and the more likely still others are to certify it. Conversely, the more the consensus appears to derogate its prospective value, the harder it is to attract adherents.

—*Trust and distrust effects.* Individuals involved in the work of ICC construction who represent different potential partners have good reason, at least initially, to distrust one another and the agencies they represent. They wonder about the professional competency of those alien "others," their willingness to deliver work and resources as promised, their ability to bring on board others in their agencies at the appropriate moments, and so on. Over time, however, experience accumulates, and the distrust either dissipates in favor of trust or else it grows until complete disintegration occurs. In either case, the dynamic is an emergent, self-reinforcing one.

—*Enthusiasm effects.* The ICC construction process is a human milieu that provides its own rewards for work well done and personal relationships established. Alternatively, it is a milieu in which people frustrate and disappoint one another. In either case, the dynamic is emergent and self-reinforcing.

SEQUENCING. The successful construction of an ICC does not happen overnight. Dozens or more individuals are in motion, sometimes continual and sometimes intermittent. As time goes on, the number thus engaged increases. What tasks are they working on? And, taking the long view of months or even years, is there a normal sequence of ICC construction tasks? Is there an optimal sequence? Are there sequences that pose significant risks? "We missed some steps [trust building]," said an ICC advocate in the Maryland integrated family-services case (the Systems Reform Initiative), "and we paid a heavy price for doing so."

Sequence almost certainly makes a difference. For one thing, it bears on momentum effects, sketched earlier. For another, it bears on the developmental stages through which collaborative capacity passes. Some stages may make it easier to move to the successive stages, and some may have the opposite effect. I return to the question of optimum sequencing later. Here, however, for the sake of description and illustration only, I posit ten key tasks of ICC construction, although my choice of the number and their definition is somewhat arbitrary. The tasks are a combination of the technical and the political:

—Identify an opportunity to create public value through collaboration,

—Build trust among the individuals working on the ICC from different agencies and among the agencies as well,

—Develop a common vision and a common understanding of the operating system that would be able to implement it,

—Encourage and legitimize a leadership element (person or cadre or agency),

—Constitute an advocacy group to pursue resources and legitimacy in the broader political environment,

—Constitute a network of middle-level implementers who coordinate operations and resources across agency boundaries,

—Through habit and experience, develop a rapid and reliable communication network across agencies that also connects "the right people" within the agencies,

—Develop steering (governance) capacity,

—Put the operating system in place, and

—Create a mechanism for the ICC to improve through continuous learning.

Some of these tasks will proceed in parallel, and some will not be begun until considerable progress has been made on others.

LIFE-CYCLE VULNERABILITIES AND ATTAINMENTS. Although a virtual organization, an ICC may in some ways be afflicted by the same pathologies as more conventional public-sector organizations. It may have full-time staff assigned to it, and these are at some risk of behaving like turf-protecting bureaucrats. Although it is not likely to become excessively rulebound and inflexible, once people's careers begin to depend on its long-run access to funding and stable turf, it is likely to start investing in organizational enhancement at the expense of activities more in the public interest. This reallocation may be relatively minor at first—and will be indistinguishable from the kind of organizational maintenance activities needed for simple survival—but it will grow with increasing scale. Indeed, those in the ICC may also fear the bureaucratization dynamic. Some of the board members of the CYSC were concerned that they were becoming "just another agency," and there was even some talk about how it should go out of business before this process had run its course completely. Nevertheless, I do not think that in most cases the ICC is at risk of bureaucratization, mostly because it tends to lead such a precarious existence under the suspicious eyes of turf- and resource-conscious managers from the participating agencies.

A visibly successful collaborative attracts resources. It also, in effect, becomes a resource, with money and with legitimacy, and a not very well protected resource at that. As the CYSC, prior to 1994, came to be respected for its performance, its administrative capacity, and its symbolic status as a seemingly successful collaborative effort, the Marin Community Foundation began to urge it to serve as a clearinghouse for youth services proposals from Marin County agencies. The CYSC board deflected these urgings, not wanting to be thought to "play favorites." It was also continually trying to sidestep requests from various therapists in private practice to affiliate with CYSC, the applicants desiring a "seal of approval" and possible access to informal or contract-based referrals.

On the more positive side, new and perhaps unpredictable missions and goals turn up simply as a result of experience gained from working together. This experience can create new intellectual, social, and political capital (Putnam 1993; Innes and others 1994). Such capital sets up actors to see new value-creating collaborative opportunities and perhaps mobilize to exploit them. In some cases, this can become a self-reinforcing process, perhaps furthered by the actors' pleasure in the awareness of their own creativity.

Consider, for instance, the development, in the 1990s, of CeaseFire, a Boston-based ICC of more than a dozen criminal-justice agencies and an assortment of other city agencies and community groups that aimed to prevent youth firearm violence.[10] Following two years of escalating gang violence, in 1991 the Boston Police Department (BPD) and the U.S. Bureau of Alcohol, Tobacco, and Firearms jointly conducted a study tracing the flow of firearms to youth gangs in the city. In 1992, following extensive but informal conversations among officers of the BPD Anti–Gang Violence Unit and probation officers at district courthouses, the BPD and the Probation Department began Operation Night Light, a team approach to checking on high-risk probationers living in dangerous neighborhoods. The police carried arms, which probation officers did not, and the probation officers had authority to make nighttime home visits

---

10. This was not a case in my original study of nineteen cases. I came across it in the files of Innovations in American Government Awards Program winners and finalists for 1997. See John Buntin, "A Community Responds: Boston Confronts an Upsurge of Youth Violence," Kennedy School Case Program C15-98-1428.0, 1998.

without warrants, which the police did not. Collaboration concerning prosecution, meanwhile, was growing between the U.S. attorney in Boston and the state district attorney, and it became easier to threaten offenders with longer federal sentences, to be served in a tougher prison system. In 1993 the Anti–Gang Violence Unit became absorbed into the Youth Violence Strike Force, which had more agency members and a new Warrant Apprehension Unit.

Participation by community groups furnished a critical resource to the collaborative, namely, information about violent "hot spots" and about the whereabouts and conduct of particular individuals or groups. Community groups also furnished venues for officialdom to meet with gang members and with victims of violence and legitimacy for the law-enforcement strategy of "zero tolerance" of gun violence. Participation by academic researchers from Northeastern University and Harvard's Kennedy School of Government (supported with funds from the National Institute of Justice) helped at the conceptual level and at the level of interpreting empirical patterns in the youth gun market and in the profiles of offenders and victims. Academic participation also guaranteed relatively wide publicity for the remarkable success the CeaseFire approach was enjoying. In 1995 all the various partners constituted themselves as a working group led by the BPD Youth Violence Strike Force. In 1997 President Bill Clinton chose Boston as the site from which to announce a juvenile crime control bill.

Success and the attendant publicity reinforced the collaboration. The site visitor sent by the Ford Foundation and the Kennedy School's innovations awards program to evaluate CeaseFire reported in July 1997 that "all those participating bend over backward to share the credit, either because they treasure the success too much to jeopardize it with competitive claims or they realize that this is a success that may well support 'a thousand fathers.'" The idea of a collaborative approach to complex social problems came to have a life of its own in Boston. Thus, the site visit report observed that the same group of actors who had worked together on the youth violence problem were turning their attention to new issues, such as domestic violence, school safety, and youth unemployment.

Prolonged Environmental Exposure

The normal course of events is also an important source of disturbance. Over the long run, political support can leak away as a result of leadership turnover; trust can be as fragile as individual relationships (which can be disrupted by career mobility); fiscal stress can deplete funding; large-scale formal reorganization can displace informal collaborative processes; and macro-level shifts in the policy agenda (such as a spike in concern about climate change) can draw attention away from what can seem like a minor-league bureaucratic agenda.

Chance and Entropy

These technical, institutional, and political difficulties of ICC construction are exacerbated by the fact that though there are few ways to succeed, there are a great many ways to fail. The main reason is that the ICC is an integrated system, and failure of any of the functions—or any of the elements that are critical to performing those functions—means serious performance degradation or even failure of the whole. In most of the cases I studied, resource insufficiencies by themselves threatened or killed several ICCs (New York State contract administration; Del Paso Heights Neighborhood Services Agency; California Healthy Start). This was also true of failures of leadership (Tennessee's children's services; Oregon's welfare-to-work in one region of the state; Oregon's family services).

From the point of view of the entrepreneurial cadre pushing for an ICC, the problem is similar to a darts game. The rules, let us say, are that you need 500 points to "succeed," the bull's-eye is worth 200, you have three throws, and the values of the rings around the bull's-eye begin at 100 and decrease. There are only two ways to succeed (all throws score bull's-eyes or two score bull's-eyes and one scores 100), but many ways to fail. It is of some comfort that the two ways to succeed can be achieved by four different combinations of scores achieved by the three darts—but not much.

Many of my interviewees during the 1990s remarked that their efforts at collaborative action were favored by a situation in which "all the planets were in alignment." This is a realistic, if colorful, way of describing the role of chance in the process of ICC construction. The planets they had in mind were usually political demands, institutional needs, budgetary resources, and cooperative personalities. How each of the planets had come to be where it was also reflected chance: a legal crisis here (Memorandum of Understanding on Biodiversity, following a federal court decision ending logging in large parts of Oregon and California in order to protect the spotted owl), a budgetary hemorrhage there (Tennessee and Maryland children and family services), a zealous governor somewhere else (multimedia environmental enforcement). Thus, not only was chance at work but it was at work in a certain way: the chances of favorable combinations turning up and persisting in the face of entropy were relatively small.[11] One could reasonably say that chance alone is an enemy of success.

11. On the surface, this analysis is similar to that of Jeffrey L. Pressman and Aaron Wildavsky in their classic work on programmatic failure during implementation (Pressman and Wildavsky 1979). They stopped their calculations at this point, however, without taking into account all the things that implementers do to try to manage the challenge.

Smart Practices in the Management of Process

In the face of such challenges, entrepreneurs managing an ICC construction process do not simply collapse. They act and react with varying degrees of insight, foresight, creativity, and resolve, the combination of which I call, for the sake of simplicity, *adaptiveness*. A purely positive (analytical) model of the building process needs to take account of such actions.

Exactly how to do so is unclear, however. The first difficulty is that we must make assumptions about the degree of adaptiveness that informs the ICC entrepreneurs' actions. We must then make assumptions about the levels of political risk and of cost that they are willing to impose on the ICC project, since most actions will entail some of each. Third, we must make assumptions about the effect that a chosen action will have. Finally, in cases where the ICC builders face active opposition (whether open or covert), we need to imagine what countermoves will be made and with what effect. The cumulative uncertainty from all of these assumptions is very high and makes the testing of any model by the usual mode of successful prediction (or, more commonly, retrodiction) in which entrepreneurial adaptiveness plays a large role a dubious undertaking.

One possible strategy for dealing with these problems is to omit entrepreneurial adaptiveness altogether from models of the collaborative process (Alter and Hage 1993). This is no worse than omitting hard-to-assess variables from models of many other phenomena, except that it leaves unexamined practices that would probably be of interest to ICC entrepreneurs, a group that at least some public management scholars would like to serve. A second strategy is simply to make assumptions (explicitly or implicitly) about adaptiveness that seem right "on average" and work from there. This seems reasonable to me and is to some extent the strategy I have followed in *Getting Agencies to Work Together*. A third strategy is to look at adaptiveness through normative rather than positive lenses: What practices would probably work well under what conditions and at generally acceptable (or low) costs and risks? I followed this strategy in my book and do so here as well. Unfortunately, although the conceptual advantages are plain (Barzelay and Thompson 2007; Weiss 1994), there are also clear disadvantages: the empirical work to establish the value of these practices has generally not been done. Hence, the value of such a speculative discussion, if it has any, is mainly conceptual.

Smart Practice

The practices at issue I call *smart practices*. I have discussed them elsewhere, so here I may be brief.[12] By *smart practice* I mean a practice that takes advantage of

12. See Bardach (2004; 2005, pp. 91–105).

some latent potentiality in the world in order to accomplish something in a relatively cost-effective manner. In the physical world, a good example would be a seagull taking advantage of gravity to open a shell by dropping it on a rock or a human being exploding some energy-packed hydrocarbon molecules in an enclosed chamber in order to move a two-ton truck. In the social world, we take advantage of the natural forces of competition to generate price signals, at a low cost, that in turn allocate myriad goods and services to their most valued uses, and we take advantage of easily induced fear and uncertainty to deter unwanted behavior on what can sometimes be a very large scale. To put it another way, smart practices are smart because they exploit some latent potential generously furnished by Mother Nature to get a lot of bang for very few bucks.

For what problems or opportunities in the construction of an ICC are smart practices needed or otherwise useful? They range from such technical matters as facilitating teamwork among frontline workers from different agencies to the development of leadership capacity to political matters such as arranging whole or partial compensation for agencies whose resources are used by the ICC. Here I discuss only a few, and these all pertain to the dynamics of the construction process, to the emergent threats and opportunities I sketched in the preceding section. It is not that these emergent threats and opportunities are necessarily more important than the more static kind, only that they are analytically interesting and relatively understudied.

Building Momentum

As I said earlier, ICC construction, like building construction, occurs in a sequence of steps. Some sequences are more effective than others—for instance, those that can create and take advantage of momentum effects.

Many smart practices might create or intensify momentum effects (Bardach 1998, pp. 276–92). One of the best known is picking some relatively easy near-term targets—"plucking the low-hanging fruit," some call it—so as to create a few "small wins"(Weick 1984).

What counts as "low-hanging fruit"? For one thing, targets with "win-win" possibilities, that is, targets that entail changes favored by all of the important stakeholders. A majority of the nineteen cases I studied for my book had this characteristic. Another is prominence. The choice of the New York State master contracting group, The Door, is a case in point. If success is achieved, it is better that it should be widely noticed and that early confidence in the ICC should be expressed by parties that enjoy respect.

The Door was also unusually competent, and this, too, can be a desirable characteristic, particularly if there is a risk that small failures, as opposed to small wins, will effectively kill any further ICC development. In fact, this is probably the characteristic uppermost in planners' minds when they choose sites for pilot or demonstration projects. It is worth noting the corollary drawbacks of unusual competency, however. It is very risky to generalize from the most competent sites to more normal sites, much less to sites of dubious competence. For this reason, a second, and perhaps a third, round of experimentation is necessary. But because such new trials cause delay, which brings its own dangers, at some point it becomes worthwhile to mount projects in many sites at once. In partial compensation, at least some of these will probably illuminate the difficulties collaboration will face in mediocre or worse circumstances.

Sometimes strategizing about how to reach targets in the future by aiming at particular targets in the near term can pay off. In Oregon, service integration strategists in the state Department of Human Services encouraged innovative collaborative projects at the local level throughout the state, along with systematic feedback to themselves about barriers that they believed state systems had created. The strategists' intention was to use the feedback, and the momentum created by local expectations, to press for changes within the department.

Sequencing and Platforming

If an effective political sequencing of ICC construction steps takes advantage of momentum effects, an efficient technical sequencing takes advantage of *platforming* effects. *Platforms* are emergent features of a developmental process that come about as follows: Each component of capacity added to the overall structure potentially serves a dual role, the first being its functionality in the performance of the yet-to-be-completed structure itself and the second being a *platform* of use in the building process. Thus, in building a physical structure, a completed frame will eventually help to hold the entire structure, but it is also a platform from which to work on the roof. Efficient platforming reduces aggravation and delay and enables participants in the steering process to envision new goals and operational approaches. Because delay also increases the risks of collapse, efficient platforming also reduces the vulnerability of an ICC during the construction process.

What are the most efficient platforming sequences? This is an empirical question on which little work has been done. As an example of what an efficient sequence might be, though, I took the ten tasks previously listed and organized them as an ensemble of platforms and suggested which should be put in place earlier, which later, and which simultaneously.

Because the model shown in figure 7-1 is essentially normative, there is no guarantee that ICC processes observed in social nature, so to speak, would fit it. However, allowing for impressionistic interpretation and the fact that it is hard to tell when steps are begun or are accomplished to some successful degree, in

Figure 7-1. *Each New Capacity a Platform for the Next*

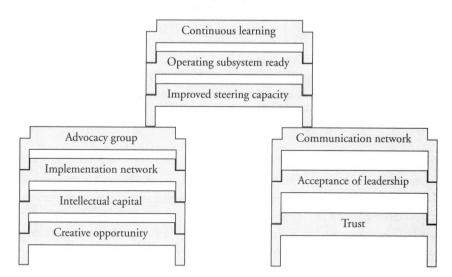

my own research on ICCs in the 1990s I found at least six cases out of nineteen that appeared to match this model.[13]

Sequencing may or may not be highly thought out. Probably sequences involving trust building and communications need to be organized with more foresight than others, simply because they are less obvious and seem to take a lot of time without creating obvious forward motion. However, certain kinds of tasks almost cry out for work to proceed in a certain sequence. Here I use an example not drawn from my book but documented in the files of the Innovations in American Government Awards Program, for which it was a 1997 finalist. The Common Vision Program of jurisdictions along the Trinity River near Dallas–Ft. Worth began as a regional response to perceived hazards in the Trinity River floodplain. An obvious first step was to build common intellectual capital by commissioning technical studies describing and evaluating alternative approaches to reducing flood damage. The Corps of Engineers district office, which received applications for land reclamation permits, came to suspect that overbuilding was a serious problem and, in the early 1980s, prepared a regional environmental impact statement documenting the immense magnitude of it. A few years later, the regional Council of Governments, in keeping with its underlying ICC-like mission, adopted a policy statement affirming the need for local

13. See Bardach (1998, p. 275). In most cases I did not know enough of the historical details to evaluate the fit. In a few cases I thought that clever leaders may have managed to short-circuit the full developmental process to some degree.

stewardship along with inter-locality cooperative management. The corps then did another study identifying various alternative plans to reduce or prevent flood damage and pointing out the associated water quality, recreational, and environmental benefits. With the aid of a detailed geographic information system and computer-based models of storm and flood scenarios, a river corridor–based permitting plan was developed. Each jurisdiction was assigned particular implementation responsibilities, and a combination of peer pressure and the threat of court action sufficed to enforce these responsibilities.

Preventing and Buffering

I referred above to four common exogenous shocks: turnover of key individuals, loss of political support following election turnover, adverse change in fiscal circumstances, and the onset of large-scale and disruptive efforts to reorganize formally. These cannot be prevented per se, but the ICC can take measures to prevent itself from being exposed to them. Briefly stated, it can accelerate the pace of its development so that it reaches some threshold level of institutionalization before it has to face too many such shocks or, more commonly, so that it can outrace some identifiable oncoming hazard, such as an election that might oust a significant political supporter.

It is also possible to buffer the ICC against likely adversity. One method is to build a broad and hopefully bipartisan consensus behind the ICC that persists in the face of electoral changes and, better still, to have it strategically located in the political structure. Maryland's Systems Reform Initiative, its mid-1990s effort to better integrate services to children and families, had allies in every county who were receiving state funds from a special account in effect bearing the label "savings from out-of-home placements the state has avoided." The New Jersey School-Based Youth Services Program saw to it that some state monies for the program flowed into all twenty-one counties. SBYS also created a council of representatives from the collaborating agencies that reported to the governor so that it would have a forum to speak for the program when the governorship changed hands.

The turnover problem can be mitigated by not allowing the ICC to become dependent on relationships or leaders that cannot be easily replaced. Roberta Knowlton, one of the two top state managers of School-Based Youth Services, spoke not just of multiple leaders but of multiple sources of leadership: "There are seven sources of leadership in School-Based [Youth Services], so that you can lose some and still not have catastrophe!" They are the lead agency and the way it manages things; the school itself; the management capacity of the director of the program; the staff hired to work for the director (which ideally should be ethnically and linguistically appropriate); the community advisory board; the parent advisory board; and an evaluator. "There is a lot of instability in local programs. It's a matter of chance which of these seven factors are up or down at any time." Here indeed is a rich example of the vulnerability of ICCs to chance and an equally rich example of a smart practice for trying to cope with it.

Seizing Opportunity

Let us acknowledge that "chance" is not only a dark-cloaked character perennially menacing the ICC construction process. Chance has another face as well. Sometimes it benevolently furnishes opportunities to initiate and successfully sustain development of an ICC. As Machiavelli wrote in *The Prince,* "I think it may be true that fortune is the ruler of half our actions, but that she allows the other half or thereabouts to be governed by us" (Machiavelli 1950, p. 91). As noted, many of my interviewees during the 1990s remarked that their efforts at collaborative action were favored, if not initially motivated by good fortune, by a situation in which "all the planets were in alignment."

What they usually meant by this was that there was a temporal, and perhaps temporary, coincidence between what they had wanted to do all along (further interagency collaboration) and what the political environment and the fiscal situation were now demanding or at least permitting. They did not necessarily mean that they themselves were at a point in their careers, or the competing pressures on their organizations were now such, that they could attend to the long and time-consuming process of building a collaborative. But I believe the presence of motivated and, in most cases, creative personalities such as themselves was an important element in the "alignment." They were prepared to seize the opportunity and make what they could of it.

Related to the seizing of opportunity is the adaptation to adverse surprise. This typically happens by scanning for substitute resources (California Healthy Start), doubling back to redo failed steps in the developmental process (Maryland Integrated Family Services), retreating on objectives (CYSC), and reconfiguring governance structures (CYSC, Memorandum of Understanding on Biodiversity).[14]

Summary and Conclusion

In this chapter I have pursued three nested themes. They all have to do with *process:* (1) the conception of process as endogenous change over time, (2) a particular type of process: the back-and-forth, challenge-and-response, dialectical

---

14. See the previous note and also the discussion of cases in Bardach (1998, pp. 69–72, 104). The question of how an evolving ICC adapts to negative surprises is intriguing and especially deserving of further research.

process involved in most organizational and political changes, and (3) the particular challenges and responses that emerge in a developmental process involving interagency collaboration.

The outermost theme, the most encompassing, has had to do with appreciating the nature of *process* as endogenous change over time. Although many political scientists and public management scholars use the term *process*—for instance, the policy process, the administrative process, the governmental process, the electoral process—the usage typically connotes merely sequences of actions or events that are structured by institutional rules and by the strategies of the attentive interests. For instance, representatives from interests A, B, and C get together and draw up a bill; the bill is heard in subcommittee; it passes, and then is heard in full committee, where it is opposed by interests D, E, and F who have recently mobilized in opposition.

But this is a relatively thin and passive view of *process,* in that it is driven primarily by exogenous forces and constraints and contingencies. A livelier sense of process would be desirable, one that is more realistic and more penetrating, a conception of process that emphasizes endogeneity, positive as well as negative feedback loops, the creative role of chance, and emergent phenomena.[15] This livelier sense of process is evident in the work of the Systems Dynamics Group at MIT, the Center for the Study of Complex Systems at the University of Michigan, and the Digital Government Research Program at SUNY–Albany, to name only three of the most prominent university-based groups.[16] It is no accident that computer simulation (computational modeling) is the preferred analytical tool in these settings, since the phenomena at issue are too complex to be modeled verbally, graphically, or mathematically. What I have offered here (for example, developmental technical sequences, momentum effects, life-cycle effects) is very superficial compared to what might be done with simulation tools. I hope it will prove suggestive, however.

The next most-inward thematic layer explored here concerns a substantive type of process, a dialectical process. The dialectic here is between an emergent set of challenges (and some opportunities) and responses (some reactive, some proactive) by individuals intent on mastering them, in some cases by employing what I call *smart practices.* I invoke a dialectical process partly because the challenges/response phenomenon is a realistic and important building block of political and managerial processes but also because a dialectical model explicitly

15. See Bardach (2006).

16. See, for instance Forrester (1969, 1968); Axelrod (1997); Axelrod and Cohen (1999); Richardson (1991). For a conception of organizational innovation that greatly respects the creative role of chance, see the work of Van de Ven and his colleagues (Van de Ven 1993; Van de Ven, Angle, and Poole 1989).

accommodates an explanatory role for adaptive entrepreneurship and a variety of smart practices.

What generates these challenges and opportunities? What creates the raw material for *smart practice* or other adaptations? One must look to the institutional particulars of the change process in question. In our case, a developmental process is taking place, one that involves the construction of interagency collaborative capacity. Such a developmental process is our innermost thematic layer. Most of this chapter has been devoted to the details of this process, for example, the challenge of sequencing construction tasks and the potential for entrepreneurial insight about which sequences would be more or less efficient than others, the challenges of emergent vulnerabilities, and the opportunities to exploit momentum processes.[17] I would also note here the effort to build chance into the causal structure that lies behind the emergence of both opportunity and vulnerability.[18]

I would reiterate, in closing, that the scenarios on display in this chapter are exceedingly preliminary and are intended more as suggestive examples than as rigorous and testable models. The case of ICC construction is, of course, only one instance of the possible applicability of dialectical and developmental models to the world of politics and institutions. Many others readily come to mind, from the construction of legislative coalitions to the life-cycle of nonprofit organizations.

17. I have not attempted to break down the ICC developmental process into phases, as is sometimes done in the literature on interorganizational collaboration, for example Gray (1989) and Roberts (1992).

18. I have found the work of Andrew H. Van de Ven inspiring in these regards.

8

The Adoption of Innovation: The Challenge of Learning to Adapt Tacit Knowledge

ROBERT D. BEHN

In 1986, the first year of the Innovations in American Government Awards, one of the winners was the program One Church, One Child. Recognizing that many black children were languishing in foster care, the Illinois Department of Children and Family Services and a group of African American ministers, under the leadership of a Catholic priest, the Reverend George Clements, undertook to have every African American church adopt one black child (Altshuler, Warrock, and Zegans 1988).

A few years later, Stephen Jenkins, a Kennedy School graduate student, in an analysis of the replication of One Church, One Child, reported the following disagreement in North Carolina about what actually was the core of this innovation (Jenkins 1989, pp. 27–28):

> North Carolina's program, called "Friends of Black Children," developed concurrently with One Church, One Child in the early 1980s and maintains its separate identity. It, too, has been enormously successful, gaining access to the black community not just through ministers, but through black leaders in all walks of life—small business, government, and others.
>
> Though program coordinators in North Carolina were aware of Illinois' efforts, they were committed to their own broad-based approach and did not seek to establish contacts with One Church, One Child staff. The state did, however, invite Father Clements to be the keynote speaker for a

commemorative ceremony it held in 1985. While in Raleigh, Clements engaged a Friends of Black Children district coordinator in a good-natured but heated debate about whether a minority adoption program not based on the One Church, One Child model was "the real thing." The black church, he [Clements] argued, was the proper access to the black community. "But ours works!" the district coordinator protested.

This story suggests a major disagreement about what the innovation really was. Was it—as Father Clements believed—getting *black churches* to take responsibility for the adoption of black children? Or was it—as North Carolina believed—getting *a variety of black organizations* to take on this responsibility? What really was *it*?

This debate dramatizes some fundamental questions about any innovation and thus its adoption: What is the innovation? What is the core concept? What needs to be faithfully "replicated"? What variations of the basic concept will "work"? What kind of adaptations are acceptable, desirable, essential? From the story, it appears that Father Clements had too narrow a definition of his own innovation. If the purpose is to ensure that more black children are adopted, why should the concept be permitted to work through only one type of black institution. Yet, if the innovators themselves do not really discern what is the core concept of their innovation—if, for example, they are constrained by a too narrow, operational notion of their idea—how will others grasp it? If the innovators are so controlled by the tactics that they employed to implement their innovation that they fail to remain focused on its real purpose—and to recognize that some variations in the concept that can still achieve the same purpose—how will others not get caught up with a fixation on these administrative details?

What Is *It?*

The "What works?" movement in public policy—the effort to make evidence-based policy choices—focuses on the "works?" component of the question: That is, does this policy work or not? This is a question that the traditional evaluation methodologies are designed to answer (Davies, Nutley, and Smith 2000; Pfeffer and Sutton 2006).

The "What works?" question has, however, a second component: "What?" *What* is it that is doing the working? Assuming that something is, in fact, working (so that things are somehow improving), *what* is doing this working? What, exactly, is causing the results that the evaluation concludes are being produced by the policy? This may appear obvious; after all, how can you evaluate a policy until you have decided what the policy is? At the same time, the key active ingredients in policy may not be all that obvious. It is not like the polio vaccine—a single, well-specified intervention that can be given to some and withheld from others.

In any innovation in policy, management, or leadership, there are undoubtedly a lot of *whats* embedded in the complex combination of practices, rules, behaviors, tactics, and strategies that have been mixed together as *the* policy. Of all of these *whats*, which one is the causal factor? Or, more likely, which are the key *whats*, and how have they been combined and how do they interact to cause the desired result? This may be not at all that obvious.[1] Elsewhere, I have called this the *definitional dilemma*: "What exactly is the innovation" (Behn 1997, p. 32).

In California, one attempt to answer the "What works?" question focused on efforts to educate elementary school students with limited English proficiency. This research analyzed five different "models" (from "Double Immersion" to "Sheltered English") that reportedly had worked to see whether they did, indeed, improve students' English. And despite their quite different pedagogical strategies, all seemed to pass the test of being "exemplary." Still, what aspect of each strategy produced the students' educational improvement? Was it the specific components of the strategy? Or was it something else? In their analysis of these approaches, Paul Berman and Beryl Nelson of RPP International wrote: "Significantly, the student outcomes for various exemplary schools appeared to depend less on the model adopted and more on the extent to which the schools practiced team teaching or created a preschool program" (Berman and Nelson 1997, p. 328).

For a policy, practice, or innovation that has proved successful, what exactly is the *what*? What is the component of the innovation that is causing the improvement in performance? Is it what the original innovators think it is? Or is it something different that was added to keep someone happy? Is it something else that was included as part of a political compromise necessary to obtain permission to experiment with the presumed innovation? Or is it a new organizational routine that was introduced at the same time for entirely unrelated reasons? Maybe a different *what* is actually producing the result.

Maybe the result was produced by an inactive ingredient added to make the medicine taste good (or less bad), to make it fizz, to give it a more appealing color, or do whatever people think it "should" look like. Maybe the key ingredient is just a placebo. As the medical profession is quite aware, placebos can be quite effective (Wampold, Imel, and Minami 2007).

1. In the introduction to their book focusing on "what works" in improving public services, Huw T. O. Davies, Sandra M. Nutley, and Peter C. Smith note that the traditional "gold standard" of evaluation—the randomized controlled experiment—"rarely offers useful insights into *why* a particular intervention performs better than another" (emphasis in the original). Further, they note that the context may influence whether the what will indeed work (Davies, Nutley, and Smith 2000, pp. 14, 9–10).

Maybe it isn't the amount of lighting at all; maybe it's all about the personal attention.

Causal Ambiguity

Even *within* an organization, the adoption of an innovation happens less frequently than the organization's executives would like (or outsiders might predict). "Experience shows," reports Gabriel Szulanski of INSEAD, in Fontainebleau, France, that "transferring capabilities within a firm is far from easy" (Szulanski 1996, p. 27). And if adoption is difficult *within* a business firm for which the definition and measure of success is well established, known, and accepted, how much more difficult is it *within* a public organization buffeted by conflicting definitions (but few, if any real measures) of success, *between* different public organizations, or *between* different public organizations in different government jurisdictions?

Some of the reasons for this lack of intra-firm adoption include many of the usual characteristics of human and organizational behavior. Carla O'Dell and Jackson Grayson of the American Productivity and Quality Center offer several: The people who created the innovation failed to realize that others could use their innovation. The people who could have used the innovation failed to realize that others had it; these people had no ongoing professional or personal relationship. The people who created the innovation realized that others could use it but had no incentive to help them (and, indeed, had an incentive not to help them). The people who could have used the innovation had, indeed, learned about it but saw no pressing reason for employing it. Or the people who could have used the innovation had indeed learned about it but lacked some important operational quality necessary to implement it. As a result, O'Dell and Grayson conclude, "In most organizations, the left hand not only doesn't know what the right hand is doing, but it also may not even know there is a right hand" (O'Dell and Grayson 1998a, p. 157; O'Dell and Grayson 1998b, pp. 17, 18).

There is, however, an additional barrier to adoption within a business firm—a factor that has nothing to do with organizational behavior and everything to do with the innovation that might be a candidate for adoption. Maybe it isn't clear exactly what the innovation is. Maybe the cause-and-effect connection isn't clear. Maybe it isn't clear what aspects, features, characteristics, qualities, or details of the innovation are causing the desired effect.

Indeed, maybe even the innovators themselves do not clearly appreciate which of the many components of their innovation are interacting in what ways to cause their effect. Maybe they don't know. Maybe they have a guess—a good guess, but still only a guess. Or maybe they understand the complicated connections but cannot fully and clearly explain them to others (at least without having these others live with them professionally for days or weeks or months). Steven Lippman and Richard Rumelt of the University of California at Los Angeles call this *causal ambiguity*—"a basic ambiguity concerning the nature of the causal connections between actions and results." Moreover, they argue, "The ambiguity surrounding the linkage between action and performance in large firms virtually guarantees the existence of substantial uncertain imitability" (Lippman and Rumelt 1982, pp. 418, 421). And if the causal linkage within a business firm can be ambiguous, how much more likely is there to exist causal ambiguity about such linkages when those involved in either the actions or the consequences include numerous outside stakeholders?

The Vocabulary of Adoption: Diffusion, Transfer, Propagation, and Replication

How does an innovation that has proved useful in one organization come to be adopted in others? A variety of words can be used to describe this process including *diffusion, transfer, propagation,* and *replication.* Each of these words comes with its own connotations. Yet these (and other) words, though they are usually used interchangeably, do suggest different processes that might work in quite different ways.

In particular, these words might suggest passive or active mechanisms by which potential new adopters of the innovation learn both about the innovation and how they might utilize it, as well as who might be actively encouraging such learning. Thus, let me suggest four different types of processes, with these four ordered (at least as I use them) from most passive (diffusion) to most active (replication):

—*Diffusion* suggests an unintentional, spontaneous, hidden-hand process by which others somehow hear about the innovation and conclude it is worthwhile to try it. (This might be called the *somehow-people-will-learn-how-to-get-better* approach.)

—*Transfer* suggests an informal trading of ideas and practices by a network of individuals—often a professional network of peers and colleagues working in the same business or policy area but in different organizations or jurisdictions. (This might be called the *friends-will-tell-friends-about-how-they-are-getting-better* approach.)

—*Propagation* suggests a more premeditated effort by some (perhaps the innovators, perhaps outside individuals or organizations, perhaps higher levels of government) to create a deliberate strategy of education and assistance to transfer the innovation to others. (This might be called the *we-ought-to-help-people-learn-how-to-get-better* approach.)

—*Replication* suggests a conscious effort by organizations (or individuals within organizations) that strive to improve by actively seeking out successful ideas, policies, programs, and practices that they can adopt. (This is the *we-want-to-learn-from-others-who-know-how-to-get-better* approach.)

Each of these four processes is, of course, an "ideal type" (Weber 1947, p. 329)—a formal, simplified construct designed to accentuate important differences and to provide a basis for comparisons. Many of the actual processes by which one organization's innovation is adopted by another may have the features of two or more of these ideal types. Nevertheless, for analytical purposes, these four ideal-type processes may prove quite useful.

Is, however, this differentiation among these four words worthwhile? Have I captured the connotations correctly? Is my approach to ordering them meaningful? This isn't clear. After all, most of the literature on the diffusion, transfer, propagation, and replication of innovations uses these words almost interchangeably without much of an effort to distinguish different ways in which an adopter learns about an innovation. For example, in his landmark study *Diffusion of Innovations,* Everett Rogers defines "diffusion" as "the process by which an innovation is communicated through certain channels over time among the members of a social system" (Rogers 2003, p. 5). This suggests a combination of my "diffusion" and my "transfer"—not quite as passive as my *diffusion,*[2] but not quite as active as my *transfer.*

Jean Hartley and John Benington from the University of Warwick, in an article examining how inter-organizational networks engage in knowledge sharing, employ *share* or *sharing* sixty-four times, *transfer* twenty-one times, *disseminate* or *dissemination* eight times, *diffusion* or *diffusing* six times, *replicate* or *replication* three times, and *promote* three times. Hartley and Benington (2006) write about "professionals sharing knowledge across a network" and of "relatively open networks of knowledge diffusion"—concepts that appear to be very similar to my *transfer* process. But they are specifically interested in a number of formal networks, such as the Beacon Scheme (Rashman, Downe, and Hartley 2005; Downe, Rashman, and Hartley 2004; Rashman and Hartley 2002), that have been explicitly created to foster the sharing and transfer of ideas. The Beacon Scheme emphasizes such words as *network* and *transfer,* yet it also is explicitly designed to be a propagation process. (Though Hartley and Benington

2. I think of diffusion as a passive process, neither guided nor encouraged nor facilitated by humans, because my first introduction to this word was in the natural sciences. In biology, a molecule can diffuse through a cell membrane from a region of high concentration to a region of low concentration. No human actively does anything; the diffusion just happens. Similarly, in physics, molecules concentrated in one region of a fluid will diffuse throughout the fluid. Again: No one does anything; the diffusion just happens.

never use any variant of the verb *to propagate;* rather, they employ a horticul-tural metaphor: to graft and transplant.)

In their survey of the "diffusion" literature, David Strang of Cornell Univer-sity and Sarah Soule of the University of Arizona write: "Diffusion refers to the spread of something within a social system. The key term here is 'spread,' and it should be taken viscerally (as far as one's constructionism permits) to denote flow or movement from a source to an adopter, paradigmatically via communi-cation and influence." And this "something" that is "spread" is a "practice," which includes "a behavior, strategy, belief, technology, or structure," and that spread can happen through passive communication or active influence. Strang and Soule describe diffusion as a "causal process," one "embracing contagion, mimicry, social learning, organized dissemination, and other family members" (Strang and Soule 1998, p. 266). And certainly all diffusion processes are "causal," in the sense that something "caused" an adopter to learn about, think about, and try out an innovation. Yet, this causal process might still be quite casual. And perhaps the success of the adoption of an innovation by others may depend upon how deliberate or serendipitous the process is.

Clearly, the research suggests that an innovation can come to be adopted by others as a result of anything from pure random luck to a conscious, calculated effort—with an active endeavor undertaken by the innovator, by an adopter, by some other entity, or through a network. Yet (as far as I can tell), little effort has been made to distinguish among these processes, let alone to establish an explicit vocabulary for discussing and analyzing them.

Diffusion. This passive process involves the transfer of information in a man-ner that is quite unintentional by all involved. This fits within what Strang and Soule call "contagion"—"irrational, spontaneous transmission" with the idea moving "grape-vine like from prior to potential adopters" (Strang and Soule 1998, pp. 268, 272). The concept of the innovation is communicated through what Mark Granovetter of Stanford University has called "weak ties" (Gra-novetter 1973). Potential adopters learn about the innovation not because any-one tried to convince them (or anyone else) of the value of the innovation, or because they sought out any new ideas. Rather, whoever is offering the informa-tion about the innovation does so with little intention of advocating that some people ought to adopt it. For example, the information might be contained in a report by a journalist who is motivated not by a desire to spread the good word, but simply by the professional benefits of writing a good story. (For *diffusion,* the key medium is the "ether.")[3]

---

3. I draw the word *ether* from the mystical medium through which physicists once thought light was propagated. Because light was (at least in part) a wave, not merely a particle, physics needed a medium through which this light could be transmitted. This ether (or aether) was invisible (without

Transfer. This still-mostly-passive process is nevertheless facilitated by regular contact among innovators and potential adopters.[4] Professional organizations and informal networks provide, in Strang and Soule's words, the "strong ties" that create the opportunity for such transfer through "face-to-face interaction" (Strang and Soule 1998, p. 272). When these innovators and potential adopters get together for a beer (and after they finish their inevitable discussion of the latest victory of the Red Sox over the Yankees), someone might mention a new practice that her organization has just tried, and someone else might note that this practice might solve one of his problems, and from this initial discussion might flow a series of subsequent discussions, communications, and visits. (For *transfer,* the key medium is beer.)

Propagation. This active process is driven by some individuals who are actively promoting the innovation.[5] For example, the U.S. Agricultural Extension Service energetically seeks to identify new, effective agricultural practices and then to convince American farmers to employ them. Management consultants and gurus make a living doing the same thing (Micklethwait and Wooldridge 1996). Indeed, Strang and Soule note that a variety of "professional change agents" work in what they call "vibrant diffusion industries" (Strang and Soule 1998, pp. 267, 286). Some businesses do the same thing internally, report O'Dell and Grayson; these businesses identify best practices in one part of the firm and then attempt to get other units to adopt them. O'Dell and Grayson call this the *bumble bee* or *pollination model* (O'Dell and Grayson 1998a, p. 159). And within a government jurisdiction, a legislature or central regulatory

---

either charge or mass) but omnipresent throughout all space and served the function of conducting electromagnetic waves. You might want to call the mechanism for diffusion the network, though I think of this concept as a little too formal, a little too mechanistic to actually capture the difficult-to-detect mechanism for diffusion. The network—the active, conscious network—is what serves for transfer (with beer connecting the nodes).

4. Note that others use the word "transfer" to refer to a process that is much closer to the active end of my scale (Rashman and Hartley 2002).

5. The Innovations in American Government Awards Program, sponsored by the Ash Institute for Democratic Governance and Innovation at Harvard's Kennedy School of Government, is such a propagation effort. This awards program is designed not merely to identify outstanding innovations but also to publicize the winning innovations and support efforts of the innovators to publicize their ideas and practices. In fact, one of the four criteria for winning this award is:

Its transferability, the degree to which the program or initiative, or aspects of it, shows promise of inspiring successful replication by other governmental entities

—To what extent can this program or initiative be replicated in other jurisdictions?

—To what extent can this program or initiative serve as a model that other jurisdictions will seek to replicate?

—To what extent are program or initiative components, concepts, principles, or insights transferable to other disciplines or policy areas?

For additional information go to www.ashinstitute.harvard.edu/Ash/awards.htm.

agency may use its power to require subunits within the jurisdiction to adopt the innovation.[6] (For *propagation,* the key medium is propaganda.)[7]

Replication. This active process is undertaken by the would-be adopters who are constantly and actively seeking new ideas, new policies, new practices, new strategies that they themselves can employ to improve. They are not mere adopters, but ambitious replicators who want to be known as innovative (at least locally) and thus are always alert for the latest ideas that can make them stand out. (For *replication,* the key medium is the programmatic kleptomania.)

Whether you accept the specific connotations that I have assigned to these four words, let alone the ordering I have given them on my passive-to-active scale, you ought to accept that an original innovation can come into wider use through a variety of processes some of which are purely fortuitous while others are carefully calculated. And this calculation can be made by the innovator, the adopter, or by some facilitating broker (who exercises influence through official power, acknowledged status, or convincing persuasion).

The Constraints of Vocabulary

Note the word *replication.* It suggests that the objective is the production of a perfect duplicate. In fact, the verb *to replicate* suggests that the objective is to create an exact "replica"—and that the original innovation consisted of a sequence of replicons that can and indeed do replicate themselves as a unit.

The biological metaphor is subtle but clear. It is as if the original innovation was encoded in some organizational DNA that contains all of the necessary instructions for replication and development. Indeed, it is as if, by some biological-like process, the original innovation could split itself into two, with each of the two DNA strands containing precisely the same information. This replication process may not be perfect—the new organization that has been created through the splitting of the DNA strand may not be an exact duplicate of the original. But that is only because of some imperfection in the process, some random but unavoidable mutation.

In fact, whether the verb is *replicate, propagate, transfer,* or *diffuse,* the traditional implication is the same. Here is something new, something wonderful,

6. Historical note: I owe this point about the use of power to impose an innovation on others to my colleague Eugene Bardach. This came about through the ideal-type process of "transfer"—an informal lunch of several scholars, during which I mentioned these four processes, and Gene suggested that I was ignoring power. One further historical note: during this lunch, Gene did have a beer, though I did not.

7. I could have chosen the word disseminate here. After all, the phrase *dissemination of innovation* is used more frequently than *propagation of innovation,* and the phrase *innovation dissemination* is more common than *innovation propagation.* Nevertheless, I chose *propagate* because I thought its connotation was more active, more aggressive than *disseminate.*

something effective, something brilliant. It works. Others ought to do it, too. Others ought to copy it. And to get it right, they ought to copy it precisely.

The choice of words such as *replication,* or *propagation,* or *transfer,* or *diffusion* may simply be a product of our limited vocabulary. This choice may also be restricted by our inability to coin new words that more accurately capture the concept we are seeking to describe. The words are not, however, inconsequential. Each word comes not only with its formal dictionary definition but also with the common connotations that we assign to the word—both individually and collectively. This is why Hartley and Benington argue that the "copy and paste" or "the drag and drop" metaphor are inappropriate ways to think of the process and suggest as a replacement "an active process of grafting and transplanting" (Hartley and Benington 2006, p. 104).

Consider the now discredited phrase "the one best way." The founders of "scientific management" argued that they could—through, for example, time-and-motion studies—determine *the* one best way to carry out an organizational task.[8] Today, however, no one advocates a one best way to do anything (Burnes 1996; Burke and others 2005).

Rather, "the one best way" has been morphed into "best practice." This more up-to-date phrase comes, however, with precisely the same connotation: There, indeed, exists a *best way* to do something. Moreover, it comes with a second connotation: Every organization (at least if it is *au courant)* ought to employ this "best practice."

Consequently, once a policy or a management practice has been certified as an "innovation," it automatically and immediately becomes yet another best practice. And—just as automatically—a "best practice" comes with the not so subtle connotation that any organization that seeks to implement this innovation needs to replicate it—and faithfully. Otherwise, how could it claim to be employing this new, improved "best practice"?

The Vocabulary of Adaptation and Evolution

But what, exactly, is this new, innovative best practice? What exactly is this innovation's DNA? What are the key sequences in the DNA strand that produce the desired outcomes? What are the extraneous (unused and unuseful) segments that keep popping up but really contribute nothing? How, in fact, does this new organism/innovation function? What is the environmental niche in which it thrives? What are the environmental niches in which it will whither? In

---

8. The concept of "the one best way" was originated by Frank and Lillian Gilbreth (see, for example, Gilbreth and Gilbreth 1917). Nevertheless, the phrase is most frequently associated with Frederick Winslow Taylor (see Kanigel 1997).

what ways does it need to adapt to survive in these other environments? How much does it need to adapt? Is such adaptation possible? Or can the innovation prove productive in only a limited political, organizational, and cultural environment? If so, what are the environmental conditions in which the innovation can (after its inevitable if modest adaptation) thrive and prosper?

The vocabulary of evolutionary biology is much more helpful than the vocabulary of diffusion, transfer, propagation, and replication.[9] After all, if we believe that there is no universal one best way—or even only a locally superior best way—then the language of adaptation seems more accurately descriptive and more usefully evocative.

Some innovations have tough shells and, like cockroaches, may be able without much adjustment to survive and thrive in widely divergent climates. Others may be quite sensitive to local conditions and may require frequent modifications in response to the ever-constant changes in the environment. Indeed, this may be particularly true of the latest innovations in policy, management, and leadership. Why did they take so long to evolve? Or have they evolved numerous times before, only to be crushed by some cantankerous committee chair or some outraged stakeholder group? In fact, today's innovations are more likely to be sensitive to their environment than those organizational cockroaches that have figured out how, despite recurrent stompings, to survive fiscal year after fiscal year.

Initially, an innovation evolves in a single environmental niche—the one for which the original innovators specifically designed it. Still, the innovation has the potential to be effective in its larger "fundamental niche"—the much broader and more diverse environment in which it would be theoretically (though never completely) possible to thrive and operate. In the end, however, the innovation may be able to survive only in a narrower "realized niche" (Roughgarden 1974). In some environments, the innovation may offer a value that is immediately obvious. In other environments, it may find an effective champion. In still other environments in which the innovation is quite capable of proving successful, it will, however, lose out to competition from other policies and practices that seek to achieve the same (or contradictory) purposes, to resistance grounded in cultural norms, to the inability to find any way to get an initial toehold, or simply to the inability of the adopters to figure out what kind of adaptations the new environment requires.

Thus, the evolution of an innovation is a chancy affair. Under the right circumstances it might expand rapidly and flourish—proving effective in a variety

9. Nonaka (1991) argues that the machine metaphor for an organization, which has been employed by such Western thinkers as Frederick Winslow Taylor and Herbert Simon, fails to capture its full capabilities. Instead, he advocates a Japanese metaphor—the organization "is not a machine but a living organism" with the capacity to evolve (pp. 96, 97).

of organizations and jurisdictions. But if the conditions are not at all propitious, the same innovation might be confined to its original narrow niche. The extent to which an innovation evolves into additional settings is hard to predict.

Of course, this metaphor of biological evolution goes too far. It is not the pure chance of random mutation that alone determines an innovation's future. Nor are random mutations the only source of modifications that permit the innovation to survive in other environments. Rather, it is humans—conscious, clever, calculating people—who determine whether a truly effective innovation will expand beyond its original niche and how large its realized niche will inevitably be. But for these conscious humans to make calculations that are indeed clever, they need a clear understanding of the key components of the innovation's DNA. They have to understand what aspects of the innovation cause the effects it has been credited with achieving. And, at least initially, this requires that the original innovators offer an accurate and robust explanation of what they have done, of why they have done it, of what they have accomplished, and of what the cause-and-effect connection is between their actions and their results.

Baltimore's CitiStat

In 2000, Mayor Martin O'Malley of Baltimore created CitiStat, an adaptation of the CompStat performance strategy created by the New York City Police Department in the early 1990s. To understand the concepts underlying this innovative effort to get all city agencies to produce better results, I have visited a variety of cities that have adopted the CitiStat approach (and talked with others). And I have been amazed how many cities appear to have replicated the most visible features of Baltimore's CitiStat room and technology but not the core characteristics that (I, at least, think) will have the biggest impact on the performance of city agencies. There are, I believe, several reasons for this:

—The room, the technology, and the meetings are the most obvious features of CitiStat. They are also the easiest to replicate.

—Visitors to Baltimore can easily be mesmerized by the room and the technology. Moreover, Baltimore proudly shows off both.

—Baltimore has not developed a carefully constructed cause-and-effect theory that explains what core characteristics of its CitiStat strategy have what effects on the behavior of whom.

—Traditional, explicit knowledge about the visible features of CitiStat—the features that are easiest to observe, easiest to describe, and easiest to adopt—fails to capture the tacit knowledge that Baltimore's CitiStat team has created (but cannot easily explain).

—Visitors to Baltimore lack the "absorptive capacity" to comprehend what they are observing, and (if they do) their own organization back home lacks the "absorptive capacity" to implement it.[10]

Thus, many CitiStat adopters either implement a superficial version of the visible features of Baltimore's performance strategy or try to figure out for themselves what the innovation really is, what it is trying to accomplish, how it works in Baltimore, and how it might work with some changes in their own situation.

Observing Practice or Outcomes

Strang and Soule note that what adopters of an innovation decide to do can depend upon whether they are observing the practice to be adopted or the outcomes of that practice. If the potential adopters can observe the outcomes, they have the ability to engage in some "social learning." If, however, they can only observe the practice, they are forced to resort to "mimicry" (Strang and Soule 1998, p. 269).

How much of an opportunity do the potential adopters have to engage in some social learning? How much effort are they willing to devote to serious thinking about what the practice is (or might be) and—more important—*how* that practice produces (or might produce) better outcomes? What is the nature of the potential adopters' thinking? Have they reflected seriously on the true value *to them* of the innovation—deliberated about what outcomes the innovation might produce? Or are they merely attempting to show that they are up on the latest whatever.[11] In one study of the diffusion of innovation, Jack Walker found that a 1931 fair trade law enacted by California was adopted—literally "copied"—by ten other states, including, from California's original legislation, "two serious typographical errors" (Walker 1969, p. 881).

Unfortunately, for many innovations in leadership and management the would-be adopters can only observe the practice—and often not even all of the essential elements of that practice. Certainly this is true for CitiStat. Yes, numerous potential adopters can visit a CitiStat meeting. This, however, is necessarily a short visit, and it misses a key component of the practice—the follow-up. And although these potential adopters often get a briefing on this performance strategy that includes some discussion of outcomes, they can neither observe nor verify these outcomes.

10. For a discussion of *absorptive capacity*, see Cohen and Levinthal (1990) and Zahra and George (2002).

11. Some of the literature on diffusion, transfer, propagation, and replication of innovation examines this behavior of mindless mimicry. See, for example, Abrahamson (1991, 1996) and Banerjee (1992).

In Baltimore, neither a single direct observation of the practice (most visitors spend less than a day and see no more than two CitiStat sessions) nor the briefing provide much understanding of any cause-and-effect theory. Consequently, potential adopters can either mimic what they see at CitiStat or try to create their own CitiStat process by consciously thinking through their own cause-and-effect approach. Unfortunately, the anchoring and adjustment heuristic of cognitive psychology suggests that the would-be adopters will be so anchored by what they observed and were told in Baltimore that they are unable to do much more than make small adjustments to this established "model."[12]

Strang and Soule write that "we typically know that potential adopters are brought into contact with the diffusing practice but do not know quite what they see" (Strang and Soule 1998, p. 269). And for an innovation in management and leadership, these potential adopters may not even see all that there is to see. If the propagators of an innovation—be they the innovators themselves or other advocates—want to have an impact not only on the adopters' practices—their formal procedures, systems, structures, and behaviors—but also on their creative adaptation of these practices to their own unique needs and circumstances, these propagators need to do more than facilitate the opportunity for the potential adopters to observe the innovation. They also have to provide an opportunity for social learning. This might involve permitting the would-be adopters to observe outcomes; for an innovation in leadership or management, however, the relevant outcomes are apt to be changes in the behavior of agency directors, middle managers, frontline workers, and collaborators outside the organization (and the changes in these behaviors are difficult for even the original innovators to observe directly).

Many cities have adopted Baltimore's CitiStat but then dropped it; others have created what might be called CitiStat lite. In contrast, many public agencies in New York City have taken the New York Police Department's CompStat concept and adapted it to their own use—and sustained it over many years. Why? What might explain the more effective adoption and adaptation by Baltimore and by New York City agencies?

In Baltimore, the effort to create CitiStat was in part driven and organized by Jack Maple, one of the key individuals in the creation of NYPD's CompStat. Consequently, Maple did not merely give the people in Baltimore his cookbook. He did not merely tell people what they should do. Rather, he was

12. For example, when people are asked to estimate a number and given some kind of small hint or even meaningless suggestion, they will unconsciously start with this suggestion and make an adjustment from it; the suggestion, however, will be too much of an anchor and thus the adjustment will be insufficient. The classic citation for the "anchoring and adjustment" heuristic is Tversky and Kahneman (1974). The original introduction of this concept is Slovic and Lichtenstein (1971). For a more recent discussion, see Epley and Gilovich (2006).

actively engaged in the process of setting up CitiStat, and thus was able not only to convey his explicit knowledge about the CompStat process but also to help the mayor's team in Baltimore adapt this performance strategy to their own needs and to develop their own tacit knowledge of their own innovation.

In New York, the managers of city agencies had the ability to observe multiple versions of CompStat, to have multiple interactions with key NYPD managers, and to learn about how CompStat really worked through multiple sources. Consequently, it may well be that the various versions of "AgencyStat" in New York City reflected less mimicry and more learning and adaptation. City agencies in New York have had much more of an opportunity (compared with organizations that can make only one or a few visits) to learn not only the explicit knowledge about the police department's formal practices of CompStat. They also have even many more ways and opportunities to learn about the sophisticated tacit knowledge that the police department has generated as it has developed its CompStat strategy.

The Tacit-Knowledge Problem

Michael Polanyi was, perhaps, the first to divide knowledge into two classes: explicit and tacit. Explicit knowledge can be codified and communicated in formal language such as words, procedures, blueprints, instructions, equations, algorithms. In contrast, tacit knowledge is personal, reflecting an individual's experience and his or her own unique way of understanding and representing that experience. Tacit knowledge is difficult to explain. As Polanyi expressed it, in his most widely quoted eight words: "We can know more than we can tell" (Polanyi 1967, p. 4).

Further, to adopt an innovation, we need to know more than we can observe. Gordon Forward, the chief executive officer of Chaparral Steel, a minimill based in Midlothian, Texas, that makes structural steel, was once asked why he was willing to take competitors on tours of his plant. Forward replied that he was prepared to show visitors practically "everything and we will be giving away nothing because they can't take it home with them." Dorothy Leonard-Barton of the Harvard Business School observes that such visitors only see the pieces, yet this "knowledge management organization is comprehensible only as an organic whole" (Leonard-Barton 1995, p. 7). Site visitors can observe explicit knowledge, but they will be oblivious to the tacit knowledge that is at work before their very eyes.

Moreover, the original innovators, in attempting to communicate the value and content of an innovation, are apt to devote most of their effort to describing its explicit features. After all, these features are (by definition) the easiest to explain. Yet the tacit aspects of an innovation—those that are least amenable to telling—may be more significant. Writes Ikujiro Nonaka of Hitotsubashi University: "Knowledge that can be expressed in words and numbers only represents the tip of the iceberg of the entire body of possible knowledge" (Nonaka 1994, p. 16).

O'Dell and Grayson (1998b) make a similar argument, suggesting that explicit knowledge accounts for only 20 percent of useful knowledge—approximately the percentage of a floating iceberg that is above the water line (p. 109):

> Tacit knowledge—the know-how and judgment that come from experience, intuition, tricks, rules of thumb—is often 80 percent of the valuable knowledge in a process. But because such tacit knowledge is typically very hard to express and difficult to codify, the really valuable stuff remains 'between the ears and behind the eyes' of the source. The recipient gets only the explicit (20 percent) portion of the valuable knowledge, and then wonders why the transplant failed.

Yet, conclude O'Dell and Grayson, within business firms there exists "an over-reliance on transmitting 'explicit' rather than 'tacit' information" (O'Dell and Grayson 1998a, p. 157). Unfortunately, they continue, "The problem is that most of the important information people need in order to implement a practice cannot be codified or written down. Practices have to be demonstrated and 'recipients' engaged in interactive problem solving before the knowledge 'sinks in'" (O'Dell and Grayson 1998b, p. 19).

It would, of course, be nice if the innovation could be fully described in a report. It would be even better if instructions for implementing the innovation could be completely outlined in a step-by-step cookbook. Unfortunately, most of the innovations in policy, management, and leadership that can be adequately taught through a step-by-step cookbook have been discovered and replicated long ago. Thus, most of the remaining worthwhile innovations—that is, most of the innovations for which it is worth devoting significant resources to adoption—involve a significant amount of tacit knowledge. Today's significant innovations—the ones that government agencies and jurisdictions need most to replicate—cannot be codified in a report, let alone a cookbook or algorithm (Behn 2003). "The really important and useful information" required to make an "improvement," argue O'Dell and Grayson, "is too complex to put on-line" (O'Dell and Grayson 1998a, p. 164).

If an innovation can be captured exclusively (or mostly) with explicit knowledge, the diffusion, transfer, propagation, or replication of that innovation is relatively easy. Someone writes a manual, someone goes around giving speeches, or a few consultants make money explaining the innovation in clear (if glorifying) English.

For an innovation that depends upon tacit knowledge, however, all this is much more difficult. It requires the adopters to acquire much of this tacit knowledge. And to do so, they need to spend quite a bit of time listening to and working with the original innovators. O'Dell and Grayson are emphatic about this point: *"Tacit knowledge is best shared through people; explicit knowledge can be shared through machines. Or, the more tacit the knowledge, the less high-tech the solution"* (O'Dell and Grayson 1998b, p. 88; emphasis in the original).

After all, the original innovation was not a single, coherent idea that one individual conceived while contemplating a sunset. Yes, there may have been that original insight. But that insight was stimulated by a history of experiences, numerous false starts, a variety of metaphors, and interactions with numerous individuals.[13] Still, it is the innovation's original "brain storm" that gets the credit through the retelling of organizational history, even though it is more likely to have been a slight sprinkle in the prefrontal cortex that was preceded by a variety of apparently inconsequential and certainly forgotten neuron flashes. For the original insight needs to be nurtured, tested, revised, and reconceptualized by a variety of people working together—all of whom contribute through their suggestions, their actions, their wisdom, their prudence, and their audacity to the evolution of something that is both new and effective.

Each of these individuals contributed something significant to the final innovation, yet few (or maybe even none) of them have a complete understanding of all of the aspects of the tacit knowledge that it reflects. Thus, if asked to describe the innovation in detail, none would offer an identical description, and many would have a very difficult time explaining it on paper, even though they have witnessed the innovation in action—indeed, made the innovation work themselves multiple times. The difficulty is that we humans (including the original innovators) aren't particularly good at what Nonaka calls *articulation*—the skill of "converting tacit knowledge into explicit knowledge," of "finding a way to express the inexpressible" (Nonaka 1991, p. 99).

Maybe this description of the innovation process is only partially accurate. Maybe it is only partially accurate for only some innovations. Nevertheless, even if it is only partially true, we need to think differently about how we attempt to adopt those for which it is true or merely somewhat true. For any adoption of such an innovation will require an adoption of the tacit knowledge on which it is based. And because at least some of that tacit knowledge is situational—that is, it reflects the specific circumstances in which the original innovation evolved—any adoption requires not only a transfer of that tacit knowledge to a new environment but also an adaptation of some aspects of that tacit knowledge so that it reflects the inherently different realities of the new environment.

---

13. I have often described the process of producing my Ph.D. dissertation (Behn 1968) as consisting of three stages: (1) nine months devoted to defining the problem correctly, (2) one morning to guessing at the answer, and (3) nine months to proving that my guess was correct.

The Imperative of Adaptation

Innovators in public policy, management, or leadership do not create a generic innovation. Rather, they create an innovation that fits their particular needs, their particular problems, their particular organization, their particular circumstances, and their particular desires. Thus, the innovation is very particular to the innovators and their situation. It might be completely irrelevant to many people in other circumstances. It might be helpful to some other people in some other circumstances—but only if the core concepts of the innovation are appreciated and modified to reflect the particular needs, problems, organization, circumstances, and desires of the adopters. This is why Berman and Nelson offer their "adaptation hypothesis": "no adaptation, no success" (Berman and Nelson 1997, p. 327).

If the innovation is a piece of hardware, perhaps the modifications required are minimal. When, however, the innovation involves some software—and thus when much of the actual operational knowledge about the innovation is tacit, reflecting the context in which the innovation evolved and those individuals who effected this evolution—adaptation is necessary. For the new setting is different, and the people who will replicate the innovation in that setting are different, and thus the tacit knowledge must be transferred, understood, and employed in a way that reflects these new and different realities. Moreover, the adopters may need to build through consultation (and perhaps more adaptation) a coalition that supports this innovation, its implementation, and also its adaptation.

Any description of an innovation that is contained in some kind of technical format—whether it is a conference presentation, instruction manual, or motivational video—permits would-be adopters to infer two things:

1. To implement this innovation, we do not need to adapt it very much; the technical manual contains all the necessary instructions.

2. To implement this innovation, we do not need much tacit knowledge; the technical manual contains all the necessary—that is, explicit—knowledge.

The innovators never say this, of course. They don't even imply it. They do, however, permit the would-be adopters to infer it. And that is sufficient.

Yet, the original innovation was, inevitably, situationally specific. Thus, to work in a new (if only slightly different) situation, the adopters need to make some modifications. Moreover, the adopters need help in acquiring the tacit knowledge that contributes to the effectiveness of the innovation—knowledge that the original innovators, unfortunately, simply cannot tell.

To help the adopters learn how best to adapt, and to help the adopters acquire tacit knowledge, O'Dell and Grayson offer four "'basic' truisms" that a firm can use internally to improve the prospects for the intra-organizational transfer of an innovation (O'Dell and Grayson 1998b, 201–2):

1. "Face-to-face is critical—at the outset." The idea is to start exchanging tacit knowledge very early.

2. "A one-shot deal is never good enough." And you won't exchange much tacit knowledge if you do it only once.

3. "Facilitators will earn their 'money's worth.'" These brokers can nurture the exchange and keep the process on track.

4. "Do everything possible to achieve early, visible results." Otherwise, people will lose interest or decide to experiment with an even more *au courant* fad.

O'Dell and Grayson are not interested in racking up replication points. Rather than have a large number of organizations adopt something badly, they prefer to have a few do it well. And that may, indeed, be the trade-off, for preparing the technical manual and distributing it to hundreds of would-be replicators may take less time and energy than helping one adopter learn how to make the necessary adaptations intelligently.

And if O'Dell and Grayson are correct—if this is what needs to be done to move an innovation from one unit to another unit *within* a business firm—just think what needs to be done to accomplish the same movement across public agencies in different jurisdictions.

You Have to Reinvent the Wheel

Perhaps the most pernicious phrase in replication is the oft-repeated, never-challenged, invariably simplistic four-word admonition "Don't reinvent the wheel."[14] This phrase is harmful because it implicitly encourages unthinking mimicry: Why bother to do any thinking; someone else has already done it for you.

Unfortunately, for those seeking to adopt—and adapt—an innovation, the exact opposite is true. They have to think. They have to decide whether they need a wheel, or a helicopter, or a saxophone, or a rainbow. Moreover, whatever they decide they need, they also have to think about how they will adapt this wheel or the rainbow to their own use.

If the innovation to be replicated can be clearly described in clear words, definitive procedures, detailed blueprints, comprehensive instructions, mathematical equations, and explicit algorithms, there is no need to reinvent it. A perfectly serviceable adoption can be achieved by faithfully following the explicit guidance offered by these words, procedures, blueprints, instructions, and algorithms. If knowledge of the innovation is completely and thoroughly explicit, there is, indeed, no need to reinvent the wheel.[15]

14. I first said "You have to reinvent the wheel" in Behn (1995). The sentence "Don't reinvent the wheel" (in quotes) produced 110,000 Google hits on April 14, 2007.

15. Actually, Polanyi would not accept even this. He argues that even mathematical knowledge cannot be made completely explicit since, at the minimum, the mathematician needs some tacit knowledge to know when to use what mathematics (Polanyi 1967, pp. 20–21).

Suppose, however, that the innovation involves not only explicit knowledge but tacit knowledge as well. Suppose that the innovation was not created by just a single, brilliant insight that, once articulated, was obvious to everyone who managed to pass the latest high school graduation examination. Suppose that the innovation had evolved over time as a group of diverse individuals, with diverse skills, diverse knowledge, diverse interests, and diverse policy preferences experimented, learned, talked, thought, and experimented some more. Suppose that through this evolutionary process of experimentation, discovery, failure, learning, success, and still more learning the individuals who were working on this innovation had evolved their own tacit knowledge. Suppose that some of this tacit knowledge had become—as a consequence of an evolving consensus— something close to explicit knowledge that could, indeed, be written down in words that all of the individuals involved would agree were accurate and that outsiders could comprehend and use. Suppose, however, other components of this tacit knowledge might be captured only by a word, acronym, phrase, proverb, or story. And suppose, further, that not every member of the group attached precisely the same meaning to each of these metaphors (Behn 1992).

In this case, there is no wheel. There is no manual, no equation. All that the innovators really can offer are some hints of about how the wheel behaves, or why it might behave that way, or in what circumstances it might behave that way, or who has to do what to get it to behave that way, or why it sometimes doesn't behave that way, or . . . . And if there is no wheel, the replicators will be forced to reinvent it. They have to redesign what others once thought was a wheel but that they now don't quite recognize as such, so that this new hweel, or wehel, or leewh (whatever it is) works effectively to help achieve their organization's mission.

This is the bad news.

It is also the good news. For if there is no wheel to replicate, no one can complain that the agency's leaders failed to replicate it. If there is no wheel to replicate, no one can claim that they tried but weren't smart enough to replicate it faithfully and flawlessly. If there is no wheel, no one can complain that these leaders are imposing an inappropriate technology on the agency. If there is no wheel, no one can complain that the leaders are trying to reinvent it.

You Also Have to Reinvent the Sledge

Even if the innovation is a piece of hardware that needs little adaptation to work within the organization, it may be necessary to adapt the organization to the innovative piece of hardware. In fact, if the organization is to make the best possible use of the innovative hardware, it is going to have to behave somewhat differently, if only by assigning some individuals to operate the hardware. Thus, Berman and Nelson write that "the organization itself must adapt to the demands" of the innovation that it is trying to adopt. They call this "mutual adaptation"—the adaptation of the innovation to the organization and the adaptation of the organization to the innovation (Berman and Nelson 1997, p. 327).

If we are prepared to accept, intellectually and emotionally, that there is no wheel to replicate, then we can get about the serious business of experimentation, discovery, failure, learning, adaptation, some success, followed by yet more experimentation, discovery, failure, learning, and subsequent adaptation. Of course, we need to make a serious effort to understand the original innovation—what it did and didn't accomplish and, even more important, why. We can look to the original innovators for guidance and insight. We can probe their thinking and learning. But we cannot expect that they will be able to reveal in words or numbers the true, inner secret of the innovation. For despite all of our probing and all of their explanations, the innovation will still remain an enigma.

Moreover, through this process of experimentation, discovery, failure, learning, and success, we will not only adapt the innovation to the organization. We will also adapt the organization to the innovation. Even if there exists a wheel, the organization cannot simply and instantaneously and universally replace every sledge and travois with a wheeled vehicle. Some people possess real expertise in the organization's sledges and can't figure out how to work with the wheel. Others fear losing the status that they have obtained by controlling the fanciest sledge. Others fear losing their job as the expert sledge mechanic. Still others are emotionally attached to their own personal travois. Even with a wheel that we don't have to reinvent, we still have to reinvent multiple units of the organization so that they can make effective use of the wheel.

The organization can't simply swallow the innovation whole; it has to absorb it slowly, thinking carefully about each bit and how it will incorporate it into the organization. And, the organization has to learn. It needs to learn about the innovation—its underlying cause-and-effect theory. And it needs to learn about itself—about how it can make the best use of this theory within its own aptitudes and limitations. What is the organization trying to accomplish, and how might the innovation help it do that? And what are its capabilities, culture, and constraints, and how might it need to adapt the innovation? What kind of tacit knowledge do the members of the organization need to acquire so that they can make the best use of this innovation?

It's time to accept that most innovations worth replicating contain much tacit knowledge. It's time to accept that most innovations cannot be adopted unless we are willing to engage in the long, complex, and uncertain process of learning and adapting that tacit knowledge.

9

Does Innovation Lead to Improvement in Public Services? Lessons from the Beacon Scheme in the United Kingdom

JEAN HARTLEY

This chapter examines whether and how innovation is related to improvement in local public services. Globally, the development of award programs has become a distinctive and sometimes explicit feature of attempts by governments to improve public services or accelerate reform (see Bouckaert 2001; Löffler 2001). However, there is a need to understand the "theory of change" that underlies the use of awards programs by governments and other agencies. Until recently the idea that awards led to public service improvement had been assumed, without a clear framework for analyzing the causal mechanisms (Hartley and Downe 2007).

I use the Beacon Scheme, a U.K. governance awards program (in Britain, *scheme* is another word for *program*) as a means to explore a number of questions about innovation and improvement of public services. What do organizations hope to gain from participation, and what are the perceived disadvantages and risks of making an application? How do "learner" organizations become involved, and how does learning take place between the innovative organization and the learner organization? Does learning lead to change and improvement in public services? This last is important because, though inter-organizational

This chapter draws on research evidence produced by the Warwick team, consisting of Jean Hartley, Lyndsay Rashman, Zoe Radnor, Erin Withers, and Christoph Ungemach. Former members of the team are James Downe, Kevin Morrell, and Jim Storbeck.

learning and sharing good practice is admirable (see Easterby-Smith and Lyles 2005), the crunch issue is outcomes.

The Beacon Scheme is a national awards program to encourage innovation and excellence in local government (and a small number of other local public services such as fire, passenger transport, and police services). The Beacon program has twin aims: first, to reward high performance in service provision through a high-profile award, and second, crucially, to share good (sometimes called "best") practice with the aim that average- and low-performing organizations can learn from Beacons (as award winners are called), adopt or adapt the innovation, and thereby improve the quality of their services. Award and dissemination programs such as Beacons are a central strand of the U.K. government's agenda of public service reform and improvement, as indicated in several policy papers (see, for example, Department of Transport, Local Government, and the Regions 1998; United Kingdom, Cabinet Office 2006). So the Beacon Scheme provides a valuable site of inquiry about awards, learning, change, and improvement in public service organizations.

There are several reasons for including an analysis of the U.K. Beacon Scheme in this volume. First, the Beacon Scheme is widely regarded by academics and practitioners as the "gold standard" of award schemes in the United Kingdom in that it is seen to be both rigorous as a competitive award and prestigious for the organization as an outcome (Hartley and Downe 2007; Hartley and Rashman 2007). It is also seen to be a key means to support innovation in U.K. public services (Audit Commission 2007) and thereby to achieve rapid and major improvement (Cabinet Office 2006). In a world where public service awards have proliferated (Borins 2000; Hartley and Downe 2007), this is no small achievement.

Second, it is useful to compare innovation and improvement through Beacons and the Innovations in American Government Awards Program, because both are long-standing, high-profile national schemes for public services. What are the similarities and differences between the two schemes in their focus, applications, and impact, and what might that tell us about innovation awards schemes more generally? In particular, the location of the two award schemes in different countries, the United States and the United Kingdom, means that they are located within different institutional architectures, and this provides insights into the impact of the institutional arrangements on the motivations and the perceptions of risk and reward of public service organizations in applying for and gaining a national award.[1] The policy context may therefore have an impact

---

1. The territorial terminology in the United Kingdom can be somewhat confusing since the devolution arrangements of the late 1990s. In broad terms, the comparison is between the Innovations in American Government Awards Program in the United States and the Beacon Scheme in the United Kingdom; technically, however, the Beacon Scheme actually applies solely to England.

on how leaders and managers act in relation to the awards program and the dissemination of particular practices.

Third, and very important, the research reported here on the Beacon Scheme, conducted by a large team at Warwick University, is based on the population of all 388 English local authorities, or local governments. (Local government organizations in the United Kingdom tend, on the whole, to be larger than their U.S. counterparts, covering a range of local public services, and with powers derived from, rather than ceded to, national government).[2] The Warwick research focused not only on all the authorities that make applications and gain the award, but also on those that are not engaged either in applying for or learning from Beacons. Surveys and interviews have been undertaken with skeptics and enthusiasts; with engaged and non-engaged local authority politicians and managers; and with observers from outside local government as well as those within. The research also classified all local authorities on the basis of the extent of their engagement in the Beacon Scheme in terms of applications, shortlisting, and awards (Withers and Hartley 2007); has tracked their applications or failure to apply over a seven-year period (Hartley and Downe 2007); and has examined engagement or non-engagement in the dissemination and learning element of the Scheme (Rashman and Hartley 2002, 2006). The availability and analysis of a population not just of award applicants or winners is particularly significant. Sandford Borins (see the introduction to this volume) and Steven Kelman (chapter 3, this volume) both comment on the fact that much innovations research in the public service sector in the United States has been limited by "selection on the dependent variable" of an award. In other words, there is a problem of inferences about innovation when only successful

---

Wales, Scotland, and Northern Ireland each have their own Beacon-equivalent schemes with broadly similar objectives. The research cited in this chapter is based on research with the population of 388 English local government organizations, but many of the issues are relevant across the whole of the United Kingdom.

2. Local (municipal) government has a number of functions—providing a voice for the local community, supplying a number of local services, and working with (or against) central government. In the United Kingdom, local government generally serves larger populations than the equivalent institution in the United States and is more strategic. The population served may vary from 85,000 to over 1 million residents. So size therefore also varies: the largest authorities employ around 50,000 full-time-equivalent staff and the smallest may employ only 400. The functions of the local authority (also called "local council") vary according to type (county, district, metropolitan, unitary, or London borough), and Beacon themes may be relevant to some authorities and not others. Local politicians are the democratic core, being representatives of the community and leading the organization. The most senior politician is the leader, or elected mayor (mayor in the United States), who is likely to be full time. Managers have career appointments and are expected to be politically independent. The chief executive is the most senior manager (compare the role of city manager in the United States), who works to the leader. In the surveys reported here, local politicians are sometimes referred to as *members* and managers as *officers*. For an overview of English local government, see Wilson and Game (2006).

innovations are examined (on research design, see Robson 2002; Bryman and Bell 2003). The analysis of the Beacon Scheme gives an opportunity to look beyond this limitation to the complete set of organizations that potentially could apply for or benefit from the awards program. The population in the Beacon Scheme is also large for these purposes: 388 local authority organizations.

Fourth, the research evidence gathered by the Warwick research team on the Beacon Scheme is extensive—in fact, it is possibly the most extensive existing data set on innovation and improvement in public services. The Warwick University team started research on the Beacon program and its impact within a year of its inception, in 1999, and has undertaken both quantitative and qualitative data collection until 2007, in phases, resulting in longitudinal data. It includes both extensive surveys and intensive case studies, with multiple respondents (local politicians, strategic and operational managers, managers from partner agencies in the public, private and voluntary sectors, and central government civil servants). It includes "hard" performance measures derived from the national collection of performance indicators and "soft" measures of learning. As noted earlier, it includes both engaged and non-engaged organizations in relation to the Beacon Scheme. The data sources are summarized in table 9-1.

Fifth, Kelman (chapter 3, this volume) has argued for the necessity of understanding the "performance turn," that is, how innovation can contribute to a marked improvement in performance. George Boyne (2003) also notes that there is a need for research that investigates management practices not in isolation but in regard to performance improvement. So, the data set on the Beacon Scheme is particularly pertinent (and rare) in that it examines both process and outcomes—innovation and its varied relationships with improvement (see also Hartley, forthcoming).

The English Beacon Scheme

The Beacon Scheme (called the Beacon Council Scheme until 2005) for local government was established in 1999 to help raise standards of services across all English local authorities. (Somewhat similar award schemes for local government exist in Wales, Scotland, and Northern Ireland.) It was first introduced in a white paper of the central government that suggested that "Beacon Councils—the very best performing councils—will set the pace of change and encourage the rest to innovate and to modernise" (Department of Transport, Local Government, and the Regions 1998, p. 4). It was described by central government as "special because it is at the heart of a national programme to

Table 9-1. *Research and Data Methods for the Warwick Research on the Beacon Scheme*

Research method	Population and sample
National survey of all English local authorities, 2001	Multiple respondents from 180 authorities (N = 314; 47 percent response rate by authority)
National survey of all English local authorities, 2004	Multiple respondents from 191 authorities (N = 448; 49 percent response rate by authority)
National survey of all English local authorities, 2006	Multiple respondents from 174 authorities (N = 360; 45 percent response rate by authority)
Focus groups and telephone interviews, 2001	59 local politicians and managers from 37 local authorities
Case studies, 2001	12
Followup of half of those cases two years later	6
Case studies, 2004	13
Case studies, 2005	11, of which 6 revisited and 5 new case study organizations
Survey of frontline staff	Staff from all frontline services in 15 councils (N = 1,933)
Construction of database of all applications, shortlistings, and awards over six years and analysis of who applies and who does not apply	388 authorities over 7 rounds (years) of award
Analysis of performance indicators relevant to context, corporate improvement, and service improvement in four themes	69 variables for 388 authorities
Data envelopment analysis of performance indicators at population, application, shortlisting, and award stages in four Beacon themes	25 indicators across 4 service themes
Participant and nonparticipant observation of some panel meetings and annual review meetings with the minister for communities and local government	At least annually
Interviews with civil servants in central government about their engagement in and learning from the scheme	13 civil servants in 6 U.K.-based service departments

spread best practice across the whole range of council business" (Department of the Environment, Transport, and the Regions 1999, p. 18).

The Beacon Scheme for English local government and a small number of other local public services such as police, passenger transport, and fire authorities is in its eighth year and is now one of the longest-standing policy instruments of the U.K. Labour Government.

Jean Hartley and James Downe (2007) examined the criteria and processes of several significant award programs across the globe, in both the public and private sectors, and proposed a critical conceptual distinction between two forms of award program: the threshold award and the competitive award. The distinction is valuable because whether the award is threshold or competitive fundamentally affects both the use of a program by applicants and the degree of risk in making an application. In threshold award schemes, a standard or criterion is defined. Any organization or service unit that attains the standard, as judged by assessors, gains the award. To some extent this can be seen as an accreditation as well as an award. The number of "winners" is based on those who exceed the standard set by the award panel. The competitive awards scheme takes a quite different approach to assessment. Award categories are outlined (such as service themes, or types of staff or organization) and a competition is held, with a closing date and assessors or a judging panel who select the "best." Best is defined in terms of performance (quality of service or "excellence" of staff or organization) or in terms of innovation. Awards of this type are particularly interesting in that they are high profile and often attract media attention. However, the downside, from an organization's point of view, is that it has to manage the risks to reputation and morale that may occur if an application is made and is available in the public arena, but the organization fails to win the award. There is also the risk of achieving the award but then having further to fall if things subsequently go wrong.

The Beacon Scheme is a competitive awards program. Virtually all 388 local authorities throughout England are eligible to apply in particular service-theme categories in each year.[3] In addition, in 2003 the program was extended to include a small number of other local public services, though these still remain a small minority of applications, and awards, compared to local authorities (Hartley and Downe 2007). Several years ahead, the award panel makes recommendations to ministers on service themes, normally suggesting ten themes each year. For example, the themes for awards in 2007 were delivering cleaner air, electoral services, emergency planning, healthy schools, increasing voluntary and

3. Authorities with the lowest national performance rankings cannot apply. In technical terms, this is an authority with a Comprehensive Performance Assessment of zero; these assessments are made by the national Audit Commission.

community sector service delivery, neighborhood and community champions (the role of elected members, or local politicians), preventing and tackling anti-social behavior, promoting financial inclusion and tackling overindebtedness, promoting sustainable communities through the planning process, and school improvement. The themes are carefully chosen after a consultation exercise with local and central government, and with other interested stakeholders. They are often, though not exclusively, related to national policy priorities and designed to be in service areas where innovation may be both expected and important to public services, and where the themes ensure that all eligible authorities, both across local government and across the wider set of public services, have some choice of themes for which they can apply.

Applications can be made by single authorities or joint applications can be made in partnership with other authorities or with partners in the public, private, or voluntary sectors. All applications are assessed by the Advisory Panel of the Beacon Scheme, which consists of both general members and specialists in specific services relevant to that year's themes. The panel is a nondepartmental public body with an advisory role on Beacons policy, applications, and awards to the central government minister responsible for local government.[4]

Applicants have to meet three criteria to be considered for the award. They must be judged to have an excellent or innovative service in the nominated theme; they must have good overall corporate performance judged on the basis of a range of evidence, including national performance measures and the results of recent service inspections across the board (the so-called corporate hurdle); and they must show how they will offer opportunities for others to learn from their good practice—the "dissemination" criterion.

The shortlist is publicly announced by the advisory panel of the Beacon Scheme, which is responsible for the assessment. Following further assessment through interviews and site visits by small groups of advisory panel members supported by civil servants, the panel makes recommendations to the minister for local government for a number of awards in each service theme—generally two to five authorities gain the award per theme. Awards are announced at a glitzy gala dinner for around 600, including all shortlisted authorities, with

4. Nondepartmental public body (NDPB) is a classification applied to certain types of public bodies. An NDPB is not an integral part of a government department and carries out its work at arm's length from ministers, although ministers are ultimately responsible to Parliament for the activities of NDPBs sponsored by their departments. An advisory body, such as the advisory panel of the Beacon Scheme, advises the minister on particular policy areas. The advisory panel is supported by a small secretariat from the parent department and from the Improvement and Development Agency for Local Government, a national body concerned with organization development for local government. As an NDPB, the panel can continue to exist for as long as needed, which establishes the scheme as a relatively permanent feature of public service reform.

ministers of the U.K. government making the announcement for the service theme in the area for which they have national-level oversight or responsibility.

The obligations of a local council that becomes a Beacon award winner extend beyond attending the gala dinner, because of the commitment to dissemination. Each authority appoints or seconds a Beacon coordinator, whose job it is to lead the dissemination plans, set up site visits and open days, and deal with queries from other bodies. There are four types of Beacon events designed to promote the sharing of good practice, which can be conceptualized in knowledge creation and transfer terms, with differing opportunities for the sharing of tacit as well as explicit knowledge (Hartley and Rashman 2007). National (and sometimes regional) learning exchange conference events include all award holders. These events provide attendees with a broad presentation and information about each Beacon Council (award-winning council) within the award theme, so that further learning opportunities can be selected. The second type consists of open-day visits, hosted by a Beacon Council on-site, and this offers exchange of knowledge, information, and ideas, based on more intensive learning, for example, through site visits and discussions with staff and sometimes with local politicians, partners, and community groups. The actual format of the open day is arranged by the Beacon Council, and those who have won an award in more than one year tend to improve their capacity to share in ways that help others learn, tailoring the event to address the needs of visitors to help adapt ideas to their own context rather than solely presenting features of the service (Withers and others 2007). Third, web-based materials (for example, performance data, short vignettes about the Beacon service in particular councils) are available through a national agency concerned with local-government improvement.[5] Fourth, a visitor may request a tailored exchange of knowledge and experience with a Beacon authority, or award-winning council, for example, through peer support, mentoring, shadowing, or secondment, though this approach can be quite intensive and is used less frequently than the other methods—though it is seen to be valuable when used (Rashman and Hartley 2006). Visits to individual Beacon authorities through the open days are reported by learners to be the most conducive to learning by visitor organizations (Hartley and Rashman 2007). This underlines the importance both of tacit knowledge in innovation diffusion and also in viewing diffusion as an active process of sharing and exploring good or promising practice through social interaction (Hartley and Benington 2006), rather than as a mechanical process of adoption of existing practice (see also Behn, chapter 8 of this volume). The Improvement and Development Agency also has a role in alerting local authorities to good or

5. This is the Improvement and Development Agency for Local Government, which supports organization development initiatives.

promising practices in Beacons as well as advising on the dissemination plans of individual authorities.

Beacon status is awarded for one year. The local authority may use the Beacon logo on promotional materials and stationery, and is given a modest financial award to contribute toward the costs of dissemination, though interviews show that the financial reward is insufficient to cover the costs of application and dissemination (Downe, Rashman, and Hartley 2004). In 2003 the government added some further funding to enable "current Beacons to work directly with authorities to improve areas of performance related to the theme for which they achieved Beacon status" (Office of the Deputy Prime Minister 2003, p. 8) and later again, some additional funding could be applied for by Beacons for additional "peer-to-peer support." The announcement of Beacon themes was also extended for three years ahead, giving authorities longer to link themes to their own corporate priorities and to prepare an application (this was particularly important for smaller, less well-resourced authorities).

Although the scheme is rigorous and research evidence shows that it is valuable (discussed later in this chapter), it is a voluntary scheme and is the "poor cousin" to the target-driven approaches to performance management and measurement approaches to service improvement that characterized the Blair years. J. Hartley, Z. Radnor, and K. Morrell (2006) note that the Beacon Scheme attracts about one-tenth of the funding of audit and inspection of local government, and they contrast the voluntary approach of the scheme with the coercive approach of inspections, which can result in central government intervention if performance is deemed to be inadequate.

Up to and including the seventh round of awards, a total of 182 authorities had been awarded Beacon status. By 2004 most of the local authorities in England had participated in Beacon events in the dissemination process as learners in one or more rounds (Rashman and Hartley 2004).[6]

Comparison with the Innovations in American Government Awards Program

This overview of the Beacon Scheme provides sufficient material to compare it to the Innovations in American Government Awards Program, the other major awards program, on the other side of the Atlantic. The comparison is shown in table 9-2. The evidence base for the comparison consists of the Warwick research on the Beacon Scheme (see table 9-1), combined with informal conversations with a number of the American researchers, observation of one of the

6. The research is based on local authorities, not on other local public services, which make up a minority of applications and awards.

Table 9-2. *Comparison of Key Features of the Innovations in American Government Awards Program, and the English Beacon Scheme*

	Innovations in American Government Awards Program
Policy context	Reinventing government Concern about loss of trust in government
Purpose	Celebrate innovation Share "best practice" Improve the reputation of government organizations
Year of foundation	1985 (first awards announced 1986)
Type of award	Annual, competitive
Criteria for award	Novelty: the organization or service shows a leap in creativity Effectiveness: there is evidence of results Significance: it addresses a problem of public concern Transferability: there is capacity for other organizations to learn from and use the innovation Efficiency and effectiveness of the organization overall Dissemination plans
Funding	Major voluntary body (Ford Foundation)
Administration of award	University (Harvard)
Panel	Innovations National Selection Committee, chaired by an academic and appointed by the dean of the Kennedy School of Government, Harvard
Applications	Open to all U.S. public organizations at federal, state, and local level
Categories	None—open to all innovations
Scale	Approximately 1,000 applications per year from a population base of about 80,000 public organizations, representing a small percentage of a large base
Applicants	Single organizations and partnerships Single organizations, or partnerships, or joint applications
Application evidence	Submission with narrative covering key criteria and performance evidence where available
Selection process	Paper application and initial selection, secondary application to long list; shortlisted applicants receive site visits and report by academics and are invited to present at university with final decisions by panel
Award ceremony	Gala dinner in Washington, D.C.
Reward for organization gaining the award	$100,000
Dissemination	Seminars, conferences, and site visits encouraged by university Web material on university portal Newsletters and websites Dissemination supported by Ash Institute

---

Beacon Scheme

New Labour government's drive to rapidly and substantially improve public services

Reward innovation and excellence
Spread "best practice" to low and mediocre performing local authorities

1999

Annual, competitive

Theme-specific criteria concerned with innovation and/or excellence

Central government (Communities and Local Government)

Local government peak organization (Improvement and Development Agency)

Beacons Advisory Panel, appointed by Minister for Communities and Local Government, a nondepartmental public body (see note 4 for explanation of NDPB)

Open to all English local authorities and other specified local public services

10 different service themes per year

Around 200 per year (varies by year, see Hartley and Downe 2007 for detailed analysis) out of a population of 388, representing a large percentage of a small base

Submission with case study of making a difference plus national performance indicators

Paper application and initial selection; site visit by two members of panel supported by central government officials; long list invited to present in London (at central government offices); shortlisted and final suggestions by Beacons Advisory Panel put to minister for approval

Gala dinner in London with about 10 ministers present

Financial reward of $150,000 (equivalent)

Beacon logo for use on corporate stationery

Beacon coordinator in each award-holding organization

Four main mechanisms of dissemination: learning exchange conferences; open days at site; web materials; tailored interactions between award-holder and learner.

Supported by Improvement and Development Agency

shortlisting days of the American program, and reading of the American literature (see also Walters, chapter 2 of this volume).

The comparison reveals a number of interesting features. First, there is a high degree of similarity in that both programs are annual and competitive and provide high recognition and modest reward (modest in the sense that the award is reported not to cover the full costs of application and dissemination). They both involve detailed and rigorous investigation and probing into the application claims and a concern to ensure dissemination of the practices of award holders.

There are, however, also some important differences. Crucially, the Beacon Scheme is tied to the government's program of public services improvement. It is sponsored by central government and run in consultation with local government, but central government retains control over the policy priorities and direction of the scheme. The Beacon advisory panel is independent as an NDPB but is advisory to the minister for communities and local government. In recent years, the minister has accepted all of the recommendations of the panel, but in the first two years of the program's existence, there were some differences between the panel and the minister. At issue was whether the high performance of some applicants was sustainable; if not, this could represent a risk to the scheme's reputation because an authority might gain an award that was later undermined by service quality. Consequently, a small number of authorities were excluded from receiving the award at a late stage. This was highly problematic initially. (Interestingly, it was not an issue about the political affiliation of the local authority but was evidence of anxieties as to whether high performance was sustainable—and the risks of embarrassment if an authority gained an award that was later vitiated by negative press coverage.) However, since that initial period—when the program was still, inevitably, somewhat experimental—the minister has accepted all the recommendations from the panel. The United Kingdom has a more centralized government system than the United States, and the U.K. program is led and underpinned by central government funding and support. Thus, the institutional architecture may create a substantially different climate for each of the two schemes, and possibly a different calculus for organizations as they decide whether or not to apply for an award. For U.K. local authorities, the award earns prestige and reputation with central government as well as the kudos of high performance (as we will see in the next section). However, the learning element of the program may be less affected by this institutional architecture (compare Behn, chapter 8 of this volume; Hartley and Rashman 2007).

The institutional context has also created an emphasis in the United Kingdom on both innovation and "excellence" (or high performance), which is more ambiguous than the U.S. program, which concentrates on innovation (though in the United States the issue of performance is addressed in the criterion of showing evidence of results, so that a link is sought between innovation and improvement). In the United Kingdom, in recent years, public services reform has been heavily driven by performance targets, measures, and indicators, so that although the rhetoric has given scope for innovation, authorities have had to demonstrate concretely (through standard performance measures and indicators collected nationally) that they are improving as well as innovating. This is likely to have driven out some "promising practices," or not-yet-proven innovations. John Benington (2007) notes this tension between experimentation and performance across a range of policy initiatives, and it is at the heart of the exploration-exploitation dichotomy in approaches to organizational learning noted by James G. March (1999) and Steven Kelman (chapter 3, this volume).

There are similarities but also differences between the two programs in relation to *dissemination*. (Both use this language, despite some of the problems inherent in this term; see Behn, chapter 8, this volume, and Hartley and Benington 2006. The U.S. program also speaks of *replication*, which is a term not used in the United Kingdom because it undermines the sense of local conditions and practices.) Both programs are concerned not only to recognize innovation (through the award) but to share good or promising practices. The learning processes behind the sharing of good practice are similar, but they are undertaken with different institutional emphases. For the Beacon Scheme, the award criteria are not only about innovation and excellence but also about dissemination plans. An applicant can fail to gain an award where the dissemination plans are insufficient (though this happens less than in the early days, given how much has been learned about sharing good practice in the lifetime of the program). The scale of dissemination is very important for the U.S. program, and careful attention is given to this, but it is downstream from the award and for many years was led by a different agency from the one that leads the application process. Dissemination is also a very different proposition given the potential U.S. "learner community" of 80,000 organizations from all levels of government and all public services, compared with 388 English local authorities and a small number of other local public services. Overall, the diffusion of innovation appears to be stronger in design terms in the Beacon Scheme in that the award and dissemination are closely linked, though the actual level of diffusion is dependent on a range of factors (Hartley and Rashman 2007).

I now turn to examining the three key themes of applications, learning, and improvement, based on the Warwick University team's empirical research on the Beacon program.

The Beacon Award: Which Organizations Apply and Which Do Not?

The role of "players" (applicants and potential applicants) is critical to public service award programs. There is a need to understand who "plays" and who stays out of the game, and also to examine how and why such choices are made. Examination of the types and range of applications, both across groups and over time, can help to establish whether there are systematic biases in a given scheme and what barriers have to be overcome if genuinely innovative organizations are discouraged from applying for any reason. The attractiveness of a program to applicants and potential applicants is a necessary (though not sufficient) element in the programs' effectiveness. By *effectiveness* is meant the contribution of an awards program to improving public services. Examining attractiveness is a critical first step to understanding the operation of these programs more widely.

The Warwick database of all local authorities over seven rounds of Beacons was analyzed and a sample of non-applicants, applicants, and winners was examined in greater depth, using interviews and case studies. In addition, detailed statistical analyses of performance measures and indicators were undertaken to determine whether or not the "best" authorities apply for the Beacon award.

By the sixth year of the Beacon Scheme, there were relatively few large authorities that had not made an application.[7] There are 150 large authorities in England, and only two had not made an application. However, among the smaller, less well-resourced authorities, called district councils, 59 out of 238 had not made an application. District councils have made fewer applications than larger authorities for Beacon awards on several dimensions; a higher proportion have made no application at all; a lower percentage have made applications in any particular round; and they have been underrepresented among award winners (Hartley and Downe 2007). In the multiple regression analysis of variables explaining applications, being a small council (district council) is the major predictor (Withers and Hartley 2007). The scheme therefore seems to meet the criteria of attractiveness for large local authorities, but not for small ones. The barriers are systematic, but they are not insuperable, because there are more district council Beacons than districts that have never applied, suggesting that a substantial number of districts have found ways to overcome barriers to

---

7. A large authority is a county council, a metropolitan council, a unitary council, or a London borough. A small council is a district council. County, metropolitan, unitary, and London boroughs run large strategic services such as children's services including education, adult social services, and strategic planning. District councils are the second tier of government in county areas only and cover more localized services such as social housing, libraries, and sports facilities. The difference in size, due to the nature and range of services provided, is considerable. A district is likely to employ under a thousand staff, sometimes considerably less than this, whereas the larger authorities are likely to have at least 7,000 staff and often many more.

application, though they find it much harder than larger authorities. This is comparable to Marta Ferreira Santos Farah and Peter Spink's finding (see chapter 5, this volume) that the frequency of applications to the Brazilian innovation awards program was directly related to the size of the municipal governments that were applicants.

The database analysis also showed that authorities that have won a Beacon in the past are more likely to make an application in the future (under a different service theme). There are several reasons why Beacon Councils continue to make applications. These authorities have passed the "corporate hurdle" element of the application assessment, which reduces some uncertainty about the judgment outcome. They have also been through the assessment process and are more familiar with the criteria and the techniques that may favor a strong application. Authorities value "winning" (Downe, Rashman, and Hartley 2004), and doing so makes them more confident and more motivated to make applications in future rounds. They also have a higher self-reported organizational capacity (Rashman 2007), which may be related to "absorptive" capacity (Cohen and Levinthal 1990)—in other words, they are better able to use their existing knowledge to gain further advantage through knowledge transfer and utilization.

Conversely, do organizations that have made an unsuccessful application tend to be discouraged from applying in future years (assuming that they have a quality service to put forward)? Evidence shows that the application rate for those that have applied but not won is higher than the rate in the overall population in the following year (Hartley and Downe 2007). This suggests that earlier rejection does not act as a barrier to later applications; in fact, some authorities report that they profit from the feedback received after making an unsuccessful application.

Examining trends over time shows that application levels fluctuate somewhat according to the policy context. There was a very high level of applications in round 1, partly because of the enthusiasm to engage in a new initiative that rewarded high and innovative performance under a new government (the first-round year was 1999, after the Labour win in May 1997). In addition, there was an initial suggestion from central government that authorities that gained the Beacon award over a few years might "earn" extra funding, along with freedom from some central government constraints. Some authorities remained skeptical about the Beacon Scheme and awards, or saw other strategic priorities as more important (Rashman and Hartley 2002). In round 3, the Beacon Scheme had the lowest level of applications, due in part to perceptions of ministerial interference and because additional funding and freedom from constraint had not been granted to the Beacon Scheme. Applications picked up substantially when the advisory panel was given greater independence (although it was still advisory), criteria for applications were clarified, and feedback to applicants improved. This shows that an award scheme benefits from analysis in its larger policy context.

There is evidence that the "best" authorities apply for Beacons. Performance analysis of the population, applicants, shortlisted group, and Beacons by four service themes showed that there was a clear mean increase in performance as the application process proceeded (Downe and others 2002). This tendency toward increasing average performance scores as the selection process unfolds lends support to the notion that the advisory panel is, in general, making the "right" decisions from the applications pool.

Why do authorities make applications for the Beacon award? What do they gain or lose, both from the process and the award? Evidence from interviews (Hartley and Downe 2007; Rashman and Hartley 2002) with local politicians and corporate and service managers suggests that considerable political judgment goes into the decision about whether to make an application. One local politician felt that the award can have political benefits that will help the council in the future. He suggested that "the award has put the authority on the map with [central government department]." Another local politician explained that having a Beacon award showed other local authorities and central government that a lot of good work has been undertaken. The way the council presented itself was important: "We have three Beacon awards in two years—this gives out a good message about how we are performing." These comments, among others, suggest that enhancing the organization's reputation is an important element in the decision to make an application. This is also borne out by the survey research.

The 2006 national survey asked respondents (corporate and service managers and senior local politicians) from Beacon award–winning councils about the benefits and the costs of having a Beacon award. The responses are shown in table 9-3.

There is a high level of agreement and strong net agreement (on a five-point scale in the survey) that the benefits of Beacon status raised the council's national profile (87 percent agree), boosted staff morale (87 percent agree), and facilitated acquisition of knowledge from other councils (76 percent agree). Among all the benefit statements presented there is more agreement than disagreement. In interviews, too, the key reported benefits of the Beacon award relate to national profile and reputation and staff morale. These results are also consistent with the results found for the earlier survey, in 2004. The award is clearly much more than "badge collecting."

The reported impact on staff morale is interesting. It is known that organizations that develop the capacity for innovation often continue to be innovative (Newman, Raine, and Skelcher 2000; Hartley, forthcoming) and suggests

Table 9-3. *National Survey 2006: Benefits and Costs of the Beacon Award*[a]

Base: All Beacon Councils answering	Number responding	Net agree (percent)	Agree or strongly agree (percent)	Disagree or strongly disagree (percent)
Benefits				
Beacon status has raised the council's national profile	62	87	90	3
Being a Beacon has boosted staff morale	62	87	89	2
We gained knowledge and ideas from other authorities	62	76	79	3
Beacon status motivated further service improvement	62	73	79	6
Beacon status has had a positive lasting effect	62	65	71	6
Being a Beacon has helped relationships with partners	61	64	70	7
Beacon services have benefited the whole council	62	61	76	15
Being a Beacon enabled a focus on specific aspects of the service	62	58	66	8
Being a Beacon has boosted elected members' profile	62	56	61	5
Beacon status has improved perceptions of the council locally	62	44	61	18
Beacon status gave the authority influence with partners	62	40	55	15
Costs				
Being a Beacon took resources away from service delivery	62	−8	31	39
It is hard to sustain innovation during the Beacon year	60	−15	28	43
The human resources costs outweighed the benefits	61	−18	25	43
The financial costs outweighed the benefits	61	−34	18	52
Beacon services have overshadowed other council departments	62	−58	8	66
Beacon status made the authority less receptive to further change	62	−81	5	85

Source: Rashman and Hartley (2006).

a. Question asked of award holders only: We are interested to know about the costs and benefits of being a Beacon Council. Please indicate whether you agree or disagree with the following statements.

that staff morale may be one of the causal links. Evidence from the staff survey also showed that frontline staff from authorities with a higher "strike rate" in terms of Beacon awards had more positive attitudes to personal and service innovation, corroborating this evidence from leaders and managers (Morrell and Hartley 2007).

But there are disadvantages, too. Concerning the costs of having a Beacon award, there is more disagreement than agreement for all the statements put forward, but this margin is quite small for some statements. In particular, around a third (31 percent) of Beacon respondents reported that being a Beacon took resources away from service delivery. This indicates the high level of responsibility and activity the award brings with it in relation to dissemination. (In one interview in a particularly small district council, a corporate manager hoped that the council would be shortlisted, thereby gaining national kudos, but would not win because the dissemination would be too burdensome.)

Some applicants reported that the application process was valuable in itself, because it helped to focus attention on the service, identify gaps in performance, and improve working relationships internally across departments and externally across partnerships with other councils and organizations. Some respondents appreciated the feedback from the advisory panel, which helped service managers concentrate on a specific area, pay attention to key dimensions, and identify potential improvements.

Interviews and performance analysis indicated three possible reasons for an authority's not applying for an award (Downe and others 2002; Downe, Rashman, and Hartley 2004). First, the authority did not have high-quality or innovative services. Second, some authorities have a reputation for and evidence of high-quality services but have chosen not to apply for their own strategic reasons. These included the pursuit of recognition by central government and improvement of services through other channels; different local strategic priorities; and being more concerned to achieve other elements of the national improvement agenda set by central government than those spotlighted in the themes. Third, some authorities believe that the costs of diverting resources into making an application are too high.

Inter-Organizational Learning

The "dissemination" element of the Beacon awards has been central to the program's design and implementation. So how can effective learning be conceptualized? And how much and what kinds of learning take place? This theme shifts the focus from the Beacon Councils themselves to the learner organizations—though the research also shows that Beacons continue to learn and in fact report at least as much learning as their visitors. Inter-organizational learning (knowledge creation and transfer) through the Beacon Scheme may be conceptualized as one of the links intended to contribute to performance improvement. This is shown in figure 9-1. This section of the chapter focuses on the learning element.

How does learning take place? Earlier, four main approaches to sharing good practice were outlined: national exchange conferences; open days at the Beacon

Figure 9-1. *Suggested Links between Knowledge Creation and Transfer and Service Improvement*

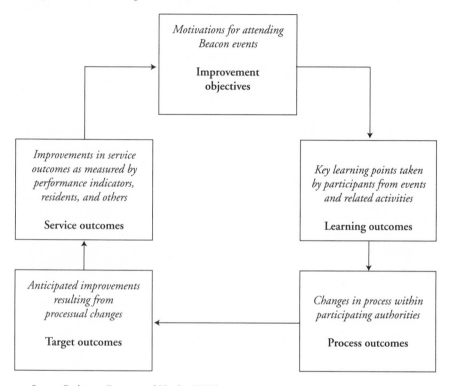

Source: Rashman, Downe, and Hartley (2005).

Council; written and electronic resources; and tailored exchanges of knowledge. Taking the view first from the Beacons that have organized dissemination activities, these councils reported that most successful dissemination mechanisms were all face-to-face methods: open days, including site visits and study tours at the Beacon Council. Over 93 percent of Beacon Councils found open days to be a successful mechanism. Mechanisms such as videos and CD-ROMs and council websites were the least successful (though 61 percent and 62 percent, respectively, found these to be successful). It appears that methods that include the sharing of tacit knowledge and that are based on social interaction rather than the transfer of explicit knowledge through paper and electronic materials are more valuable as the latter focus largely only on explicit knowledge (Rashman and Hartley 2006; see also Hartley and Rashman 2007; Behn, chapter 8, this volume).

Turning to the views about dissemination from the "learner" perspective, nearly two-thirds of respondents (64 percent) have taken part in Beacon dissemination events or activities since 2004. Beacon open days are the most popular, with 70 percent of those engaged in dissemination having attended one. Around half had seen written articles, features, and guides (54 percent); had attended a workshop, seminar, or study tour (49 percent); or had seen Beacon Council material on the web (47 percent).

Beacon events and learning activities are seen by learners to be valuable, with 92 percent reporting learning a great deal or a fair amount about one or more aspects of innovation and service improvement. "Best practice" and innovation are at the forefront of the learning experience.[8] Seventy-nine percent of attendees said that they had learned a great deal or a fair amount about how best practice has been achieved by Beacon Councils, two-thirds (66 percent) said that they had learned how to develop new solutions to problems, and 61 percent said that they had learned how to actively seek innovative practices (Rashman and Hartley 2006). The same percentage learned how challenges for improvement could be identified. These results and others are shown in table 9-4.

Beacon events and activities were also useful at a strategic level, though to a lower degree. A third (34 percent) reported that they learned about the processes of organizational change used by Beacon Councils, and 30 percent said that they had learned at least a fair amount about the role local politicians could play in supporting change. Just over a quarter, 27 percent, learned how to improve corporate performance. This suggests that although the focus of the award is on a particular service or set of practices, in fact, visitors come with a set of lenses through which to look at the Beacon Council. Other evidence shows that operational managers were more inclined to seek out information about "best practice" in the service area, whereas strategic and corporate managers, as well as politicians, are more inclined to focus on how organizational change was led and mobilized.[9] Beacons therefore have a wider remit than is implied by the award. Although the award is for the service, in fact, the Beacons can be informative about how to lead and manage change, and a number of managers use the Beacon in this way. This links well with the reflections of Robert D. Behn (chapter 8, this volume) on what the "it" is that is diffused where there is an innovation. The contribution of Beacons not only to the sharing of best practice but also to the building of organizational capacity to adapt to change is being increasingly recognized by both local and central government (Rashman 2007; Rashman and Hartley 2006).

8. The author is skeptical of the notion of "best practice" (Hartley and Benington 2006), but the questionnaire uses this language because this is the concept that is used in government policy regarding the Beacon Scheme, and so this is the language with which managers and local politicians are most familiar.

9. This has also been found through interviews (see Rashman and Hartley 2002; Hartley and Rashman 2007).

Table 9-4. *National Survey 2006: Extent of Learning from Beacon Events*[a]

Base: All participating in Beacon events and answering	Number responding	Learned a fair amount or a great deal (percent)
How best practice has been achieved by Beacon Councils	193	79
Developing new solutions to problems	191	66
Actively seeking innovative practices	189	61
How challenges for improvement were identified	190	61
Practical details of how to implement specific improvements in service delivery	191	57
Partnership working for mutually beneficial outcomes	190	56
The level of resource deployed by Beacon Councils	190	52
Consultation and feedback with staff, customers and stakeholders	190	46
How to overcome barriers to change	189	45
Leadership of change	192	43
Measuring and monitoring performance	192	40
Facts and figures about service performance in other authorities	190	38
Processes of organizational change used by Beacon Councils	189	34
The role of elected members in supporting change	191	30
How to improve corporate performance	191	27

a. Question: We are interested to know whether the Beacon event/s that you attended measured up to your expectations. Thinking about the most recent Beacon event that you attended, please indicate the amount that you learnt in the following areas.

Learner organizations vary in their capacity to prepare for, learn from, absorb, and adapt the ideas and practices they see, experience, and talk about with Beacon Councils, and how much contact they have also seems to matter. Greater engagement in the Beacon program is associated with more reported learning about improving corporate performance, which is one element of the building of organizational capacity. Half of those with a high level of involvement in Beacons through learning reported learning how to improve corporate performance (50 percent) compared to around a quarter of those with a fair amount of involvement with Beacons (25 percent) and one in five of those with only a little involvement (22 percent). This is important because it suggests that a one-off trip is less likely to lead to substantial learning about the identified practices. Preparation prior to the event also seems to be important, particularly preparation geared toward clarifying the purpose of the visit and the needs of the learner authority (Rashman and Hartley 2006).

Councils that submit more award applications were also more likely than those with fewer or no applications to have learned how to actively seek out innovative practices. Eighty-two percent report this result, as compared to

58 percent of those involved a fair amount and 45 percent of those involved a little. Interestingly, the percentage increases for those who are not engaged at all in applications: 67 percent report that they have learned how to actively seek out innovative practices. There are two important conclusions to draw from this analysis. First, the higher level of reported learning among those with no engagement in applications is counterintuitive but may represent an overconfidence in their capacity to learn and innovate, given that it has not been tested out in the competitive setting of the award application. Second, and of particular importance, is that the higher level of learning by those with greater engagement in the Beacon Scheme appears to support the view that having the capacity to innovate includes the capacity to learn, and this is an important link (Rashman 2007).

The irony in policy terms, however, is that although the Beacon Scheme aims to improve the performance of poor- and average-performing local authorities by helping them learn from the best, the greatest benefits appear to be gained by organizations that already have the capacity to innovate and to learn. This is likely to have wider significance beyond the Beacon Scheme, given the idea of absorptive capacity (Cohen and Levinthal 1990) and indicates that diffusion is highly dependent on the qualities of the learner, not just the qualities of the innovative practice.

Traditional approaches to the diffusion of innovation, or the sharing of good or "best" practices, are based on the importance of the assumption that knowledge is transferred through dissemination and relies on the spread of information among a group of individuals concerned with the uptake of new ideas. Often, such approaches work on the premise that there is a single "best practice" that can be transferred wholesale, and all at once, to a new site. Yet in practice, knowledge may be inherently difficult to transfer, and some characteristics of the transfer situation and of the knowledge being transferred may be said to be "sticky" (Szulanski 2003), requiring considerable effort to produce transfer, even where individuals or teams are motivated to share ideas and practices.

The Warwick research developed a framework of learning that is based on interaction and knowledge creation between organizations rather than the transfer of learning from one organization to another, as shown in Figure 9-2.

The model represents a major step forward in conceptualizing diffusion in several ways. First, it focuses specifically on knowledge creation and transfer, or learning, as the means to understanding how practices are shared and spread between organizations (or fail to be shared and spread). Second, it examines multiple influences on these processes in interaction, examining in particular four sets of factors. In particular, the model focuses attention on the features of both the originating and the recipient organization, reflecting the assumption

Figure 9-2. *Key Enablers of Inter-Organizational Knowledge Transfer*

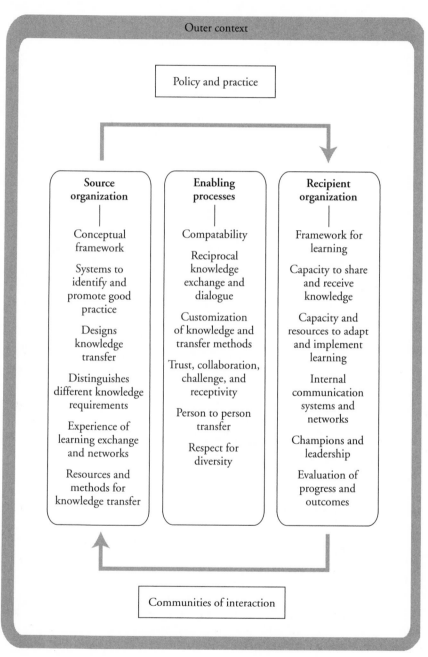

Source: Hartley and Rashman (2007).

that they are together important for understanding knowledge creation and transfer. Third, in the model the knowledge to be transferred is socially constructed and organizationally embedded rather than acontextual and ahistorical "best practice." Fourth, it highlights a range of approaches to sharing knowledge, in part based on the aims of the "learner" and the types of knowledge to be transferred (tacit or explicit; complex or simple; routine or bespoke; strategic or operational). Fifth, there is very little research that focuses on the context of public service organizations. This model is now proving to be influential in a number of settings. (For a fuller outline of the model and its features, see Hartley and Rashman 2007).

The framework for sharing knowledge between units within an organization and between organizations thus depends on four sets of features:
—Features of the source organization
—Features of the recipient organization
—The enabling social conditions between organizations
—The environmental context (including the policy context and wider environment of society)

The double arrows indicate that learning can take place in both directions, consistent with what is known about learning in networks and social settings, and also consistent with the case study interviews.

The social processes of features of the knowledge-sharing process and the nature of the relationship between organizations are important. These help to create a climate of trust, collaboration, and sense making and to reduce barriers to knowledge transfer, so that experience of mistakes made and dead ends in service improvement can be shared, alongside the successful actions. There is evidence that learners appreciate and learn from mistakes as well as from successes in inter-organizational learning networks (Hartley and Benington 2006). This evidence also helps to explain why visitors and Beacons report that learning through the open days (where interaction is at its highest and where sharing stories of success and failure can be exchanged because there is the basis for building trust) is seen to be the most popular and most effective way of sharing learning.

Does Learning Lead to Change and Does Change Lead to Improved Services?

Organizational learning has been celebrated in recent years (see, for example, Easterby-Smith and Lyles 2005) and is a significant element of those organizations that exhibit a pattern of innovativeness, not just one-off innovations (Tidd, Bessant, and Pavitt 2005; Utterback 1996). A critical issue for public service organizations, however, is not just learning but whether learning leads to improvement. Improvement can be considered at the service or corporate level (it could also include improvements to the broader public sphere, but that is beyond the scope of this chapter). There is still relatively little research that connects learning processes with outcomes (Rashman, Withers, and Hartley 2006). Therefore, a key measure of the success of the dissemination of the Beacons' award-winning innovations is whether "learner" councils actually implemented changes to their services or corporate practices as a result of the lessons they learned from Beacons.

In the 2006 national survey, respondents who had participated in Beacon dissemination activities were given a list of eighteen possible organizational changes (the option of adding something to the list was also offered) and asked whether their organization had implemented any of the changes as a result of the visit. There was a high level of endorsement of changes implemented. Two-thirds of respondents (66 percent) who attended an event implemented at least one of the eighteen changes, or another change not listed. Only 34 percent stated that they had not implemented any change. One caution is that reporting may be affected by recall, because interviews showed that respondents sometimes could not clearly attribute change ideas to a particular event or activity, which is to be expected, given the overall pressure for public service reform in the United Kingdom and the attendant raft of initiatives.

Table 9-5 (on p. 184) shows the type of changes that were implemented, shows whether the changes were judged to be successful, and also shows the extent to which the changes represented adaptation or adoption of the good practice.

Starting with the question of whether change was introduced as a result of the dissemination process, the evidence shows that Beacon events have led to changes being taken forward on diverse fronts. Fifty percent of the learner entities revised their service policy or strategy as a result of attending an event. The next most commonly implemented changes, instigated by about a third of respondents, were a change in approach to working with partners (33 percent), introducing new working practices (31 percent), conducting a review of the service (29 percent), and introducing or working toward performance standards (28 percent). Managers were least likely to implement a review of a support function (implemented by just 14 percent), a change in service procurement (14 percent), and a change in approach to working with central government (13 percent); these changes are more likely to be undertaken by corporate managers, who form only part of the respondent group.

Where changes were implemented and attributed to the Beacon program, typically there was more than one change. Two-thirds (66 percent) of those attending a Beacon event subsequently implemented at least one change. Eight percent implemented one change, whereas 58 percent implemented two or more changes. Half of the managers introduced six or fewer changes (51 percent), and one in eight reported at least ten changes.

Table 9-5. *National Survey 2006: Changes Implemented as a Result of Ideas Generated from Beacon Events*[a]
Percent

Base: All respondents who have attended a Beacon event (N = 231)	Imple-mented change	Successful (score of 4 or 5)	Base: All respondents who have implemented change in area		
			Based closely on Beacon	Adapted from Beacon	Accelerated existing plans
Revised policy/strategy	50	53	6	39	55
Change in approach to working with partners	33	42	12	32	57
Introduce new working practice	31	43	13	40	47
Review of service	29	46	8	33	60
Introduce/work toward performance standards	28	41	3	14	83
More consultation with community groups and users	27	44	3	29	68
Change in customer service	24	44	7	40	53
Integrate service with others	23	40	6	30	64
Change in organizational structure	22	40	8	35	57
Review/improve work processes and work flow	22	36	8	43	49
Change in monitoring and evaluation	20	46	9	24	67
Introduce new technology	18	41	10	39	51
Changes to staff training and development	17	35	8	28	65
Change in approach to member-officer relationship	16	35	5	27	68
Change in approach to working with staff	15	32	17	37	46
Review of support function	14	27	3	44	53
Change in service procurement	14	37	6	27	67
Change in approach to work with central government	13	22	3	35	62

a. Questions: Did you implement any changes in your service as a result of ideas generated by the Beacon Scheme? To what extent were the changes that you made successful?

Were the changes seen to be successful? Respondents were asked to rate the degree of success of each of the changes implemented on a five-point scale, and this is also shown in table 9-5. Success rates varied from a reported high of 53 percent (for introducing new technology); 46 percent for changes in organizational structure and changes to staff training and development; and 44 percent for review of service or change in customer service to the lowest success rates reported for changes in service procurement (32 percent) and revising policy or strategy (27 percent). The overall success rate hovers in the mid–40 percent area, which is actually slightly higher than is generally reported in studies of organizational change, where a 30 percent success rate is commonly reported (Hartley 2002; Burnes 2004).

Other data exist that go beyond self-reported improvement. The Warwick researchers made detailed visits to six case studies two years after these organizations had made changes as a result of a visit to a Beacon. The evidence from the cases showed that practical changes had been made that had resulted in measurable improvement showing up in national performance indicators (Rashman, Downe, and Hartley 2005).

Table 9-5 also shows the extent to which the promising practice of a Beacon is "replicated" or adapted. It has already been noted that replication is extremely rare (Behn, chapter 8, this volume) and is confined to very particular organizational circumstances that are almost laboratory-like. Rather than adopting an innovative design or practice wholesale, organizations are likely to adapt the new ideas and practices to fit local circumstances, whether the idiosyncratic features of the latter concern political control, resource base, geographical circumstances, organizational culture and capacity, or other factors. Hartley and Benington (2006) have argued that *graft and transplant,* a horticultural metaphor, is more accurate than *copy and paste.*

This point is shown very forcefully in the Beacons evidence. Only 17 percent of event attendees adopted a change wholesale and based their borrowing closely on the practices of the Beacon. Instead, the proportion of "learner" entities who adapted Beacon ideas to their own circumstances ranged from 27 to 44 percent of the changes. Only the change in work standards is lower, perhaps understandably, though even that is reported to be 14 percent of those who make adaptations.

In addition, a high proportion report that visiting a Beacon accelerated their own existing plans for change. Across all changes, between half and two-thirds (46 percent to 68 percent) were found, and only the item on work standards was higher (83 percent).[10] This is also very interesting, providing another angle and motivation to the adoption versus adaptation debate. The acceleration of existing plans suggests either that the visit to a Beacon was made specifically to explore how another local authority had tackled a particular issue or that the visit gave leaders and managers the confidence to engage in their own changes; they sometimes used the argument that they were not taking as much risk in innovating as might otherwise be thought or mobilized support for their own

10. The percentages of adoption, adaptation, and acceleration are different in the 2004 survey, where more respondents claimed that they were adapting Beacon ideas and fewer said they were accelerating ideas. The proportions of those that closely adopted the Beacon idea have remained similar. The shift from adaptation to acceleration may reflect the policy context.

changes on the grounds that they would otherwise be left behind. There is evidence of both these mechanisms in the case studies (Withers and others 2007; Rashman, Downe, and Hartley 2005).[11]

Thus, sharing good practices of innovation is much more than replication. First, there is much more adaptation to local circumstances; second, part of the role of an award holder vis-à-vis other organizations may be to give the latter the confidence and the arguments to push ahead with existing plans for improvement. Thus, award holders may serve in a number of capacities for learner organizations. Diffusion of innovation is more complex—and more full of opportunity—than perhaps has been conceptualized to date, and this has broad relevance for award schemes.

Conclusions

The Beacons program is small compared with the Innovations in American Government Awards Program, but there are valuable insights to be gained from it because of the richness, variety, and breadth of data about the population of public service organizations that are eligible to engage in the program. The research provides evidence on three key issues: why and whether organizations apply for the award; how much learning takes place through the program; and, critically, whether learning leads to change, and change to improvement. There are wider lessons for any program concerned with celebrating innovations in public service organizations and ensuring the diffusion of good practices to improve public services.

The comparison with the American program is instructive. Both programs are competitive awards, run annually. Both feature rigorous application and assessment processes in order to select the best and have a strong interest in the diffusion of good practice with the aim of improving the quality of and trust in government and its services. Yet they start from different institutional contexts: the Beacon Scheme is an instrument of central government and tied very closely to the central government's policy objectives of public service improvement. The institutional architecture of democracy and public services means that the calculus for organizations to engage in the scheme is likely to be somewhat different in each country, and the risks and rewards of gaining an award may vary. This suggests the need to consider the impact of the policy context on innovation and the diffusion of innovation in a more direct way than has happened in

---

11. Of course, in the survey evidence there is the possibility of an attributional bias, where a claim is made that the organization has preexisting plans. However, this would not explain the extent to which respondents reported this, and the attributional bias was not found to be widespread in interviews.

the literature to date, and may be particularly relevant for an awards program with international dimensions.

In both countries, the award is financially modest compared with the costs of applying and disseminating, yet the evidence in the United Kingdom is that organizations continue to apply because the reward confers a good reputation (particularly relevant in the U.K. policy context, but possibly relevant in other settings, too) and because it has a significant impact on staff morale (this has been confirmed in research with frontline staff). Smaller organizations often lack the capacity to apply to the program and to host the follow-up, knowledge-transfer events, though having a strategic focus helps to overcome this.

Dissemination is key to both programs, though this aspect is organized somewhat differently in the two programs. Yet, perhaps *dissemination* is a misleading concept. It tends to focus attention on what has been called *innovation push* (what the innovative organization has to offer) rather than *learning pull* (what the learner organization needs) or, more crucially, the need to ensure close interaction between the host and the recipient organization to facilitate the exchange of tacit as well as explicit knowledge. Learning depends on a clear model of how inter-organizational learning takes place—and this requires a socially interactive model, not just a replication model. The Hartley and Rashman model focuses attention on four main features: the policy context; the characteristics of the host organization; the characteristics of the recipient organization; and also the learning processes that enable knowledge creation—since new knowledge is continually being created as it is adapted to new conditions and contexts—and not just knowledge transfer.

Engagement by learners in the Beacons program appears to result in quite a high level of change and even improvement. This may be an influence of the overall policy context, in which there is a strong and centralized drive for "modernization" and improvement of public services. However, the evidence shows very clearly that only a minority opts for simple adoption of innovations—much more likely is the adaptation of Beacon ideas to the new context. In addition, the influence of award schemes on acceleration of existing plans has been underemphasized in the literature, yet this appears to be an important aspect of change. It underlines that change and improvement are political as well as technical processes, because building and mobilizing support for change is important, as is having good or promising ideas to work with. This suggests that both Beacons and American Innovation awards can inspire and mobilize as well as provide practices and ideas to be diffused.

10

Innovations in Government: Serving Citizens and Strengthening Democracy

GOWHER RIZVI

In what is often regarded as a pathbreaking collection of essays, *Why People Don't Trust Government,* Joseph Nye, Philip Zelikow, and David King (1997) pointed to numerous surveys and opinion polls that repeatedly show that citizens' trust in democratic government has diminished. People seem to have lost confidence in the political and electoral processes as evidenced by the dwindling number of people casting their votes. Politicians and bureaucrats are held in low esteem, and there is a widespread perception that government corruption around the world is increasing; more often than not the voters are using their power of the ballot to throw out incumbent governments for their perceived failures to honor their campaign pledges. And it is perhaps no less disturbing that the best and the most idealistic young women and men no longer are attracted to government service.

The evidence also indicates that the American people are losing their confidence in the federal government. Trust in the U.S. federal government appears to have declined steadily in the last half century. In the 1960s well over three-quarters of Americans trusted their government to do the right thing. But the handling of the Vietnam War and the subsequent Watergate scandal eroded that trust, and by the end of the century only a quarter of Americans admitted

Without the help of my colleagues Bruce Jackan, Susan Valaskovic, and Christina Marchand this chapter could scarcely have been written. To them I am most grateful.

to trusting the federal government to do the right thing. A recent poll revealed that the United States Congress enjoys even less confidence than President George Bush, arguably the most unpopular president in the history of the country (Jones 2007). The surveys and anecdotal evidence from other countries point to conclusions that are not too dissimilar.

Perhaps even more disconcerting is the fact that, as Nye, Zelikow, and King (1997) point out, not only have people lost confidence in their governments, but they are also distrustful of other public and corporate institutions. The evidence from the United States makes for a painful reading. The universities—where scholars are supposedly engaged in the pursuit of the truth—no longer enjoy the same prestige that they once did. Public confidence in universities has dropped from two-thirds to one-third. The legal profession, though never held in particularly high esteem, has slipped to an all-time low. Surprisingly, the medical and health-care profession has also fallen into similar disrepute—citizens' trust in them has fallen from three-quarters to less than a third. The media—the watchdog of democracy—are seen to have become the handmaiden of corporate America and appear to have virtually forfeited the public's esteem. Media support has dropped from a low of 29 percent to an all-time low of 14 percent. The private sector, although never seen as the paragon of virtue, has been plagued by scandals and white-collar crimes, so it is not surprising that only one in five persons expresses faith in private-sector companies.

While a degree of wariness and skepticism about the government may be healthy, the erosion of trust is clearly a danger signal in a democracy. The erosion of popular confidence in the government has important societal consequences that are not always fully grasped. It denudes the government of its legitimacy, hinders its ability to govern, and paves the way for demagogues and authoritarian rule. Not surprisingly, military intervention, which at the turn of the century many had believed had become a thing of the past, has once again surfaced in a number of countries. In extreme circumstances the lack of trust in government spurs secessionist tendencies and the breakup of a country. The importance of trust in the new public management arrangements is even more crucial. Today, governments increasingly depend on the combined resources of all three sectors of society—the civil society, the market, and the government—for the co-production of governance (Keohane and Nye 2005).

Cynicism in the political process and in elected officials not only reduces citizen participation and undermines government accountability and individual liberties but can also adversely impact the quality of democracy. Trust and confidence in government matter for all sorts of practical reasons as well. If governments cannot perform, citizens will become more distrustful and dissatisfied, thereby undermining institutional confidence and regime stability. The erosion of trust in the government also affects the willingness of the public to provide resources through taxes, the willingness of bright people to enter government service, and the willingness of citizens to comply with the law.

Confidence in government is also an indicator of political stability, which has many important consequences. Citizen engagement in public policy debate is essential to ensure accountability and safeguard liberties. Trust in government is also essential for the provisioning of public goods, the building of transport infrastructure, the creation of educational institutions to build human resources, and the advancement of science and technology. In a global economy, confidence in government is essential for attracting capital and foreign investors and protecting intellectual property. While some of the claims of the erosion of trust in government may have been exaggerated, there is no doubt that many of the complaints have a sound basis. Restoring confidence in government is central to the survival of democracy itself.

The Innovations in American Government Awards Program at the Kennedy School's Ash Institute for Democratic Governance and Innovation was originally set up in 1985 in response to these concerns about the dangers to democracy arising from citizen apathy and consequent loss of trust in the government (Behn 1997; Borins 1998). The institute has sought to restore citizen confidence and trust in government through the Innovations in American Government Awards Program, which recognizes, celebrates, and replicates the best innovations in government. Over the twenty years since the program was launched, the institute has recognized over 400 innovations and awarded in excess of $20 million to disseminate and replicate these innovative ideas. Perhaps it will be no exaggeration to claim that the attempt to make governments effective through innovations is fast becoming a worldwide movement toward effective good governance. The program has also been replicated in a large number of countries, including sister programs in Brazil, Chile, China, Kenya, Mexico, Peru, the Philippines, and South Africa; and awards programs have emerged as a major tool for promoting government innovations. The awards program has also initiated and supported numerous research projects to deepen our understanding of government innovations, and in the process it has contributed to the growth of an entirely new subfield of study and teaching: government innovations. And there is no denying that the program's advocacy for innovations has had a transformative impact on the way the public purpose is realized and governance delivered.

At the turn of the new century, with the decision of the Kennedy School to extend the work of the institute to government innovations globally, it was increasingly apparent that although innovations were important instruments in making governments effective and in problem solving, they did not fully address the challenges faced by many emergent and fledgling democracies. Making governments effective and innovative was a necessary but not sufficient condition to deal with the challenges faced by many countries. Roy L. Ash, the founder of the Ash Institute, called for concentrated scholarly attention to the very nature of democracy. The institute would have to address itself not only to making government more effective and responsive but also turn to the critical issue of strengthening democratic governance, institutions, and processes, both globally and in diverse societies. Democratic constitutions, institutions, and processes would have to be adapted to meet the specific conditions of each individual society. One size would not fit all. The importance of context was obvious and so was the necessity of building knowledge through a two-way flow of ideas and experiences through North-South and South-South exchanges. Going forward, the Ash Institute's challenge will be to ensure that innovations contribute to the strengthening of democratic governance and institutions globally (Rizvi 2003).

Democracy has become a near-universal aspiration of all people, and today there are more countries that claim to be democratic or aspire to it than at any other time in history. We desire democratic government because a government that reflects the popular will is better equipped to advance the aspirations of the people and create an even playing field that enables citizens to develop their full human creativity. Democratic government is more likely to respect the rule of law and human rights, support freedom of expression and religion, give minorities an effective voice in the governance of their society, and respect the diversities and particularities of the different communities. And because such governments are popularly and freely elected by the citizens, they have a popular mandate and enjoy the confidence and trust of the people.

Now, however, at the very moment when democracy appears to have triumphed, grave dangers threaten to undermine the very future of democratic governments. There is a large gap between the aspirations and the realities. Whether it is in advanced societies or in the emerging democracies, there is a widespread perception of malgovernance and a popular sense of betrayal by elected governments. Increasingly, we hear that democracies are not working or they are ineffective in delivering what citizens demand, or that democracy is incompatible with the aspirations of the majority of the people in developing countries. A multitude of challenges appear to be confronting democracies.

The people of the United States have enjoyed uninterrupted democratic government for so long that they take democracy for granted. In much of the developing world democracy is an innovation, and democratic institutions, norms, and values have yet to grow firm roots. The concepts and principles of reinvented government need to be meaningfully transposed to developing societies, which will require making democratic governance, political processes, and institutions more effective. Constitutional, institutional, and structural arrangements will have to be modified to enable more effective participation by all citizens in diverse conditions, especially in plural societies. And perhaps most important, the overt and often uncritical enthusiasm for market-based reform of government has weakened democratic accountability and in the process may have led to the casting aside of a central concern of the government as the guarantor of social justice. Democracy is valuable not only in itself, but also because it provides the best potential for advancing human welfare, development, and social justice, and for distributing equitably the benefits of development. An explicit effort to ensure that the marginalized and historically disadvantaged groups are not excluded from the purview of the government must remain integral to any government reform.

Ironically, democracy is also being endangered by its very champions and advocates. Democracy is an end in itself. In our euphoria for democracy, quite often we have loaded democratic governments and institutions with tasks and expectations that they were not designed to solve. The advocates of democracy have created expectations that democratic governments and institutions can neither deliver nor manage. While admittedly democracy is the best of all forms of government, it is not a means for the realization of all sorts of desirable ends—social, economic, or political (Grindle 2007; Keyssar 2007). Democracy is at best a project, a goal, and a continuous process, constantly in need of perfection. Free elections are absolutely necessary but are not a sufficient condition for democracy; and each generation must reinvent and nurture democratic values, beliefs, institutions, and processes. Central to democratic governance are the rule of law, a vibrant free press, and dense civil society organizations, freely competing political parties, universal adult suffrage, freedom of expression and belief, a respect for human rights, the ability to organize and participate in political and economic activities, guarantees of civil and political liberties and constitutionally safeguarded fundamental rights of life and liberty, and, above all, a societal agreement on a set of rules by which political differences are resolved. The democratic values and practices cannot be created merely by enshrining them in a constitution but must be carefully nurtured and grown organically. Through the deliberations of the Global Network of Government Innovators and the research it has supported, the Ash Institute is seeking to introduce a non-American perspective into the academic discourse in this country (Rizvi 2007).

Even though certain democratic principles and values are universally accepted and recognized, democracy can neither be exported nor foisted on other societies. It must be homegrown. Each society must develop its own democratic constitution, institutions, and governance processes on the basis of its own values and aspirations and its specific circumstances. The attempts to build mirror images of our own democratic institutions in diverse societies not only are problematic but also tend to undermine the very principle of sovereignty of popular will on which democracy rests. In seeking to export democracy not only do we fail to take into account the diversities and specificities of other societies, but very often we undermine the democratic process by seeking to secure a particular outcome through the electoral process, as was done in Iraq; or we unwittingly undermine a government created through a fair and transparent democratic process if it fails to conform to our perception, as in Palestine. The essence of democracy is the free will of the people expressed through a legitimately recognized electoral process and the principle of one person, one vote. Implicit in this principle is the right of the people to elect a government of their own choice. The Ash Institute, committed to advancing democratic principles, values, and concepts, also facilitates research that recognizes societal diversity and the need for each society to develop democratic practices and methods specific to its own needs (Cheema and Rondinelli 2007).

There is no question that innovation has made government efficient, solution-driven, and cost effective. The decision to expand the Ash Institute activities and academic focus beyond the United States to the larger world, and especially to developing countries, made the study of government innovations with an understanding of the history, philosophy, and practice of democracy in all its diversities a logical progression. In the context of developing countries, innovations must go hand in hand with the strengthening of democratic institutions. To do this requires a deeper and more complex understanding of the developing societies. But comparative research conducted from an American vantage point is not enough to understand the developing societies; rather, we must strive to understand other countries and societies from their own perspectives. The research supported by the Ash Institute is informed by a belief that developing societies are no longer mere consumers of knowledge but also producers of that knowledge (de Jong and Rizvi 2008, forthcoming). The Ash Institute, although itself a northern institution and based at Harvard University, does not see its role as merely the purveyor of northern knowledge to the rest of the world. Rather, the Ash Institute sees itself as a forum where "theory and practice" and "North and South" come together. All work and activities of the institute are firmly informed by its belief and commitment to building knowledge through a two-way exchange of ideas and experiences. The Ash Institute's Global Network of Government Innovators provides a regular forum where scholars and practitioners, from north and south, come together, learn from each other, and build knowledge.

The task for us in the twenty-first century is to secure the future of democracy by adapting and strengthening democratic institutions so that they are not only able to deliver government more effectively but are also capable of addressing the needs of diverse and plural societies. Innovation is not just about enhancing performance but also about institutions, policies, and processes that put citizens and social justice at the center of our governance efforts. Innovation is central to enabling societies to build anew the models of government and governance now needed to address the dramatic challenges of the twenty-first century. In short, governments must reinvent themselves—become smarter, flexible, and innovative. The challenges for governments are enormous, but the evidence from twenty years of the innovations awards program leaves no doubt that governments are also capable of addressing these challenges.

It is easy to see why government innovation has caught the imagination of governments and citizens alike around the world. Unlike earlier attempts such as the idea of structural adjustment reforms (SAR) with its emphasis on managerial solutions, which were viewed with suspicion and perceived as mechanisms to weaken the government and expand the power of the market, government innovations have several advantages.[1] Innovations are not exported from donor countries but, rather, are homegrown in response to local problems; they are ideologically unencumbered and not necessarily tied to market-based solutions nor hostile to the market; and because innovations deal with real problems facing citizens, they usually confer a perceptible and immediate benefit to the citizens. It is not surprising that government innovations are fast becoming a global movement. The acknowledgment that public problems may best be solved by combined societal effort has transformed our views of how society is governed, and it also opens up enormous new possibilities and opportunities (Goldsmith and Eggers 2004). In the last two decades or so numerous innovations in governance have made governments not only more effective, but also more citizencentric.

Government innovations have had a transformative impact on the way governance is conducted and delivered today, and cumulatively these innovations have helped to bring about a paradigm shift and have fundamentally altered the way we think of societal governance. Governance is no longer the top-down execution of government fiat. It is both diffused and at the same time focused and integrated from the perspective of the citizens and service users; governance is produced collaboratively through the pooling of resources, personnel, and capacities. Old-style silo-like bureaucratic structures no longer fit the needs of societies and are being replaced by an interlinked web or network of agencies within the government, and often linked beyond it to civil society organizations and the market.

The introduction of collaborative arrangements, as well as the adoption of certain market principles and practices in the conduct of government, has been beneficial. These arrangements have introduced flexibility, cost consciousness, and responsiveness that were lacking previously. In particular, the incorporation of the idea of competition in the delivery of government services and

---

1. For more information on structural adjustment reforms, see Jolly, Cornea, and Stewart (1987) and Sobhan (1991).

procurement policies has helped to reduce the indifference and callousness that had typically characterized the behavior of public servants because of the government's monopoly on service delivery.

Another successful innovation has been the concept of citizens as customers. Taxpayers pay for the services and the salaries of public servants, so it is only proper that citizen satisfaction should be the yardstick for judging government performance. The citizens have certain legitimate expectations of the standard and quality of services, and there is no reason why the government should not be able to deliver them. A number of governments have employed instruments such as "citizens charters" to set out in a transparent way the standards and types of services that are being offered to them with a clear mechanism for redress if those commitments are not fulfilled. This is a major innovation that is now widely used (Kelman 2007b; Kettl 2007).

Governments are also importing from the private sector innovative concepts such as productivity ratings, performance-based budgeting, cost accounting, and flexible budget accounts that allow agencies to roll over and retain savings from one fiscal year to another, and generally encourage and reward productivity (Behn 2004). Like their counterparts in the private sector, government managers have adopted the practice of setting goals and targets; the powers of the treasury and finance departments to micromanage have been trimmed; and audit rules have been changed to allow shifting money between accounts and budget lines. Consequently, departments work more flexibly to achieve their goals and are not always constrained by rigid compliance requirements of finance ministries. In Singapore, for instance, a department is allowed to borrow up to 10 percent from its budget allocation of the following year in order to facilitate some restructuring that requires up-front expenditures.

Governance today is no longer what it was twenty years ago, even though the public purpose of the government has remained the same (Moore 1995). Today, the combined resources and expertise of the government, civil society, and market are harnessed in co-producing the governance of the society. It bears repeating that these innovations in government have helped to bring about a paradigm shift and have fundamentally altered the way societal governance is delivered. They have demonstrated that the governance of the society is no longer the sole prerogative of the government—the public purpose is today being advanced through the combined effort of all three sectors in society.

Governments have adopted the principle of competition and are now outsourcing many of their tasks to leverage the comparative advantages of the private sector. Instead of creating new bureaucracies to deliver governance, governments are using market incentives to advance public policy and to change public habits (Kamarck 2002). Departments and agencies now cut across their bureaucratic jurisdictions in order to provide seamless service to citizens. They have become flexible and cost effective by introducing activity-based costing and simplifying procedures that now emphasize outcomes and not merely outputs. They are delivering quality services through the introduction of the International Standards Organization (ISO) benchmarks and have unleashed a plethora of innovations such as citizens' charters, public-sector service report cards, and participatory budgeting. Governments are vigorously delegating, devolving, decentralizing, and de-concentrating their power and their control of the purse in recognition of the principle that problems are best solved by those who are closest to them (Fung and Wright 2003). Through the extensive application of information technology the costs of transactions have been cut and government is being delivered to citizens' doorsteps.

To be sure, in the past couple of decades governments have responded to the challenges by what is popularly referred to as "reinventing government." The obvious recognition that "government" and "governance" are not the same thing helped to reinvent or reengineer the way government functions. This reconceptualization of government has enabled us to conduct governance in ways very different from how it has been done in the past. The appropriate role of the state is to regulate, facilitate, and create an enabling environment that fosters development and empowers citizens but does not stifle initiative or enterprise, leaving citizens the room to manage and shape their own communities. *The public purpose of the government—solving public problems—remains the same as before.*

Government in the twenty-first century, however, has to solve problems in ways that do not create bureaucracy. The era of hierarchical government bureaucracy, the predominant organization model used for delivering public services and fulfilling public policy goals, is now slowly coming to an end. In a fast-changing world, power is more dispersed, the boundaries are more fluid, and populations more diverse and mobile—they defy simple one-size-fits-all solutions. Instead, governments have to build networks of capacities, in which the combined resources and expertise of many agencies—governmental and nongovernmental—and individuals are brought together to handle a particular public problem. Hierarchical governments are being replaced by interlinked webs or networks of agencies within government and often linked beyond government to the civil society organizations and the market. *The core responsibility of the government has shifted from managing people and programs to coordinating resources for producing public value.* In the New Public Management, governments have been transformed from operational agencies to regulatory and facilitating organizations.

In the new governance paradigm many of the activities of the government have been outsourced in recognition of the fact that private and not-for-profit sectors have better capacity and greater comparative advantage in delivering those services. But governments have not become obsolete, nor can we conceive of ordering our society without government. Even Adam Smith, who had argued for leaving much of the governance of society to the invisible hand of the free market, was constrained to acknowledge a limited but crucial role for government in justice, law and order, defense, property rights, public works, and the general well-being of the citizens. Today, the most ardent supporter of the free market agrees that the provision of public goods—education, health, product safety, workers' safety, nondiscriminatory hiring, pension funds, and pensions and laws protecting women and children—can only be done by the government. And our experience of the last century has also taught us that government is essential as a countervailing authority to the market through antitrust and regulatory roles and the regulation of business for protection of the environment. Above all, the government remains the guarantor of social justice and the social safety net.

The celebration of the Innovations in American Government Awards Program's twentieth anniversary is the occasion for both retrospection and looking forward. We are delighted that many of the government innovations that we are celebrating are now regarded as standard operating procedure for the government. The program shows that public servants are prolific innovators. And what is really remarkable is that, unlike in the private sector, public servants innovate not because of financial incentives or personal rewards but because of their ethos of public service—a desire to serve citizens. Governments are today more efficient, transparent, and accountable than they were before; they are nimble, responsive, and cost-conscious, but they are also able to solve problems and respond to the differentiated needs of diverse citizens.

Historically, democratic institutions and processes evolved and developed in homogeneous societies, and the central democratic tenet of majority rule based on one person, one vote worked well. But in plural and divided multinational societies with deep community and ethnic cleavages, the rule of the majority often precludes the effective participation of minority groups. One person, one vote often leads to winner-take-all and the tyranny of the majority. Minority groups who feel excluded from power and decisionmaking often resort to extraconstitutional means. Democratic governments must reinvent themselves to meet the needs of plural and diverse societies and developing societies. The real challenge is to retain the core democratic principle of one person, one vote and at the same time adapt existing practices while creating new institutions, instruments, and political processes to meet the realities of plural societies.

There is still much to be done. Efficiency and equity have not always gone together; we have to ensure that innovations strengthen and nurture our democratic institutions and processes and that the habit of innovation remains deeply ingrained in the culture of public service. Government innovation and New

Public Management constitute a radical departure from the way societal governance has been delivered in the past, even though, as noted earlier, *the purpose of government remains the same.* Together they have helped to make governments efficient, transparent, and cost-effective.

But ultimately, the success of both government innovation and New Public Management will be judged according to the extent they have advanced the well-being of citizens. Government is the guarantor of social justice. It is this role that gives government its distinctive character and the legitimate authority to tax or coerce its citizens. Although New Public Management may have made governance more cost-effective and efficient, there is evidence that it may have contributed to emasculating the government, especially its institutional and organizational capabilities. It has not paid enough attention to strengthening democratic institutions and processes; it takes for granted the existence of the rule of law; and, most important, it neglects government's responsibility as the guarantor of social justice. The last quarter of the twentieth century witnessed the largest economic expansion in the history of the world, but the benefits of that affluence have not percolated down to the bottom half of the population, and the gap between the rich and the poor has widened every year for the last quarter century. In absolute numbers there are more people living in poverty today than there were a hundred years ago. The challenge for government innovations and New Public Management in the twenty-first century is to find imaginative, creative, and effective ways to strengthen democratic institutions and combine effectiveness with equity. Only then will government innovations be worthy of the New Public Management name.

Harvard University's Kennedy School of Government and the Ash Institute can modestly claim to have been on the cutting edge of bringing the concept of "innovations" into government. But it needs to be stressed that government innovations are a means to an end, and not ends in themselves. The end is, and must be, to enhance the quality of life and make government responsive to the demands of the citizens. The broader well-being of the citizens and an orderly and socially just society must be the ultimate goals of innovations. All government innovations have to be viewed through a dual prism. Innovations must enhance the quality of the life of the citizens, reflecting the government's role as the guarantor of social justice, and they must strengthen democratic governance, institutions, and processes. If they fail these acid tests, their value is greatly diminished.

11

Research on Innovations in Government: What Next?

SANDFORD BORINS

The Innovations in American Government Awards Program and the Ash Institute for Democratic Governance and Innovation, both housed at Harvard University's John F. Kennedy School of Government, and sister award programs supported by the Ford Foundation can take credit for providing recognition for and supporting the diffusion of innovations in government all over the world. Similarly, the Innovations in American Government Awards Program and the Ash Institute, through the research they have supported, can take credit for enhancing our understanding of innovation in government. The "Kennedy School school" has helped us understand what is happening at the leading edge in government, provided justification for and empirical examples of initiative taking by public servants, including those at the front lines, and elucidated the dynamics of organizational change in the public sector.

An increasingly popular measure of the academic influence of a research study is its citation count, now instantly produced online by Google Scholar (www.scholar.google.com). By this standard, the books that make up the core of the Kennedy School school collectively have had considerable influence on public administration scholarship. Their citation counts (as of July 4, 2007) were as follows: Mark Moore, *Creating Public Value,* 390; Michael Barzelay, *Breaking through Bureaucracy,* 334; Eugene Bardach, *Getting Agencies to Work Together,* 158; Robert D. Behn, *Leadership Counts,* 78; Sandford Borins, *Innovating with*

Integrity, 55; and Martin A. Levin and Mary Bryna Sanger, *Making Government Work,* 35.

In retrospect, it is clear that the Innovations in American Government Awards Program, by providing data on innovation in government through its applications and by funding innovation research by scholars based at Harvard (Moore and Barzelay) and other universities (Bardach, Behn, Borins, Levin and Sanger), became a focal point for research on innovation in government in the United States during the 1990s. With the passage of time, these scholars have moved on to other interests: Moore to the governance of nonprofit organizations, Barzelay to New Public Management and strategic planning in government, Behn to democratic accountability and performance management, Bardach to policy analysis, and Borins to the management of information technology.

At the same time, other scholars in other countries, building in part on the insights of the Kennedy School school, have become interested in innovation in government. Some recent examples: In England, Jean Hartley, George Boyne, and Richard Walker have focused on innovation in public services, especially in local government, using data generated by the Beacon Scheme. Constructing databases that include all English local governments has enabled these researchers to examine issues such as the relationship between innovation and performance improvement and the diffusion of innovation (Boyne and others 2005; Hartley and Downe 2007; Rashman, Downe, and Hartley 2005; Walker 2006). In Australia, Mark Considine and Jenny Lewis (forthcoming) surveyed politicians and public servants in a sample of Australian local governments to understand the networks by which information is shared and innovative ideas are transferred. A recent European public-sector innovation project surveyed managers of third-sector health and social service organizations in eight countries to explore their views about the antecedents and consequences of government innovation (Vigoda-Gadot and others 2007). While many of the members of the original Kennedy School school have moved to new interests, two have continued to write about innovation by exploring individual innovations that are especially instructive: Behn (2005), on Baltimore's CitiStat program, and Barzelay, on the Brazilian federal government's Brazil in Action program (Barzelay and Shvets 2005).

In recent years, the Ash Institute for Democratic Governance and Innovation has used its research funds in a somewhat different way than in the heyday of the Kennedy School school over a decade ago. As would be expected by the program's changed title, the institute has put a new emphasis on research on democratic governance, both in its own right and in relation to innovation. In addition, the institute has put considerable emphasis on funding research by Kennedy School faculty (reported at www.ashinstitute.harvard.edu/Ash/research.htm). In some sense, the choice to support faculty at its own institution may be influenced by the overall funding situation for public administration research in the United States. This research is not funded by the major federal government funding agencies, such as the National Science Foundation, the National Institutes of Health, or the National Endowment for the Humanities. This state of affairs differs from that in such countries as Canada and the United Kingdom, where public administration researchers receive ongoing funding from the Social Sciences and Humanities Research Council and Economic and Social Research Council, respectively.[1]

Leaving aside the question of which institutions could fund research on innovation in government, what we can do is identify research topics that should be explored. To an extent, this book has attempted to outline a research agenda through the topics included in its chapters. An agenda can, however, be set forth more generally to stimulate further theory building and empirical testing.

What Is Happening at the Leading Edge of Governance and Public Service?

As Marta Ferreira Santos Farah and Peter Spink observe in chapter 5, innovations awards programs are an effective way of finding out what is happening at the leading edge of governmental initiatives and problem solving. This argues for the importance of research categorizing innovations and exploring their characteristics, which the innovations awards have done for the United States. Other researchers, using as their database either awards programs sponsored by NGOs or recognition programs within government, such as England's Beacon Scheme, have looked extensively at innovations in other economically advanced countries. Necessarily, the innovation agenda changes over time, and new forms and types of innovations will appear. An example of this is innovations in citizen participation in governance, which, as Archon Fung points out (chapter 4, this volume), have become increasingly evident since the nineties in many countries.

A different context for discovering what is happening is in developing countries, as shown in Farah and Spink's chapter on Brazil. The Ford Foundation

1. The Social Sciences and Humanities Research Council supports curiosity-driven research through its peer-reviewed three-year standard research grants. Public administration applications are considered, together with those in political science. In the 2007 competition, Canadian researchers in the two disciplines received forty-eight three-year grants for a total of $3.4 million (excluding institutional overhead, which is not paid by this program). Public administration projects generally account for up to ten grants and up to $700,000. The significance of a comparable funding program in a U.S. context can be determined by multiplying all these numbers by ten.

In the United Kingdom, the Economic and Social Research Council plays a comparable role, supporting the work of Jean Hartley, John Benington, George Boyne, and Richard Walker. Hartley has received funding for her research on the Beacon Scheme in the order of $1 million over three years—and this is not atypical (Hartley, personal communication [email], July 10, 2007).

has funded numerous innovation awards programs in developing countries, and the Ash Institute has established an international network of government innovators. This international network could be called on to demonstrate what is happening with respect to government innovation in developing countries, and this could serve as the basis for comparisons among developing countries and with the economically advanced countries. These comparisons could also explore the impact of both the policy context and institutional architecture of how awards are used to reward and diffuse innovation.

Sustainability and the Innovation Life Cycle

Awards programs provide recognition for innovations that appear to be well established and to be functioning effectively, and for which there is some evidence of diffusion. Then the awards program moves on to next year's new thing. The question for innovation researchers is what has happened to last year's new thing. Bardach, in chapter 7, took up that question by doing interviews with the managers of the inter-organizational initiatives he studied over a decade ago for his book *Getting Agencies to Work Together.* He used this follow-up evidence to characterize the developmental challenges these initiatives could be expected to face.

This approach could be generalized to deal with all types of governmental innovations. Initially, researchers might be interested simply in sustainability, namely, whether an innovation is still in operation x years after it was initiated. The more important question, as Bardach shows, is that of the evolutionary dynamics of the innovation, such as the internal challenges and external shocks to which it must respond, and the adaptations that, as a consequence, might have occurred. To speak of a life cycle implies that innovations may reach an end point when they become folded into an organization's standard operations, eventually to be replaced by a new innovation.

Diffusion of Innovations

A third area we can learn more about is the diffusion of innovations. In chapter 8, Robert Behn discusses the relationship between innovators and organizations that might adopt the innovation in terms of what the former must do to effectively communicate the essence of their innovation and what the latter must do to understand and then adapt the innovation to their own circumstances. In chapter 9, Jean Hartley presents a general model of diffusion according to which effective diffusion requires attention not just to "dissemination push" but also to the features of the transfer process, the receiving organization, and the policy context. She applied this model to the Beacon Scheme to evaluate the different mechanisms available for transmission and measure the extent of diffusion.

Diffusion has always been one of the key topics in the study of innovation. Indeed, Everett Rogers's classic *Diffusion of Innovation* (2003) has a Google Scholar count of 9,431! Studying the dynamics of diffusion depends on knowledge of the population within which an innovation might diffuse. One of the problems in attempting to do research based on the innovations awards—raised by Steven Kelman in his discussion of selection on the dependent variable—is that the data deal with an innovation itself, but not the population in which an innovation occurs and through which the innovation might spread. Hartley's research on the Beacon Scheme, as well as the research of other scholars such as Boyne and Walker who have looked at innovations in English local government, has the virtue that the population is small and well defined, so that the dynamics of diffusion can be observed and explained. To progress, research on diffusion dynamics must identify the population within which an innovation occurs and the dynamics of diffusion within that population.[2]

Innovation and Performance at the Organizational Level

The innovations awards focus on individual innovations, and the research of the Kennedy School school has followed that focus, either by the detailed study of particular innovations or by comparative study of groups of individual innovations. Scholars, taking what Kelman calls the performance turn, have begun measuring organizational performance and understanding its determinants. In this context, innovativeness is one aspect of organizational performance. In chapter 3, Kelman makes the point that there may be a trade-off between good performance in an organization's ongoing work and innovation. Hartley (2005) developed a four-cell matrix to theorize about the varied relationships between innovation and improvement. Organizations in a stable and unchanging environment do not need to be either innovative or effective at continuous improvement—but in practice it is very unlikely now to find any public-sector organizations in such a mythical benign environment. Other organizations may be very effective at continuous improvement but not innovative, or they may be the reverse—innovative in terms of attempting new things and learning from both success and failure, but not effective at continuous improvement. The optimum, of course, is an organization that can make continuous improvements

---

2. Kelman's recent (2005) research on implementing change within the procurement community in the U.S. federal government, based on a large-sample survey of procurement professionals, has done this admirably.

in ongoing operations at the same time it is undertaking and learning from new initiatives. As Kelman notes (chapter 3), this optimum may be difficult to achieve because the organizational and leadership challenges of managing continuous improvement are different from those of managing major innovations.

The innovation awards do not come to grips with this topic directly. If a considerable number of applications come from, and awards go to, a certain organization, it may be possible to infer that such an organization is particularly innovative, and explore it further. Donahue takes this approach in chapter 6 and argues that the U.S. Department of Labor, under Secretary Robert Reich, became an innovative organization by recruiting strong leadership at the political appointment level and promoting innovation in its management systems and organizational culture.

The topic of organizational performance and innovation shares a common methodological challenge with that of diffusion. To make progress, it is necessary to have information about an entire population, either the population of organizations through which a particular innovation might spread or the population of organizations displaying varying degrees—including the absence—of innovativeness or other aspects of good performance. The innovations awards program has provided data about individual innovations, but not data about populations. The question, then, is how to proceed on innovation research using the resources of the innovations awards, in terms of data currently available or data that could be created.

The innovation awards can provide some data for exploring the first three of these four themes about innovation. Over twenty years, the innovation awards have provided a good view of what is happening on the cutting edge in government in the United States, and these data can be used to discover new themes within the United States or to provide comparisons with other countries, especially those of the developing world—for which the sister innovations awards programs supported by the Ford Foundation can also provide data. The innovations program provides a starting point for studying the sustainability and life cycle of innovation because its staff have kept in touch with winners and finalists, so there is some knowledge of sustainability, and there are contacts who could be interviewed for more comprehensive study of the life-cycle dynamics of innovation (as Bardach does in chapter 7). In the area of diffusion, the practice of maintaining contact with previous winners makes it possible to learn about their efforts to encourage and document diffusion, as well as to learn more about organizations that have approached them with a view to adopting their innovation.

By concentrating on individual innovations at all levels of government in so vast a country as the United States, the innovations awards program has little knowledge of the populations within which the diffusion of individual innovations might occur or the population of organizations that could be studied in terms of their innovativeness, or other aspects of performance. The innovations awards and, later, the Ash Institute, by supporting research using applications to the awards, has thus picked the low-hanging fruit. Extending that research to undertake further contact with applicants and research about applications to the awards involves a greater expenditure of resources—in effect, picking fruit higher up the tree. Finally, undertaking new research on populations of organizations requires yet again more resources—in essence, picking the highest fruit.

If asked what is yet to be done, to a person the contributors to this volume would say that, when all is said and done about innovation in government, there is still more to be said and to be done. As the Ash Institute moves into its third decade, it will continue to be engaged in research about innovation in government. It could do so using solely its own resources to support research projects or by working in partnership with other institutions and other funding sources. The Kennedy School school, for which support of the Innovations in American Government Awards Program was so essential, broke important ground in the study of innovation in government. The Ash Institute will continue to play an important role in the next generation of research about democratic governance and innovation.

References

Aberbach, J. D., R. D. Putnam, and B. A. Rockman. 1981. *Bureaucracies and Politicians in Western Democracies.* Harvard University Press.

Abrahamson, Eric. 1991. "Managerial Fads and Fashions: The Diffusion and Rejection of Innovations." *Academy of Management Review* 16, no. 3: 586–612.

———. 1996. "Management Fashion." *Academy of Management Review* 21, no. 1: 254–85.

Abrúcio, Fernando L. 1998. "Os avanços e os dilemas do modelo pós-burocrático: a reforma da administração pública a luz da experiência internacional recente." In *Reforma do Estado e Administração Pública Gerencial,* edited by Luiz C. Bresser Pereira and Peter Spink, pp. 173–200. Rio de Janeiro: Editora da Fundação Getulio Vargas.

Agranoff, Robert. 2007. *Managing within Networks: Adding Value to Public Organizations.* Georgetown University Press.

Agranoff, Robert, and Michael McGuire. 2003. *Collaborative Public Management: New Strategies for Local Governments.* Georgetown University Press.

Alonso, Pablo, and Gregory B. Lewis. 2001. "Public Service Motivation and Job Performance: Evidence from the Federal Sector." *American Review of Public Administration* 31, no. 4: 363–80.

Alter, Christine, and Jerald Hage. 1993. *Organizations Working Together.* Newbury Park, Calif.: Sage.

Altshuler, Alan A. 1997. "Bureaucratic Innovation, Democratic Accountability, and Political Incentives." In *Innovation in American Government: Challenges, Opportunities, and Dilemmas,* edited by Alan A. Altshuler and Robert D. Behn, pp. 38–67. Brookings.

Altshuler, Alan A., and Robert D. Behn 1997. *Innovation in American Government: Challenges, Opportunities, and Dilemmas.* Brookings.

Altshuler, Alan A., and Marc D. Zegans. 1997. "Innovation and Public Management: Notes from the Statehouse and City Hall." In *Innovation in American Government: Challenges,*

Opportunities, and Dilemmas, edited by Alan A. Altshuler and Robert D. Behn, pp. 68–82. Brookings.

Altshuler, Alan, Anna Warrock, and Marc Zegans. 1988. "Finding Black Parents: One Church, One Child." Case Program, publication no. 856.0. Harvard University, John F. Kennedy School of Government.

Amabile, Teresa M. 1996. *Creativity in Context.* Boulder, Colo.: Westview Press.

Amabile, Teresa M., Regina Conti, Heather Coon, and others. 1996. "Assessing the Work Environment for Creativity." *Academy of Management Journal* 39, no 5: 1154–84.

Andrews, Rhys, George A. Boyne, Kenneth J. Meier, Laurence J. O'Toole Jr., and Richard M. Walker. 2005. "Representative Bureaucracy, Organizational Strategy, and Public Service Performance: An Empirical Analysis of English Local Government." *Journal of Public Administration Research and Theory* 15, no. 4: 489–504.

Appleby, P. H. 1949. *Policy and Administration.* University of Alabama Press.

Arnstein, Sherry R. 1969. "A Ladder of Citizen Participation." *American Institution of Planning Journal* (July): 216–24.

Aronson, Elliot, Phoebe C. Ellsworth, J. Merrill Carlsmith, and Marti Hope Gonzales. 1990. *Methods of Research in Social Psychology.* 2nd ed. New York: McGraw-Hill.

Arretche, Marta. 2000. *Estado federativo e políticas sociais: determinantes de descentralização.* Rio de Janeiro: Revan.

Audit Commission (United Kingdom). 2007. *Seeing the Light.* London.

Avritzer, Leonardo. 2002. *Democracy and the Public Space in Latin America.* Princeton University Press.

Axelrod, Robert. 1984. *The Evolution of Cooperation.* New York: Basic Books.

———. 1997. *The Complexity of Cooperation: Agent-Based Models of Competition and Collaboration.* Princeton University Press.

Axelrod, Robert, and Michael D. Cohen. 1999. *Harnessing Complexity.* New York: Free Press.

Baiocchi, Gianpaolo. 2005. *Militants and Citizens: The Politics of Participatory Democracy in Porto Alegre.* Stanford University Press.

Banerjee, Abhijit V. 1992. "A Simple Model of Herd Behavior." *Quarterly Journal of Economics* 107, no. 3: 797–817.

Bardach, Eugene. 1998. *Getting Agencies to Work Together: The Practice and Theory of Managerial Craftsmanship.* Brookings.

———. 2004. "The Extrapolation Problem: How Can We Learn from the Experience of Others?" *Journal of Policy Analysis and Management* 23, no. 2: 205–20.

———. 2005. *A Practical Guide for Policy Analysis: The Eightfold Path to More Effective Problem Solving.* Washington: CQ Press.

———. 2006. "Policy Dynamics." In *The Oxford Handbook of Public Policy,* edited by M. Moran, M. Rein and R. E. Goodin. Oxford University Press.

Barzelay, Michael. 2002. *Breaking through Bureaucracy: A New Vision for Managing in Government,* rev. ed. University of California Press.

Barzelay, Michael, and E. Shvets. 2005. "Innovating Government-wide Public Management Practices to Implement Development Policy: The Case of 'Brazil in Action.'" *International Public Management Journal* 9, no. 1: 47–74.

Barzelay, Michael, and Fred Thompson. 2007. "Making Public Management a Design-Oriented Science." Paper read at Eleventh International Research Society for Public Management Symposium. Potsdam, Germany (April 1–3).

Behn, Robert D. 1968. "Linear Stochastic Differential Games." Ph.D. dissertation, Harvard University, Division of Engineering and Applied Physics.

———. 1988. "Management by Groping Along." *Journal of Policy Analysis and Management* 7, no. 4: 643–63.

———. 1991. *Leadership Counts: Lessons for Public Leaders from the Massachusetts Welfare, Training, and Employment Program.* Harvard University Press

———. 1992. "Management and the Neutrino: The Search for Meaningful Metaphors." *Public Administration Review* 52, no. 5: 409–19.

———. 1995. "You Have to Reinvent the Wheel." *Governing* (November): 92.

———. 1997. "The Dilemmas of Innovation in American Government." In *Innovation in American Government: Challenges, Opportunities, and Dilemmas,* edited by Alan A. Altshuler and Robert D. Behn, pp. 3–37. Brookings.

———. 2003. "On the Delusion of: Cookbook Management." *Bob Behn's Public Management Report,* December.

———. 2004. *Performance Leadership: Eleven Better Practices That Can Ratchet Up Performance.* Washington: IBM Center for the Business of Government.

———. 2005. "The Core Principles of Citistat: It's Not Just about the Meetings and the Maps." *International Public Management Journal* 8, no. 3: 295–319.

Benington, John. 2007. *The Reform of PublicSservices.* London: Stationery Office and National School of Government.

Berman, Paul, and Beryl Nelson. 1997. "Replication: Adapt or Fail." In *Innovation in American Government: Challenges, Opportunities, and Dilemmas,* edited by Alan A. Altshuler and Robert D. Behn, pp. 319–31. Brookings.

Bertelli, A. M. 2006. "Motivation Crowding and the Federal Civil Servant." *International Public Management Journal* 9, no. 1: 1–23.

Bertelli, A. M., and Sven E. Feldmann. 2007. "Strategic Appointments." *Journal of Public Administration Research and Theory* 17, no. 1: 19–38.

Borins, Sandford. 1998. *Innovating with Integrity: How Local Heroes Are Transforming Government.* Georgetown University Press.

———. 2000. "Public Service Award Programs: An Exploratory Analysis." *Canadian Public Administration* 43, no. 3: 321–42.

———. 2001. "Public Management Innovation in Economically Advanced and Developing Countries." *International Review of Administrative Sciences* 67: 715–31.

———. 2002. "Leadership and Innovations in the Public Sector." *Leadership and Organization Development Journal* 23, no. 8: 467–76.

Bouckaert, G. 2001. "Pride and Performance in Public Service: Some Patterns of Analysis." *International Review of Administrative Sciences* 67, no. 1: 15–27.

Boyne, George. 2003. "What Is Public Service Improvement?" *Public Administration* 81, no. 2: 211–27.

Boyne, George, J. Gould-Williams, J. Law, and Richard Walker. 2005. "Explaining the Adoption of Innovation: An Empirical Analysis of Public Management Reform." *Environment and Planning C: Government and Policy* 23, no. 3: 419–35.

Bozeman, B. 2000. *Bureaucracy and Red Tape.* Upper Saddle River, N.J.: Prentice Hall.

Bozeman, B., and P. Scott. 1996. "Bureaucratic Red Tape and Formalization: Untangling Conceptual Knots." *American Review of Public Administration* 26, no. 1: 1–17.

Bresser Pereira, Luiz C., and Peter Spink, eds. 1999. *Reforming the State: Managerial Public Administration in Latin America.* Boulder, Colo.: Lynne Rienner

Brewer, Gene A., and Sally Coleman Selden. 1998. "Whistle Blower in the Federal Civil Service: New Evidence of the Public Service Ethic." *Journal of Public Administration Research and Theory* 8, no. 3: 413–39.

Brick, Philip, Donald Snow, and Sarah Van De Weterling, eds. 2000. *Across the Great Divide*. Washington: Island Press.

British Columbia Citizens' Assembly on Electoral Reform. 2004. "Making Every Vote Count: The Case for Electoral Reform in British Columbia." Final Report. Vancouver, B.C.

Brown, Trevor L. and Matthew Potoski. 2003. "The Influence of Transactions Costs on Municipal and County Government Choices of Alternative Modes of Service Provision." *Journal of Public Administration Research and Theory* 13, no. 4: 441–68.

———. 2006. "Contracting for Management: Assessing Management Capacity under Alternative Service Delivery Arrangements." *Journal of Policy Analysis and Management* 25, no. 2: 323–46.

Bryman, A., and E. Bell. 2003. *Business Research Methods*. Oxford University Press.

Burke, Brendan, Chung-lae Cho, Jeffrey L. Brudney, and Deil S. Wright. 2005. "No 'One Best Way' to Management Change: Understanding Administrative Reform in its Managerial, Policy, and Political Contexts across the Fifty American States." Paper presented at the 8th Public Management Research Conference. Los Angeles, California, University of Southern California, School of Policy, Planning, and Development (September 29–October 1).

Burnes, Bernard. 1996. "No Such Thing as . . . a "One Best Way" to Manage Organizational Change." *Management Decision* 34, no. 10: 11–18.

———. 2004. *Managing Change*. 4th ed. Harlow: Pearson Education.

Burns, James MacGregor. 1978. *Leadership*. New York: Harper & Row.

Burns, Tom, and G. M. Stalker. 1961. *The Management of Innovation*. Oxford University Press.

Cabinet Office. 2006. *The UK Government's Approach to Public Service Reform*. Pamphlet. London.

Cabrera Mendoza, Enrique. 2005. *Acción publica e desarollo local*. Mexico City: Fondo de Cultura Economica.

Campbell, Tim. 2003. *The Quiet Revolution: Decentralization and the Rise of Political Participation in Latin American Cities*. University of Pennsylvania Press.

Cheema, Shabhir, and Dennis Rondinelli, eds. 2007. *Decentralizing Governance: Emerging Concepts and Practices*. Brookings.

Cohen, Wesley M., and Daniel A. Levinthal. 1990. "Absorptive Capacity: A New Perspective on Learning and Innovation." *Administrative Science Quarterly* 35, no. 1: 128–52.

Conde Martinez, Carlos. 2005. "Policy Transfer in the EU: A Model for MENA Countries?" Paper prepared for the UNDESA Ad Hoc Expert Group Meeting on Approaches and Methodologies for the Assessment and Transfer of Best Practices in Governance and Public Administration. Tunis, Tunisia (June 13–14) (www.unpan.org/innovmed/meetins/Tunisiedoc1.htm).

Considine, M., and J. Lewis. Forthcoming. "Innovation and Innovators inside Government: From Institutions to Networks." *Governance: An International Journal of Policy and Administration*.

Crewson, Philip E. 1997. "Public Service Motivation: Building Empirical Evidence of Incidence and Effect." *Journal of Public Administration Research and Theory* 4: 499–518.

Cyert, Richard, and James March. 1963. *A Behavioral Theory of the Firm*. Englewood Cliffs, N.J.: Prentice Hall.

Davies, Huw T. O., Sandra M. Nutley, and Peter C. Smith. 2000. *What Works? Evidence-Based Policy and Practice in Public Services*. Bristol, U.K.: Policy Press.

Davis, Jason P., Kathleen E. Eisenhardt, and Christopher B. Bingham. 2007. "Developing Theory through Simulation Methods." *Academy of Management Review* 32, no. 2: 480–99.

De Jong, Jorrit, and Gowher Rizvi, eds. 2008 (forthcoming). *The State of Access: Success and Failure of Democracies to Create Equal Opportunities.* Brookings.

Deci, Edward L., and Richard M. Ryan. 1985. *Intrinsic Motivation and Self-Determination in Human Behavior.* New York: Plenum Press.

Deci, Edward L., R. Koestner, and R. Ryan. 1999. "A Meta-Analytic Review of Experiments Examining the Effects of Extrinsic Rewards on Intrinsic Motivation." *Psychological Bulletin* 125, no. 6: 627–68.

DeHart-Davis, Leisha, and Sanjay K. Pandey 2005. "Red Tape and Public Employees: Does Perceived Rule Dysfunction Alienate Managers?" *Journal of Public Administration Research and Theory* 15, no. 1: 133–48.

Department of the Environment, Transport, and the Regions. 1999. *First Report of the Advisory Panel on Beacon Councils.* London.

Department of Transport, Local Government, and the Regions. 1998. *Modern Local government: In Touch with the people,* London: Her Majesty's Stationery Office.

Dolowitz, David P., and David Marsh. 2006. "Learning from Abroad: The Role of Policy Transfer in Contemporary Policy-Making." *Governance: An International Journal of Policy and Administration* 13, no. 1: 5–24.

Donahue, John D., ed. 1999. *Making Washington Work: Tales of Innovation in the Federal Government.* Brookings.

———. "Dynamics of Diffusion: Conceptions of American Federalism and Public Sector Innovation." Unpublished paper. Harvard University, John F. Kennedy School of Government, Ash Institute for Democratic Governance and Innovation (www.innovations. harvard.edu/search.html).

Downe James, Jim Storbeck, Lyndsay Rashman, and Jean Hartley. 2002. "Are the Best Authorities Applying to the Beacon Scheme?" Report. University of Warwick.

Downe, James, Lyndsay Rashman, and Jean Hartley. 2004. "Evaluating the Extent of Inter-Organisational Learning and Change through the Beacon Council Scheme." *Public Management Review* 6, no. 4: 531–53.

Du Gay, P. 2000. *In Praise of Bureaucracy: Weber, Organization and Ethics.* London and Thousand Oaks, Calif.: Sage.

Easterby-Smith, M., and M. A. Lyles. 2005. *Handbook of Organizational Learning and Knowledge Management.* Oxford: Blackwell.

Eller, Estevão, Marco A. Teixeira, Maria F. Alessio, Marta F. S. Farah, and Peter Spink. 2005. *Inovações de governos locais: ciclo de premiação 2005.* São Paulo: Programa Gestão Pública e Cidadania.

Epley, Nicholas, and Thomas Gilovich. 2006. "The Anchoring-and-Adjustment Heuristic: Why the Adjustments Are Insufficient." *Psychological Science* 17, no. 4: pp. 311–18.

Farah, Marta F. S. 2004. "Avaliação do programa gestão pública e cidadania." Report. São Paulo: Centro de Administração Pública e Governo.

———. 2006a. "Dissemination of Innovations: Learning from Sub-National Awards Programs in Brazil." In *Innovations in Governance and Public Administration: Replicating What Works,* edited by Adriana Alberti and Guido Bertucci, pp. 60–80. New York: UNDESA.

———. 2006b. "Disseminating of Local Governments Policies and Programs in Brazil: The Contribution of the Public Management and Citizenship Program." Paper delivered at the 26th International Congress of the Latin American Studies Association. San Juan, Puerto Rico (March 15–18).

Feldman, Martha S. 2000. "Organizational Routines as a Source of Continuous Change." *Organization Science* 11, no. 6: 611–29.

Feldman, Martha S., and Brian T. Pentland. 2003. "Reconceptualizing Organizational Routines as a Source of Flexibility and Change." *Administrative Science Quarterly* 48, no. 1: 94–118.

Ferlie, Ewan, Laurence Lynn, and Christopher Pollitt. 2005. *Oxford University Press Handbook of Public Management.* Oxford University Press.

Fiorina, Morris. 1999. "Extreme Voices: A Dark Side of Civic Engagement." In *Civic Engagement in American Democracy,* edited by Theda Skocpol and Morris Fiorina, pp. 395–425. Brookings.

Forrester, Jay W. 1968. *Principles of Systems.* Cambridge, Mass.: Wright-Allen Press.

———. 1969. *Urban Dynamics.* MIT Press.

Freeman, Howard E., and Daniel A. Farber. 2005. "Modular Environmental Regulation." *Duke Law Journal* 54, no. 4: 795–912.

Frey, Bruno S., and Felix Oberholzer-Gee. 1997. "The Cost of Price Incentives: An Empirical Analysis of Motivation Crowding Out." *American Economic Review* 87, no. 4: 746–55.

Friedman, Thomas. 2005. *The World Is Flat: A Brief History of the Twenty-First Century.* New York: Farrar Straus and Giroux.

Fung, Archon. 2004. *Empowered Participation: Reinventing Urban Democracy.* Princeton University Press.

Fung, Archon, and Susan Rosegrant. 2006. "Listening to the City: What Should Be Built at Ground Zero?" In *Ethics and Politics: Cases and Comments,* edited by Dennis Thompson and Amy Gutmann, pp. 303–10. 4th ed. New York: Thompson Wordsworth.

Fung, Archon, and Erik Wright, eds. 2003. *Deepening Democracy: Institutional Innovations in Empowered Participatory Governance.* London and New York: Verso.

Galinsky, Adam D., Deborah H. Gruenfeld, and J. C. Magee. 2003. "From Power to Action." *Social Psychology* 85: 453–66.

Gaus, J. 1950. "Trends in the Theory of Public Administration." *Public Administration Review* 10, no. 3: 161–68.

Gersick, Connie J. G. 1991. "Revolutionary Change Theories: A Multilevel Exploration of the Punctuated Equilibrium Paradigm." *Academy of Management Review* 16, no. 1: 10–36.

Gersick, Connie J. G., and J. Richard Hackman. 1990. "Habitual Routines in Task-Performing Groups." *Organizational Behavior and Human Decision Processes* 47, no. 1: 65–97.

Gilbreth, Frank B., and Lillian M. Gilbreth. 1917. *Applied Motion Study.* New York: Sturgis & Walton.

Golden, Olivia. 1990. "Innovation in Public Sector Human Services Programs: The Implications of Innovation by 'Groping Along.'" *Journal of Policy Analysis and Management* 9, no. 2: 219–48.

Goldsmith, Stephen, and William Eggers. 2004. *Governing by Network: The New Shape of the Public Sector.* Brookings.

Grafilo, Pamela, ed. 2006. *Public Sector Delivery Through Innovation.* São Paulo, Brazil: Programa Gestão Pública e Cidadania/Innovations Programs Liaison Group.

Granovetter, Mark S. 1973. "The Strength of Weak Ties." *American Journal of Sociology* 78, no. 6: 1360–80.

Grant, Adam M. 2008 (forthcoming). "Employees without a Cause: The Motivational Effects of Prosocial Impact in Public Service." *International Public Management Journal* 11, no. 1.

Gray, Barbara. 1989. *Collaborating: Finding Common Ground for Multiparty Problems.* San Francisco: Jossey-Bass.

Gregory, R. 2003. "Accountability in Modern Government." In *Handbook of Public Administration,* edited by B. G. Peters and J. Pierre, pp. 557–68. London and Thousand Oaks, Calif.: Sage.

Grindle, Merrilee. 2007. "Innovation and Democratic Governance: Great Expectations and Cautionary Tales." Paper presented at Global Network of Government Innovators' Latin American Forum on Democratic Practices, Public Decisions, and Citizenship. Monterrey, Mexico (August 29–31).

Gruber, J. E. 1987. *Controlling Bureaucracies: Dilemmas in Democratic Governance.* University of California Press.

Hammer, Michael, and Steven A. Stanton. 1995. *The Reengineering Revolution.* New York: HarperBusiness.

Hannan, Michael T., and John Freeman. 1984. "Structural Inertia and Organizational Change." *American Sociological Review* 49, no. 2: 149–64.

Hartley, Jean. 2002. "Organizational Change and Development." In *Psychology at Work,* edited by P. Warr, pp. 399–425. 5th ed. Harmondsworth, U.K.: Penguin.

———. 2005. "Innovation in Governance and Public Services: Past and Present." *Public Money and Management* 25, no. 1: 27–34.

———. Forthcoming. "The Innovation Landscape for Public Service Organizations." In *Managing to Improve Public Services,* edited by Jean Hartley, C. Donaldson, C. Skelcher, and M. Wallace. Cambridge University Press.

Hartley, Jean, and John Benington. 2006. "Copy and Paste, or Graft and Transplant? Knowledge Sharing through Inter-Organizational Networks." *Public Money and Management* 26, no. 2: 101–08.

Hartley, Jean, and James Downe. 2007. "The Shining Lights? Public Service Awards as an Approach to Service Improvement." *Public Administration* 85, no. 2: 329–53.

Hartley, Jean, and Lyndsay Rashman. 2007. "How Is Knowledge Transferred Between Organizations Involved in Change?" In *Managing Change in the Public Services,* edited by Wallace M. Fertig and E. Schneller, pp. 173–92. Oxford: Blackwell.

Hartley Jean, and Z. Radnor. 2006. "Contrasts and Complementarities: Adoption and Adaptation of Promising Practices through Strategies of Voluntarism and Coercion." Working paper. University of Warwick.

Heflinger, Craig Anne, and Celeste G. Simpkins. 1996. "Modeling Utilization of Child Residential Psychiatric Treatment." Paper read at conference "A System of Care for Children's Mental Health: Expanding the Research Base," February 26–28.

Heinrich, C. J. 2000. "Organizational Form and Performance: An Empirical Investigation of Nonprofit and For-Profit Job-Training Service Providers." *Journal of Policy Analysis and Management* 19, no. 2: 233–61.

Heinrich, C. J., and E. Fournier. 2004. "Dimensions of Publicness and Performance in Substance Abuse Treatment Organizations." *Journal of Policy Analysis and Management* 23, no. 1: 49–70.

Hennessy, P. 1989. *Whitehall.* London: Secker & Warburg.

Hill, C. J. 2006. "Casework Job Design and Client Outcomes in Welfare-to-Work Offices." *Journal of Public Administration Research and Theory* 16, no. 2: 263–88.

Hood, C. 1991. "A Public Management for All Seasons?" *Public Administration* 69: 3–19.

Illich, Ivan. 1973. *Deschooling Society.* London: Penguin.

Innes, Judith, Judith Gruber, Michael Neuman, and Robert Thompson, eds. 1994. *Coordinating Growth and Environmental Management through Consensus Building.* Berkeley, Calif.: University of California, California Policy Seminar.

Jenkins, Stephen S. 1989. "Dissemination of Innovations: Lessons from the Experience of One Church, One Child." Cambridge, Mass.: Harvard University, Kennedy School of Government, Innovations in State and Local Government.

Jolly, Richard, Giovanni Andrea Cornea, and Francis Stewart, eds. 1987. *Adjustment with a Human Face.* Oxford: Clarendon Press.

Jones, Jeffrey M. 2007. "Congress Approval Rating Matches Historical Low." Gallup News Service, August 21 (www.gallup.com/poll/28456/Congress-Approval-Rating-Matches-Historical-Low.aspx).

Kamarck, Elaine. 2002. *Applying Twenty-First Century Government to the Challenges of Homeland Security.* Washington: IBM Endowment for the Business of Government.

Kanigel, Robert. 1997. *The One Best Way: Frederick Winslow Taylor and the Enigma of Efficiency.* New York: Viking.

Karkkainen, Bradley C. 2002–03. "Collaborative Ecosystem Governance: Scale, Complexity, and Dynamism." *Virginia Environmental Law Journal* 21: 189–243.

Kaufman, H. 1977. *Red Tape: Its Origins, Uses and Abuses.* Brookings.

Kelman, Steven. 1987. *Making Public Policy: A Hopeful View of American Government.* New York: Basic Books.

———. 2005. *Unleashing Change: A Study of Organizational Renewal in Government.* Brookings.

———. 2006. "Downsizing, Competition, and Organizational Change in Government: Is Necessity the Mother of Invention?" *Journal of Policy Analysis and Management* 25, no. 4: 875–95.

———. 2007a. "Public Administration and Organization Studies." In *Academy of Management Annals,* edited by A. Brief and P. Walsh, pp. 225–68. New York: Erlbaum.

———. 2007b. *The Transformation of Government in the Decade Ahead.* Washington: IBM Endowment for the Business of Government.

Kemmis, Daniel. 1992. *Community and the Politics of Place.* University of Oklahoma Press.

John F. Kennedy School of Government. 2004. "Parks and Partnership in New York City: Adrian Benepe's Challenge." Case Program, publication no. CR16-04-1743.0. Harvard University.

Keohane, Robert, and Nye, Joseph. 2005. "Introduction." In *Governance in a Globalizing World,* edited by Joseph Nye and John Donahue, pp. 1–41. Brookings.

Kettl, Donald. 2002. *The Transformation of Governance: Public Administration for the 21st Century.* Johns Hopkins University Press.

———. 2005. *The Global Public Management Revolution.* 2nd ed. Brookings.

———. 2007. *The Next Government of the United States: Challenges for Performance in the 21st Century.* Washington: IBM Endowment for the Business of Government.

Keyssar, Alexander. 2007. "Democracy as a Project: The Strange Career of Political Participation in the United States." Paper presented at Global Network of Government Innovators' Latin American Forum on Democratic Practices, Public Decisions, and Citizenship. Monterrey, Mexico (August 29–31).

Kingdon, John W. 1995. *Agendas, Alternatives, and Public Policies.* New York: HarperCollins.

Kotter, John P. 1990. *A Force for Change: How Leadership Differs from Management.* New York: Free Press.

———. 1996. *Leading Change.* Boston: Harvard Business School Press.

Lang, Amy. 2007. "But Is It for Real? The British Columbia Citizens' Assembly as a Model of State-Sponsored Citizen Empowerment." *Politics and Society* 35, no. 1: 35–70.

Langer, Ellen J. 1989. *Mindfulness.* Reading, Mass.: Addison Wesley Publishing.

Latour, Bruno. 1987. *Science in Action.* Harvard University Press.

Lawrence, Paul R., and Jay W. Lorsch. 1967. *Organization and Environment: Managing Differentiation and Integration.* Boston: Harvard Business School Press.

Lazear, E. P. 1998. *Personnel Economics for Managers.* New York: Wiley.

Leonard-Barton, Dorothy. 1995. *Wellsprings of Knowledge: Building and Sustaining the Sources of Innovation.* Boston: Harvard Business School Press.

Lepler, Susan, Kimberly Uyeda, and Neal Halfon. 2006. "Master Contracting with Comprehensive Service Providers: A Tool to Simplify Administration and Promote Outcome-Focused, Integrated Services." Report. Los Angeles: Center for Governmental Research and UCLA, Center for Healthier Children, Families, and Communities.

Levin, Henry M. 1998. "Educational Vouchers: Effectiveness, Choice and Costs." *Journal of Policy Analysis and Management* 17, no. 3: 373–92

Levin, Martin A., and Mary Bryna Sanger. 1994. *Making Government Work: How Entrepreneurial Executives Turn Bright Ideas into Real Results.* San Francisco: Jossey-Bass.

Lewin, Kurt. 1935. "The Conflict between Aristotelian and Galilean Modes of Thought in Contemporary Psychology." In *A Dynamic Theory of Personality: Selected Papers of Kurt Lewin,* pp. 1–42. New York: McGraw-Hill

Light, Paul. 1998. *Sustaining Innovation: Creating Nonprofit and Government Organizations That Innovate Naturally.* San Francisco: Jossey-Bass.

Lindblom, C. E. 1959. "The Science of Muddling Through." *Public Administration Review* 19, no. 2 (Spring): 79–88.

———. 1965. *The Intelligence of Democracy: Decisionmaking through Mutual Adjustment.* New York: Free Press.

Lippman, S. A., and R. P. Rumelt. 1982. "Uncertain Imitability: An Analysis of Interfirm Differences in Efficiency under Competition." *Bell Journal of Economics* 13, no. 2: 418–38.

Löffler, E. 2001. "Quality Awards as a Public Sector Benchmarking Concept in OECD Member Countries: Some Guidelines for Quality Award Organizers." *Public Administration and Development* 21, no. 1: 27–40.

Lowi, T. J. 1969. *The End of Liberalism.* New York: Norton.

Lynn, Laurence. 1996. *Public Management as Art, Science, and Profession.* Chatham, N.J.: Chatham House.

Machiavelli, Niccolo. 1950. *The Prince.* New York: Modern Library.

MacLaury, Judson. 1998. "A Brief History of the Department of Labor." In *A Historical Guide to the U.S. Government,* edited by George Thomas Kurian, Joseph P. Harahan, Morton Keller, Donald F. Kettl, and Graham T. T. Molitor. Oxford University Press.

Maloy, Kathleen A. 1997. "The Tennessee Children's Plan: How Do We Get There?" In *Evaluating Mental Health Services: How Do Programs for Children "Work" in the Real World,* edited by C. T. Nixon and D. A. Northrup. Thousand Oaks, Calif.: Sage.

March, James G. 1999. *The Pursuit of Organizational Intelligence.* Malden, Mass.: Blackwell Business.

March, James G., and Herbert A. Simon 1958. *Organizations.* New York: Wiley.

March, James G., Martin Schulz, and Xueguang Zhou. 2000. *The Dynamics of Rules: Change in Written Organizational Codes.* Stanford University Press.

Mattos, Janaina V. de. 2005. "Programas de disseminação de experiências de governos locais no Brasil em contexto de redemocratização e de descentralização." [Program to disseminate the experiences of local government in Brazil, in the context of redemocratization and decentralization.] Master's dissertation, Getulio Vargas Foundation, São Paulo.

Meier, Kenneth J., Laurence J. O'Toole, George A. Boyne, and Richard M. Walker. 2007. "Strategic Management and the Performance of Public Organizations: Testing Venerable Ideas against Recent Theories." *Journal of Public Administration Research and Theory* 17, no. 3: 357–77.

Melo, Marcus A. 2004. "Escolha institucional e a difusão dos paradigmas de política: o Brasil e a segunda onda de reformas previdenciárias." *Dados* 47: 1.

Merton, Robert. 1968. "Bureaucratic Structure and Personality." *Social Theory and Social Structure* 18, no. 4: 249–60.

Micklethwait, John, and Adrian Wooldridge. 1996. *The Witch Doctors: Making Sense of the Management Gurus.* New York: Times Books.

Mintzberg, Henry. 1979. *The Structuring of Organizations.* Englewood Cliffs, N.J.: Prentice Hall.

Mohr, Lawrence B. 1982. *Explaining Organizational Behavior: The Limits and Possibilities of Theory and Research.* San Francisco: Jossey-Bass.

Mone, Mark A., and others. 1998. "Organizational Decline and Innovation: A Contingency Framework." *Academy of Management Review* 23: 115–32.

Moore, Mark H. 1995. *Creating Public Value: Strategic Management in Government.* Harvard University Press.

Morrell, Kevin, and Jean Hartley. 2007. *The Role of Frontline Staff in Service Innovation and Improvement: Local Authorities and Their Engagement in the Beacon Scheme.* London: Communities and Local Government.

Naff, Katherine C. and John Crum. 1999. "Working for America: Does Public Service Motivation Make a Difference?" *Review of Public Personnel Administration* 19, no. 5: 5–16.

Nelson, Richard, and Sidney G. Winter. 1982. *An Evolutionary Theory of Economic Change.* Belknap Press of Harvard University Press.

Newman, Janet, John Raine, and Chris Skelcher. 2000. *Innovation in Local Government: A Good Practice Guide.* London: Department of the Environment, Transport, and the Regions (DETR).

Nonaka, Ikujiro. 1991. "The Knowledge-Creating Company." *Harvard Business Review* 69, no. 6: 96–104.

———. 1994. "A Dynamic Theory of Organizational Knowledge Creation." *Organization Science* 5, no. 1: 14–37.

Nye, Joseph, Philip Zelikow, and David King. 1997. *Why People Don't Trust Government.* Brookings.

Ocasio, William. 1995. "The Enactment of Economic Adversity: A Reconciliation of Theories of Failure-Induced Change and Threat-Rigidity." In *Research in Organizational Behavior* 17, edited by L. L. Cummings and B. M. Staw. Greenwich, Conn.: JAI Press.

O'Dell, Carla, and C. Jackson Grayson. 1998a. "If Only We Knew What We Know: Identification and Transfer of Internal Best Practices." *California Management Review* 40, no. 3: 154–74.

———. 1998b. *If Only We Knew What We Know: The Transfer of Internal Knowledge and Best Practice.* New York: Free Press.

Office of the Deputy Prime Minister. 2003. *The Beacon Council Scheme: Application Brochure 2003.* London.

Office of Management and Budget. 2007. *Budget of the United States Government, Fiscal Year 2008,* Table 24-1

Organ, Dennis W., Philip M. Podsakoff, and Scott B. MacKenzie. 2006. *Organization Citizenship Behavior: Its Nature, Antecedents, and Consequences.* Thousand Oaks, Calif.: Sage.

Overman, E. Sam, and Kathy Boyd. 1994. "Best Practice Research and Postbureaucratic Reform." *Journal of Public Administration Research and Theory* 4, no. 1: 67–83.

Pandey, Sanjay K., and Patrick G. Scott. 2002. "Red Tape: A Review and Assessment of Concepts and Measures." *Journal of Public Administration Research and Theory* 12, no. 4: 553–80.

Pandey, Sanjay K., David H. Coursey, and Donald P. Moynihan. 2007. "Organizational Effectiveness and Bureaucratic Red Tape: A Multimethod Study." *Public Performance and Management Review* 30, no. 3: 371–400.

Perry, James L., and Lois R. Wise. 1990. "The Motivational Bases of Public Service." *Public Administration Review* 50, no. 3: 367–73.

Peters, B. G. 2001. *The Future of Governing.* 2nd ed. University Press of Kansas.

Peters, B. G., and J. Pierre, eds. 2003. *Handbook of Public Administration.* London and Thousand Oaks, Calif.: Sage.

Peters, B. G., and V. Wright. 1996. "Public Policy and Administration, Old and New." In *A New Handbook of Political Science,* edited by R. E. Goodin and H.-D. Klingemann, pp. 628–41. Oxford University Press.

Peters, Thomas J., and Robert H. Waterman, Jr. 1982. *In Search of Excellence: Lessons from America's Best-Run Companies.* New York: Harper & Row.

Pfeffer, Jeffrey. 1992. *Managing with Power.* Boston: Harvard Business School Press.

Pfeffer, Jeffrey, and Robert I. Sutton. 2006. *Hard Facts, Dangerous Half-Truths, and Total Nonsense: Profiting from Evidence-Based Management.* Boston: Harvard Business School Press.

Pinchot, Gifford, III. 1985. *Intrapreneuring: Why You Don't Have to Leave the Corporation to Become an Entrepreneur.* New York: Harper & Row.

Polanyi, Michael. 1967. *The Tacit Dimension.* New York: Doubleday.

Pollitt, Christopher, and Geert Bouckaert. 2000. *Public Management Reform: A Comparative Analysis.* Oxford University Press.

Pressman, Jeffrey L., and Aaron Wildavsky. 1979. *Implementation.* 2nd ed. University of California Press.

Putnam, Robert D. 1993. *Making Democracy Work: Civic Traditions in Modern Italy.* Princeton University Press.

Radin, B. A. 2006. *Challenging the Performance Movement.* Georgetown University Press.

Rainey, H., S. Pandey, and B. Bozeman. 1995. "Research Note: Public and Private Managers' Perceptions of Red Tape." *Public Administration Review* 55, no. 6: 567–74.

Rashman, Lyndsay. 2007. *Capacity Building through the Beacon Scheme.* London: Communities and Local Government.

Rashman, Lyndsay, James Downe, and Jean Hartley. 2005. "Knowledge Creation and Transfer in the Beacon Scheme: Improving Services through Sharing Good Practice." *Local Government Studies* 31, no. 5: 683–700.

Rashman, Lyndsay, and Jean Hartley. 2002. "Leading and Learning? Knowledge Transfer in the Beacon Council Scheme." *Public Administration* 80, no. 3: 523–43.

———. 2004. *2004 Survey of Local Authorities.* Report. London: Office of the Deputy Prime Minister.

———. 2006a. *National Survey of English Local Authorities.* London: Communities and Local Government.

Rashman, Lyndsay, Erin Withers, and Jean Hartley. 2006. *Organizational Learning Knowledge and Capacity: A Systematic Review for Policy-makers, Policy Advisors, Managers, and Academics.* London: Communities and Local Government.

Reich, Robert B. 1997. *Locked in the Cabinet.* New York: Alfred A. Knopf.

Richardson, George P. 1991. *Feedback Thought in Social Science and Systems Theory.* University of Pennsylvania Press.

Rizvi, Gowher. 2003. "Strategic Planning–A Plan for the Ash Institute." Unpublished paper. John F. Kennedy School of Government, Harvard University.

———. 2007. "Reinventing Government: Putting Democracy and Social Justice Back into the Discourse." In *Public Administration and Democratic Governance: Governments Serving Citizens,* edited by United Nations Department of Economic and Social Affairs, pp. 89–135. New York: United Nations.

Roberts, Nancy C. 1992. "Public Entrepreneurship and Innovation." *Policy Studies Review* 11, no. 1: 55–74.

Robson, C. 2002. *Real World Research.* 2nd ed. Oxford: Blackwell.

Rogers, Everett M. 2003. *Diffusion of Innovation.* 5th ed. New York: Free Press.

Romanelli, Elaine, and Michael L. Tushman. 1986. "Inertia, Environments, and Strategic Choice: A Quasi-Experimental Design for Comparative-Longitudinal Research." *Management Science* 32, no. 5: 608–21.

Roughgarden, Jonathan. 1974. "The Fundamental and Realized Niche of a Solitary Population." *American Naturalist* 108, no. 960: 232–35.

Sah, Raaj Kumar, and Joseph E. Stiglitz. 1986. "The Architecture of Economic Systems: Hierarchies and Polyarchies." *American Economic Review* 76, no. 4: 716–27.

Salancik, Gerald R., and Jeffrey Pfeffer. 1978. "A Social Information Processing Approach to Job Attitudes and Task Design." *Administrative Science Quarterly* 23, no. 2: 224–53.

Savas, E. S. 1982. *Privatizing the Public Sector: How to Shrink Government.* Chatham, N.J.: Chatham House.

Savoie, D. J. 1994. *Thatcher, Reagan, Mulroney: In Search of a New Bureaucracy.* University of Pittsburgh Press.

Schlesinger, Arthur M. 1959. *The Age of Roosevelt: The Coming of the New Deal.* Cambridge, Mass.: Riverside Press.

Schneider, Ben Ross, and Blanca Heredia. 2003. *Reinventing Leviathan: The Politics of Administrative Reform in Developing Countries.* Iberian Studies Institute, University of Miami.

Schweitzer, M. E., L. Ordóñez, and B. Douma. 2004. "Goal Setting as a Motivator of Unethical Behavior." *Academy of Management Journal* 47, no. 3: 422–32.

Scott, Patrick G., and Sanjay K. Pandey. 2000. "The Influence of Red Tape on Bureaucratic Behavior: An Experimental Simulation." *Journal of Policy Analysis and Management* 19, no. 4: 615–33.

Seattle Public Utilities, Strategic Asset Management Division. 2006. *Curbside Recycling Report, December 2006.* Report.

Selznick, Philip. 1957. *Leadership in Administration: A Sociological Interpretation.* New York: Harper & Row.

Simons, R. 1995. "Control in an Age of Empowerment." *Harvard Business Review* 73, no. 2: 80–88.

Slovic, Paul, and Sarah Lichtenstein. 1971. "Comparison of Bayesian and Regression Approaches to the Study of Information Processing in Judgment." *Organizational Behavior and Human Performance* 6: 649–744.

Sobhan, Rehman, ed. 1991. *Structural Adjustment Policies in the Third World—Design and Experience.* Dhaka, Bangladesh: University Press.

Spink, Peter. 2006a. "A inovação na perspectiva dos inovadores." In *Inovação no campo da gestão pública local,* edited by Pedro Jacobi and José Antonio Pinho. Rio de Janeiro: Editora Fundação Getulio Vargas.

————, ed. 2006b. *Innovation Mobilizes Other Resources.* São Paulo: Program. Pública e Cidadania/Innovations Programs Liaison Group.

————. 2007. "Equity and Public Action." *Harvard Review of Latin* America 6, no. 3: 33–35.

Staw, Barry M., Lance E. Sandelands, and Jane E. Dutton. 1981. "Threat-Rigidity Effects in Organizational Behavior." *Administrative Science Quarterly.* 26, no. 4: 501–24.

Stinchcombe, Arthur L. 2001. *When Formality Works: Authority and Abstraction in Law and Organizations.* University of Chicago Press.

Strang, David, and Sarah A. Soule. 1998. "Diffusion in Organizations and Social Movements: From Hybrid Corn to Poison Pills." *Annual Review of Sociology* 24: 265–90.

Strauss, Anselm L. 1987. *Qualitative Analysis for Social Scientists.* Cambridge University Press.

Sugiyama, Natasha B. 2004. "Political Incentives, Ideology and Social Networks: The Diffusion of Social Policy in Brazil." Paper delivered at the 2004 meeting of the Latin American Studies Association. Las Vegas, October 7–9.

Szulanski, Gabriel. 1996. "Exploring Internal Stickiness: Impediments to the Transfer of Best Practice Within the Firm." *Strategic Management Journal* 17 (Special Issue: Knowledge and the Firm): 27–43.

————. 2003. *Sticky Knowledge: Barriers to Knowing in the Firm.* London: Sage.

Terry, L. D. 1990. "Leadership in the Administrative State." *Administration and Society* 21, no. 4: 395–412.

————. 1993. "Why We Should Abandon the Misconceived Quest to Reconcile Public Entrepreneurship with Democracy." *Public Administration Review,* 53, no. 4: 393–95.

Thomas, Craig. 2003. "Habitat Conservation Planning." In *Deepening Democracy: Institutional Innovations in Empowered Participatory Governance,* edited by Archon Fung and Erik Wright, pp. 144–73. London and New York: Verso.

Tidd, J., J. Bessant, and K. Pavitt. 2005. *Managing Innovation: Integrating Technological, Market and Organizational Change.* 3rd ed. Chichester, U.K.: Wiley.

Toledano, Dalit. 1999."Keeping Pensions Secure" and "Motivating Job Safety." In *Making Washington Work: Tales of Innovation in the Federal Government,* edited by John D. Donahue. Brookings.

Trattner, John, and Laura Ziff. 1999. "Shutting Down Sweatshops." In *Making Washington Work: Tales of Innovation in the Federal Government,* edited by John D. Donahue. Brookings.

Tushman, Michael L., and Charles A. O'Reilly III. 2002. *Winning Through Innovation: A Practical Guide to Leading Organizational Change and Renewal.* Boston: Harvard Business School Press.

Tversky, Amos, and Daniel Kahneman. 1974. "Judgment under Uncertainty: Heuristics and Biases." *Science* 185, no. 4157: 1124–31.

U.S. Government Printing Office. 1992. *U.S. Government Policy and Supporting Positions.* Washington.

Utterback, J. 1996. *Mastering the Dynamics of Innovation.* Boston: Harvard Business School Press.

Van de Ven, Andrew H. 1993. "Managing the Process of Organizational Innovation." In *Organizational Change and Redesign: Ideas and Insights for Improving Performance,* edited by G. P. Huber and W. H. Glick. New York: Oxford.

Van de Ven, Andrew H., Harold L. Angle, and Marshall Scott Poole, eds. 1989. *Research on the Management of Innovation: The Minnesota Studies.* New York: Ballinger.

Vigoda-Gadot, E., A. Shoham, A. Ruvio, and N. Schwabsky. 2007 (forthcoming). "Public Sector Innovation for Europe: A Multinational Eight-Country Exploration of Citizens' Perspectives." *Public Administration.*

Waldo, D. 1948. *The Administrative State: A Study of the Political Theory of American Public Administration.* New York: Ronald Press.

Walker, Jack J. 1969. "The Diffusion of Innovations among the American States." *American Political Science Review* 63, no. 3: 880–99.

Walker, Richard. 2006. "Innovation Type and Diffusion: An Empirical Analysis of Local Government." *Public Administration* 84, no. 2: 311–35.

Walters, Jonathan. 2002. *Understanding Innovation: What Inspires It? What Makes It Successful.* Washington: IBM Foundation for the Business of Government.

Wampold, Bruce E., Zac E. Imel, and Takuya Minami. 2007. "The Placebo Effect: Relatively Large and Robust Enough to Survive Another Assault." *Journal of Clinical Psychology* 63, no. 4: 401–03.

Wamsley, G. L. 1990. "Introduction." In *Refounding Public Administration,* edited by G. L. Wamsley, R. N. Bacher, C. T. Goodsell, P. S. Kronenberg, J. A. Rohr, C. M. Stivers, O. F. White, and J. F. Wolf, pp. 19–29. Newbury Park, Calif.: Sage.

Warwick, D. P. 1975. *A Theory of Public Bureaucracy: Politics, Personality, and Organization in the State Department.* Harvard University Press.

Weber, Max. 1947. *The Theory of Social and Economic Organization.* Translated by Talcott Parsons. New York: Free Press

Weick, Karl E. 1984. "Small Wins: Redefining the Scale of Social Problems." *American Psychologist* 39, no. 1: 40–49.

Weiss, Janet A. 1994. "Comment: Public Management Research: The Interdependence of Problems and Theory." *Journal of Policy Analysis and Management* 13, no. 2: 278–85.

White, L. D. 1926. *Introduction to the Study of Public Administration.* New York: Macmillan.

Wilson, D., and C. Game. 2006. *Local Government in the United Kingdom.* 4th ed. London: Palgrave.

Wilson, J. Q. 1989. *Bureaucracy: What Government Agencies Do and Why They Do It.* New York: Basic Books.

Withers, Erin, and Jean Hartley. 2007. "Predictors of Performance: Local Authorities' Use of the Beacon Scheme." Working paper. Warwick University Institute of Governance and Public Management.

Withers, Erin, Z. Radnor, Lyndsay Rashman, and Jean Hartley. 2007. "Longitudinal Analysis of Case Studies of Engagement, Learning and Improvement through the Beacon Scheme." Working paper. Institute of Governance and Public Management, Warwick University.

Wondolleck, Julia M., and Steven L. Yaffee. 2000. *Making Collaboration Work: Lessons from Innovation in Natural Resource Management.* Washington: Island Press.

Zahra, Shaker A., and Gerard George. 2002. "Absorptive Capacity: A Review, Reconceptualization, and Extension. *Academy of Management Review* 27, no. 2: 185–203.

Contributors

EUGENE BARDACH
Goldman School of Public Policy,
  University of California at Berkeley

ROBERT BEHN
Kennedy School of Government,
  Harvard University

SANDFORD BORINS
University of Toronto

JOHN D. DONAHUE
Kennedy School of Government,
  Harvard University

MARTA FERREIRA SANTOS FARAH
Center on Public Administration and
  Government, Fundação Getulio
  Vargas

ARCHON FUNG
Kennedy School of Government,
  Harvard University

JEAN HARTLEY
Warwick Business School, University
  of Warwick

STEVEN KELMAN
Kennedy School of Government,
  Harvard University

PETER SPINK
Center on Public Administration and
  Government, Fundação Getulio
  Vargas

GOWHER RIZVI
Ash Institute for Democratic
  Governance and Innovation,
  Harvard University

JONATHAN WALTERS
Governing magazine

Index

A. Alfred Taubman Center for State and
   Local Government, 21
Abramson, Mark, 13–14, 15
The Administrative State (Waldo), 40
Africa, 2, 25, 71, 86, 190. *See also* Develop-
   ing countries, innovations in
African Americans, 105, 138–39
Agency cooperation. *See* Interagency collab-
   orative capacity (ICCs)
Allison, Graham, 15
Alonso, Pablo, 47
Altshuler, Alan: influencing Innovations in
   American Government Awards Program,
   22–23, 24, 100; and innovations studies,
   25–26, 27; at Kennedy School, 21;
   scholarly references in works of, 34, 35;
   and traditional model of public sector
   management, 30
Amabile, Teresa, 47
American Indians. *See* Native Americans
AmericaSpeaks (New York City town hall
   meeting on rebuilding Twin Towers), 61
Andrews, Rhys, 45
Antismoking campaign (California), 119
Appleby, P.H., 40

Arnold, David, 14, 15, 16, 19
Ash, Roy L., 2, 26, 191
Ash Institute for Democratic Governance
   and Innovation: and non-American
   perspective in innovation research, 192,
   193, 202; and public trust, 190; purpose
   of, 26, 27, 191, 198; research focus of,
   200–01, 205. *See also* Innovations
   in American Government Awards
   Program
Audit process of awards program, 7
Australia, 38, 200
Axelrod, Robert, 102–03

Baltimore: CitiStat, use of, 11, 149–50,
   151, 200; Healthy Start initiative, 55;
   reduction in infant mortality, project for,
   55. *See also* Baltimore Project
Baltimore Project, 55, 68
Bardach, Eugene, 5, 34, 113–37, 199, 200,
   202
Barzelay, Michael, 5, 23, 29–30, 33–34,
   199, 200
Beacon Council, 162, 166, 173, 175,
   176–80. *See also* Beacon Scheme